THE IMPECUNIOUS AMATEUR LOOKS BACK

Author of

THE DREAMER OF DEVON

ROBERT BONTINE CUNNINGHAME GRAHAM:
HIS LIFE AND WORKS

MODERN BOOK COLLECTING FOR THE
IMPECUNIOUS AMATEUR

THE NATURE WRITERS

A STEPHEN CRANE COLLECTION

DON ROBERTO

JOHN SLOAN'S LAST SUMMER

THE MIND ON THE WING

REBEL THOUGHT

THE CORONARY CLUB

LEARNING MY ABC'S

WHAT PRICE TEACHING?

HERE'S TO TOGETHERNESS

HERB WEST'S FAREWELL ADDRESS

THE AUTHOR AND ROBERT FROST AT RIPTON, VERMONT

Photo: Ralph Nading Hill

HERBERT FAULKNER WEST

THE IMPECUNIOUS AMATEUR LOOKS BACK

The Autobiography of a Bookman

If a man does not keep pace with his companions,
perhaps it is because he hears a different drummer . . .
let him step to the music he hears.

Thoreau

WESTHOLM PUBLICATIONS
HANOVER, NEW HAMPSHIRE
1966

Set in Monotype Walbaum 374
Printed in England by the Shenval Press
London, Hertford and Harlow

For Gilbert and Nancy Reynolds Verney

#336

Herbert Faulkner West
in Th all me last to
Morris Cook — a great
Dobie collector
from H W.
Haworth N. H.   June 22.1966

Foreword

This book is an attempt to tell the story of the life of a man in the world of books: as a teacher of Comparative Literature, as founder and director of the Friends of the Dartmouth Library, as book collector, as traveller seeking rare books, as a rare book dealer, and as the publisher of Westholm Publications.

The world of books has given me much happiness and some enlightenment.

I want to thank Gilbert Verney, whose Foundation gave me the opportunity to visit the National Trust Claydon House, in Buckinghamshire, which resulted in the microfilming of the Verney Papers, and which allowed me leisure to work in London for a couple of summers.

I want to thank also my secretary, Mrs Karl Michael, of Hanover, New Hampshire, for her intelligent help in typing the manuscript.

Thanks to Hilaire Belloc I can say:

> When I am dead,
> I hope it may be said,
> That his sins were scarlet,
> But his books were read.

Portions of this book have appeared in small privately printed publications. However, all have been revised and rewritten.

Part of the chapter 'The Bookman in England' appeared in the AMERICAN BOOK COLLECTOR in May 1964.

Hanover, New Hampshire December 1965

Table of Contents

Prelude

Nothing is true except a few simple fundamentals everyone has demonstrated for himself. Where there is doubt, continue to doubt.

E. W. Howe in 1911

I admire Henry David Thoreau (1817–62) more than any other American writer. It was he who said that the essence of a good style is to tell the truth. I believe this, too. He dared to be an individual, he dared to say and write what he thought, he dared to live as his conscience, the voice of God within, dictated; he dared to be true to himself. These are some of the simple things that today, in our age of numbers, mathematics, space travel, science, computers, and an official and appalling disregard for the truth, we too often tend to forget.

Thoreau heard the music of a different drummer. So, in a way, have I, though not as a transcendentalist in Thoreau's meaning of the word, nor have I gained much knowledge 'in flashes of light from heaven', but only by dogged persistence along empirical lines, some thinking, and a lifetime of reading.

On the whole it has been a happy life. Not too serious a one, not at all pompous, not at all earth-shaking, but great fun most of the time.

This is the story of a bookman, as a professor of literature, writer, critic, collector, publisher, bookseller, traveller, and about the friends he made in the world of books.

Arthur Schopenhauer, in his essay *On Thinking for Oneself*, offers the suggestion that men of learning 'are those who have done their reading in the pages of a book'. He adds, however, that *thinkers* and men of genius 'are those who have gone straight to the book of Nature; it is they who have enlightened the world and carried humanity further on its way'. He concludes his essay by stating that another person thinks for us when we read and we

1

merely reiterate his mental process in a parrot-like manner. Thus he tries to demonstrate that too much reaping ossifies the human mind.

This is an over-simplification of a half-truth. Most anyone with sense, and this eliminates, of course, many pedagogues and doctors of philosophy, learns from experience, or from what Schopenhauer calls the book of Nature. This, however, does not exclude reading, though it may be true that men of genius learn more from life than from books. Henry Thoreau learned from both. It is true that many professors do live in an academic vacuum and are as ignorant of life as a child, but the more recent crop of college instructors resemble toothpaste salesmen, and are not to be confused with their European or English compatriots, or those who were teaching twenty years ago.

Inasmuch as I have always found it difficult to get anyone of any advanced age to summarize for me what he has learned in his life, I have decided to try to do so here as succinctly and briefly as possible from the point of view of a bookman.

Even though I was a pedagogue for forty-two years, I trust that what follows will indicate that I have learned both from books and from experience. I have been a nature lover all my life. I have also enjoyed the companionship of books. Many of them have *stimulated* my thinking, contrary to the learned pessimist and voluntarist, Arthur Schopenhauer, who may have been a little piqued against professional scholars, having been a conspicuous failure as a lecturer and teacher.

The question of what *is* truth is as old as mankind, and it is just about as difficult to answer today as when Pilate raised the question.

My friend, Paul Sample, the painter, asked me during the repulsive McCarthy era, just what one means today when he uses the word truth. He put the question like this: 'What do college presidents mean when they say, "We are in the business of seeking truth"?'

My answer to him simplified was this: Truth may be considered as being absolute or relative. Absolute truth, known ultimately only to God, though some of His chosen ones claim to know it, is believed in by most religions, and by all transcendent philosophies. The Christian Church, for example, of which Roman Catholicism is the purest historical form, believes that in matters of faith and morals it possesses absolute truth. Other religions make similar claims. Perhaps there is only one truth, which men seek along different paths and through various degrees of astigmatism.

Philosophical idealists also claim that absolute truth is possible to attain.

William Ernest Hocking in his *Types of Philosophy*, 1929, defines idealism as a word signifying: 'that whatever is ultimately real in the universe is such stuff as ideas are made of rather than such stuff as stones and metals are made of. That is, if we are looking for the substance of things, the ultimate being which explains all other beings, we shall find it to be mental in nature— the thinker and his thought, the will and its doings, the self and its self-expression. And whatever appears to be other than this, independent of it or hostile to it, as matter, or force or space and time, will be found to depend on the mind for its very existence.'

Later on he writes: 'The mind is a little thing, a mere item in an infinite universe; the mind is itself an infinite thing, the whole universe is mirrored within it.'

The mind is capable of finding absolute truth.

Modern man, in America more irreligious than religious as far as orthodox beliefs go, and many modern philosophies, owing mainly to the influence of the pragmatism of William James and John Dewey, the doctrine of evolution (see Bergson's *Creative Evolution*, 1912), materialism, and the ideas of relativity, maintain that truth is constantly changing and that, by the nature of things, truth must always be relative and never absolute. What was true a century ago is not necessarily true today nor will it be true tomorrow. What is true for a Russian or a Chinese may not be true for an Egyptian, Hindu, or a Rotarian from Oconomowoc.

The scientist, theoretically at least, has no axe to grind, and seeks only an impersonal and objective truth. He realizes that truth is hard to find, and that when he finally thinks he has found it, he knows that the hypothesis which he may then set up will endure but a short time. Today the scientist has taken over and the humanist resides only in cloisters and academic halls, and even there less and less.

The truths discovered by Isaac Newton were partially dislocated by Albert Einstein, and the laws of physics of only a decade ago must be now reconsidered in the light of nuclear studies. Truth for the scientist is constantly changing and being enlarged.

So today one must take his stand with the fundamentalists or with the modernists, with the absolutists or the relativists. The conception that truth is static and not dynamic, that God is Being instead of Becoming, is considered pious humbug foisted on a gullible and flatulent public, mainly by religions or organizations which have much, if not everything, to lose if the idea of the relativity of truth is generally accepted.

This conflict is one of the really great issues of our time.

I would not care to be as dogmatic as Tolstoy, who stated plainly in 1887 that man discovers truth by reason and not by faith, though I tend to agree with him. I can honestly say that as far as I am concerned truth is almost impossible to attain by *any* method, whether one uses the paths of faith or reason, induction or deduction, mysticism or ratiocination. There are no short cuts whatever to truth available to the man who is intellectually honest. It is the ignorant and the prejudiced man who is the most certain. It is the wisest man, like Socrates, who, after a lifetime of searching, is not sure that he knows anything.

I repudiate without reservation the anti-intellectualism of our century which is visible in all fields of thought and endeavour: philosophy, criticism, art, literature, morals, and politics. It is stifling, terrifying and has brought us close to disaster. I affirm my faith in reason, in common sense, and in the unlimited powers of the human mind. I am forced to regard myself as an old-fashioned rationalist, surrounded mainly by people who appear to think with their blood. I find myself living in a world notoriously totalitarian in pattern, even the college world, which disregards any truth contrary to its own dogmatic definition, and apparently fears any other and suppresses it when possible.

The stand an intellectual ought to take today is stated well by Nicola Chairomonte, dramatic critic in Rome of *Il Mondo*, when he writes: 'From the point of view of the community the only justification of the intellectual is that he persists, under the stress of circumstances, in being a free, conscious, reasoning individual when others lose themselves in the crowd. The duty that no intellectual can shirk without degrading himself is the duty to expose fictions and to refuse to call "useful lies" truths. To accomplish this duty, it is not necessary for him to think that he possesses the truth. The will to question can suffice.'

One thing I am certain of is that if we are not always vigilant we shall lose our hard won freedoms even as has more than half the human race living today under Communism. In the early 'fifties the spirit of the Inquisition was rampant in America and not until 1957 was the atmosphere such that the United States Supreme Court could restate, though not without protests by local politicians, the rights of the individual against the ever-encroaching power of the State.

Referring to the Court's delay in reaffirming the rights of man, Chief Justice William O. Douglas told me in the spring of 1957 that he felt his years on the Supreme Court had been wasted. I trust that he feels better about it now. Even the Supreme Court seems no longer safe in our society from the rabble rousing of unthinking and vote-seeking politicians.

What was most terrifying in the decade of the 'fifties was the fact that millions of well-meaning people in this country approved of hatred and intolerance and failed to see the danger, even to their own way of life, of what we then labelled McCarthyism but which is, in reality, a persistent force in American life.

I fear that this spirit is still abroad in our land, as it has always been through history everywhere, though less apparent than in the dark years of 1953–4 when we reached the lowest point in this century of spiritual degradation and intellectual timidity.

In fact, I came to believe in all seriousness, those days, that those who were strongly pro-McCarthy actually approved of lying, stealing, bullying, and browbeating as a permanent policy in our government. So did many 'good' Germans approve Hitler. Some do now.

Judge Learned Hand, a great American, wrote before he died: 'Our nation was founded on the postulate that had been long in the making, but had gained primacy about the time when we started in for ourselves. We staked our fate on the proposition that there can be a "government of the people, by the people, for the people"; and we boast that we have established that kind of government.

. . . In spite of many defeats and failures it is this that has remained our dominant tradition; it is the faith that we have over and over proclaimed and by which we say we live, though at the moment we appear to be hesitant in our allegiance, as we have often been before. Its implications are among the most unwelcome that men are called upon to accept. They are that truth is attainable only by trial and error, and a readiness ever to re-examine and re-appraise. That does violence to our deepest animal bent, which demands some immediate and positive response to any emergency. *Doubt and scrutiny*, the most serviceable of man's tools, were the last he acquired. He has never quite reconciled himself to their use; they are always repellent and painful.'

The man born to doubt, the man who wishes to examine closely our popular shibboleths and the policies of our dubious statesmen, and to test the truth by empirical standards, is now under grave suspicion. He is a hated and feared intellectual. Rewards go to those who affirm the most stupid nonsense, and who never deviate as much as a hair from what is popular, conservative, conventional, and thoroughly acceptable to the great majority of the intellectually unwashed. Honour, high position, and honorary degrees go to those who never express an idea until they are certain it will be approved of in the proper places, or is conventionally accepted by the 'right people'. Yet in history it has been the man who doubts and scrutinizes who has most advanced the cause of truth: Socrates, Lucretius, Montaigne, Descartes, Voltaire, Darwin and many others.

On the last day of December 1939, I entered into a journal the following:

My confidence and belief in the goodness or even the intelligence of man has not increased with the passing of the years. I regard him with irony and pity, much as did some of my literary loves, Anatole France, Joseph Conrad, Thomas Hardy, W. H. Hudson, and Robert Bontine Cunninghame Graham. Yet as one faces seemingly inevitable war one must believe in Man, or reach the dead end of absolute futility; one must believe in effort and struggle, or become eaten with spiritual dry rot; and one must believe in the future or regard the lives of oneself and one's children as meaningless. So I look ahead, as men have looked

ahead in every generation in recorded history, and hope that
men will eventually learn to live in peace with one another, will
learn to control their consuming passion of greed, will put their
faith in reason, and will grow personally more honest. If a man
like the late John Dewey or George Santayana can still believe
in the naturalistic point of view and in MAN, then we all can do
so, unless our beliefs are conditioned by something physiological
or psychological.

During the Second World War I wrote in my Journal: Tonight,
walking home under a sky full of brilliant stars, Venus the clearest
of all in the Western sky, I was led to think of that great French-
man, Pascal, so sympathetic to Anglo-Saxons owing to his
austerity of character. Though a God-intoxicated man, and one
who was once visibly moved by the miracle of the 'Holy Thorn',
he wrote: 'The silence of the infinite spaces frightens me.' And
well it might. Of the millions and millions of men who have for
thousands of years gazed at the heavens and thought of their own
littleness and insignificance, how many would not say the same?
The great majority would, surely, for life is a desperate ecstasy, a
quivering moment in an ocean of Time, and still and forever a
mystery. A mystery which is always being increased by literally
stunning views of the ever-shifting and changing beauties of
Nature.

We are each of us alone on a whirling speck of dust through a
vast and infinite space. Somehow at night, especially when the
atmosphere sparkles, this infinity assumes a more awesome aspect.
And yet, though frightening, how lovely is the Earth! Even in
the Northern wilderness at thirty or forty degrees below zero,
which may be at the moment freezing some lonely prospector to
death, there is still a vision of beauty for all eyes that can see.
And many perhaps have had that vision, and so closed their eyes
in peace. For as it has been said, 'You cannot perceive beauty but
with a serene mind, and it is a sure evidence of the health and
innocence of the beholder if the senses are alive to the beauty of
Nature.'

Beautiful, but not loving. Nature is as cold and impersonal as a
glacier.

The things in life that are lovely are often those which arouse in us a strange and often unaccountable feeling of sadness. It was William Cory, an already forgotten poet of the nineteenth century, who wrote wisely and truthfully: 'Life without music is despicable, with it inextricably strange. . . . Listening to pathetic songs I rebel against the death of those who sang them in the old times; the makers of those melodies are my unknown brethren; all others who speak in what we call words fail to let me know them thoroughly; music is the only communication of heart, and it alone makes one feel hopelessly empty.'

And so when alone, or with congenial company, we listen to Beethoven's *Eroica* or Sibelius' 'still, sad music of humanity', we are generally unable to share our deepest emotions with anyone, even with those we love, and yet we may feel an intense kinship with the composer . . . who perhaps has been lying for many years in a cold 'elmwood coffin'.

These thoughts produced during the war I would not alter much, if any, today. I am still aware of the tragic sense of life, visible everywhere, still conscious of the marvellous beauty of the world, and still enjoying the ever-changing scene, more often ridiculous than sublime.

More than once I have asked the very old to tell me what they had learned from life. It seemed to me strange how little they would, or could, tell me. From my mother, nearly ninety before she died, I learned only that life passes by before we are aware of it. She quoted me a passage from Stephen Leacock, the humorist: 'For the reality of life, we learn too late, is in the living tissue of it from day to day, not in the expectation of better, nor in the fear of worse. Those two things, to be always looking ahead, and to worry about things that haven't happened yet and very likely won't happen—those take the very essence out of life. If only one could live each moment to the full, in the present, intense with its own absorption, even if it is as transitory and evanescent as Einstein's "here" and "now".'

This I have found to be true.

What is the bookman to believe in his rapidly changing world?

My favourite professor, the late Irving Babbitt, M.A., with whom I studied a year at Harvard, used to declare that everyone is born either a Platonist or an Aristotelian.

William James made this clear in his distinction in his book *Pragmatism*, 1907, between the tough and tender-minded.

The position of the Platonist or the tender-minded person is roughly that thought is the creator of the universe and that rational ideas constitute its structure.

The world of experience, the empirical, scientific, pragmatic view of the modern man today, is crass and obdurate, stubbornly materialistic in character.

The modernist's position is that ideas themselves are experimentally developed in the course of actual inquiries in what William James and John Dewey called experimental empiricism.

It is difficult today, for any bookman, unless he is extremely tender-minded, to hold any position but that of a radical empiricist.

It was Winwood Reade (1838–75) in his controversial book, *The Martyrdom of Man*, really an introduction to universal history, who wrote: 'What a state of society is this in which free thinker is a term of abuse, and in which doubt is regarded as a sin!'

This appears, at times, to apply equally well three-quarters of a century later, and I am not unhappy to report that I am a grievous sinner, as I am a born doubter, and believe with the English poet Lord Tennyson that there is 'more faith in honest doubt than in half the creeds'.

Doubt, I believe, is the beginning of wisdom, but it is generally not an attitude that pays off well in worldly terms. It is the professional man of faith who gets big television fees, who writes well-paid newspaper columns, and whose books reach the bestseller lists. The doubter retains his intellectual integrity, continues to venerate such men as Montaigne and Lucretius, and he must be content with the reading audience capable of admiring such writers as Swift, William James and George Santayana. Some eighteen years ago, when I was close to death of a heart attack, I found my scepticism as sustaining for me as the most devout Christian doctrine.

I have known for many years that freedom is something that one has continuously to fight for. It is not an innate gift to mankind, nor is it a natural right. Freedom is part of our English

9

heritage, and it took centuries to win what little we possess. Government and power loving demagogues by their very nature encroach upon and ultimately, if they can, tend to deprive the individual of freedom as has happened now in countries which cover more than half the globe. You can name the really free countries today on the fingers of one hand.

After centuries the Englishman won the right to criticize, the right to hold minority convictions, the right to read, the right of habeas corpus, the right to face his accuser, the right to a fair and open trial, and the right to think independently for himself.

The great issue of our time is the freedom of the human individual. The battle for this is not won; nor will it ever be won. Each generation has had to fight for it. Ours must fight even harder than in the immediate past, as many in our country today have seen fit to confuse dissent with treason.

When Thomas Jefferson wrote: 'It is an insult to our citizens to question whether they are rational beings or not, and blasphemy against religion to suppose it cannot stand the test of truth and reason. If a book or idea be false in its facts, disprove them; if false in its reasoning, refute it. But for God's sake let us freely hear both sides.'

That these remarks were objected to as being dangerous and possibly subversive should surprise no one living today. Even President Eisenhower's famous book burning speech at Dartmouth, delivered June 14, 1953, was criticized by some superpatriots.

Philosophers have been the butt of satirists since Lucian, and before him. Too many of them, as William James said, 'Fill their bellies with the East Wind.' I consider myself a philosopher in the sense of Plato's definition, as one who desires to discern the truth, but I hold with Samuel Butler that all philosophies, that is, all genuine systems, if you ride them home, are apt to be nonsense.

The fact is that the great questions of philosophy—God, free-will and immortality—are unknowable. The one fact one can be nearly certain of is that we are surrounded by mystery, that is all we know and all we shall ever know.

Shakespeare, who expressed at one time or another most of the world's store of wisdom, put it well when Hamlet says:

10

There are more things in Heaven and Earth, Horatio,
Than are dreamt of in your philosophy.

This, after a lifetime of reading, I have come to believe.

One needs, too, in this atomic age of ours, a deep and abiding sense of the ridiculous, the ability to laugh at oneself, and a lively appreciation of what George Meredith called the comic spirit in his marvellous book, *An Essay on Comedy* (1897). Note this: 'and whenever [men] wax out of proportion, overblown, affected, pretentious, bombastical, hypocritical, pedantic, fantastically delicate; whenever it sees them self-deceived or hoodwinked, given to run riot in idolatries, drifting into vanities, congregating in absurdities, planning short-sightedly, plotting dementedly; whenever they are at variance with their professions, and violate the unwritten but perceptible laws binding them in consideration one to another, whenever they offend sound reason, fair justice; are false in humility or mined with conceit, individually, or in the bulk—the Spirit overhead will look humanely malign and cast an oblique light on them, followed by volleys of silvery laughter. This is the comic spirit.'[1]

One should never be unaware of it.

I would describe myself with the late Sir Ernest Benn, London publisher, as 'an impenitent individualist'. I was born a dissenter. I am still dissenting with majority opinions, sometimes with minority ones. I agree with the late Bernard Shaw that 'all who achieve rare distinction in life begin as revolutionists', and that the most distinguished 'become more revolutionary as they grow older'.

I believe that individualism is the crying need of our time. The spirit of the herd has overridden us long enough. Its vulgarity, its cheapness, its low standards, its shoddy values, its stupidity has made America a paradise for the mediocre and for mediocrity.

Even the American college has not escaped.

The drive for conformity is on. Those who would wish to understand how this affects American education should read W. H. Whyte's *The Organization Man*, 1956, and Beardsley Ruml's

[1] George Meredith, *An Essay on Comedy*. Westminster: Archibald Constable and Company, 1897, pp. 89–90.

11

article on the liberal arts colleges, 'Pay and the Professor', in the April 1957 issue of the *Atlantic Monthly*.

The application of big business methods and techniques to education may well destroy it. Those who subsidize have a legitimate right to call the tune. I expect that my own college, Dartmouth, will be declaring dividends in another decade. Meanwhile, the individual is having a hard time retaining his integrity.

Read the words of V. Voresayev, relating specifically to his comprehension of Tolstoy's *Anna Karenina*, but actually with a wider meaning for all:

'If a man fails to follow the deepest convictions of his heart and timidly turns away from the great gifts life has to offer, if thoughtlessly he turns against all that is best in him, who is to blame for his destruction? "Vengeance is Mine and I will repay."'

Emerson's dictum: 'Who so would be a man, *must* be a non-conformist,' is still pertinent today.

When I think of formal religion I am reminded of an episode in Dostoevski's *The Brothers Karamozov* in which a Catholic Churchman says that if Christ should return to earth the Church would throw him in chains, lest he reawaken the true spirit of Christianity, peace on earth and goodwill toward men, which it has lost sight of.

Religion is all too often an escape mechanism for people too weak in mind and spirit to face the trials of their own day. I have never been able to believe that mere acceptance of a few commonplace beatitudes, older than Christ by thousands of years, can effect a resurrection of Man. These beatitudes will be effective only when Man has conquered himself and gained complete personal spiritual and intellectual integrity.

The older I get the more astonished I am that any reasoning person can believe in historical Christianity as a fact. It obviously contains much wisdom and understanding of human nature, but it remains a fairy tale which originated in the East, was born of ignorance and fear, and has a cruel and bloody history, catering to the weaknesses of the multitudes.

It is also wise to remember that the strongest and most closely organized Churches are immensely rich in material goods and immensely strong in political power.

No sane man would deny that our foreign policy, especially during the rise of Communism, is not affected by the millions of Roman Catholic votes which represent the strongest political force of any one church in this country.

If there is one thing I am convinced of it is that God (a name we give to the Unknown) is impersonal and that there is nothing more completely indifferent to the welfare of men than the natural physical laws under which we all live and die, and which the Church chooses to call God's natural law.

Unlike that master of platitude who writes so smugly and authoritatively about 'positive' thinking, I shall have to say that I do not believe in the Christian epic. Most men apparently believe the most utter nonsense about God and the hereafter.

The professional believers become college presidents, radio and television seers, Pollyanna columnists, Christian uplifters, and often imagine themselves, particularly some of our senators, as the purest examples of patriotism and godliness extant.

The crying need in this anti-intellectual age of ours is not more religion, or more faith, but more doubt, and *more* intellectualism.

Eventually I have come to agree with Sigmund Freud that as men are so slightly amenable to reasonable argument, so completely ruled by their instinctual drive, one soon realizes that it is futile, and perhaps even wrong, to wish to take away from them a means of satisfying their interests and replace it by reasonable arguments.

Years of teaching have relieved me of any surprise at the feeble mentality of the man who has once brought himself to accept without criticism all the absurdities that religious doctrines would repeat to him,[1] and even to overlook the contradictions between

---

[1] Who would want to replace the empire of Communism by the empire of Catholicism? Not I. As Leonard Woolf, in his recent *Principia Politica: A Study of Communal Psychology*, courageously writes: 'The Church can and does, from time to time, make pronouncements on religion, morals, metaphysics, politics, or science, the truth of which cannot—for the Catholic—be questioned. The result is that Catholic doctrine has incorporated nearly all the major fantasies and delusions which have had a wide appeal to the irrational in human beings during the last two thousand years.' Mr Woolf was not running for an elective office, nor was he afraid of alienating Franco or official Catholic dogmas, so straightforwardly spoke out.

them. Men often remain for ever children as far as belief in such palpable absurdities as heaven and hell and supernatural qualities assigned to medals or rabbits' feet. As one man has written, 'Let us leave the heavens to the angels and the sparrows.'

Education should lead man to reality and not to illusion, and this is one advantage that the materialists have over the romantic idealists.

The last days of André Gide were filled with doubts. Note one of his conversations with Roger Martin du Gard: 'Have you ever thought about this, Roger? For centuries men had hardly any doubts of their double nature. . . . They knew that their bodies would perish, but as for their immortal souls. . . . And then, all of a sudden, they no longer feel sure! All of a sudden humanity no longer believes in the immortality of the spirit! Think how important it is! It's overwhelming, Roger, isn't it? Overwhelming!'

On another day Gide was concerned with the stupidity of the higher clergy. During the night he had been looking at an anthology of Cardinal Mindszenty's writings. He was disgusted, indignant, and in full rebellion—and, du Gard adds, very aggressive.

'Of course,' Gide said, 'I was horror-struck by that tragic trial in Budapest. But just look at the poor Cardinal's sermons and his pastoral letters! The platitudes! The childishness! the poverty of thought! I've never read anything—any-thing—like it. . . . No, No! The Churches and the Faith have really done too much harm! I cannot remain indifferent to that; right to the end I shall refuse to accept it! Those Churches must come down off their pedestals! We've got to outwit them! Mankind must be set free from their black magic! . . . Tolerance puts weapons in the enemy's hands. If we don't fight them, we might as well give in at once: we might as well admit our defeat. . . . I, for one, am not going to give it! While there's a breath left in me I shall cry, "No!" to the Churches!

'I don't dream,' Gide went on, 'of any after life. On the contrary: the farther I go, the more inacceptable I find the hypothesis of the beyond. Instinctively and intellectually! And I think that in saying that I prove myself much more genuinely spiritual than the believers. . . . It's an idea I often think over. I'd like to develop it a little, if I were given the time.'

And so, after years of probing, I have come to believe with
E. W. Howe, that nothing is true except a few simple fundamentals every man has demonstrated for himself.

When there is doubt, continue to doubt.

Men have been praying for centuries and look at the kind of a
world they have brought into being! The Church has been
flourishing for twenty centuries, and remember Belsen and
Dachau!

In religion what we need is more of Christ, and less of formal
religions, which all too often think for us, interfere in our daily
lives, deprive us of this and that book or play, take our money,
play politics, and often back the most fiendish men and causes. The
most backward countries, now open to Communist infiltration,
are those where religion has been all-powerful.

I believe in one God, the Incomprehensible, whose Nature man
can never know, a God closer to Spinoza than to the God of either
the Old or the New Testament.

I do not wish for a future life as no crueller punishment could
be devised than to live for ever.

W. H. Hudson expresses a modern view of immortality in his
wonderful little essay, 'The Return of the Chiff-Chaff', in his
book *A Traveller in Little Things*, 1921. He says in part: 'Spring's
immortality was in us; ever-living earth was better than any
home in the stars which eye hath not seen nor heart conceived.
Nature was all in all; we worshipped her and her wordless mes-
sages in our hearts were sweeter than honey and the honeycomb.
. . . The "naked shingles of the world" is but a mood of our
transitional day; the world is just as beautiful as it ever was, and
our dead as much to us as they have ever been, even when faith
was at its highest. They are not wholly, irretrievably lost, even
when we cease to remember them, when their images come no
longer unbidden to our minds. They are present in nature:
through ourselves, receiving but what we give, they have become
part and parcel of it and give it an expression. As when the rain
clouds disperse and the sun shines out once more, heaven and
earth are filled with a chastened light, sweet to behold and very
wonderful, so because of our lost ones, because of the old grief at
their loss, the visible world is touched with a new light, a tender-

15

ness and grace and beauty not its own. . . . It is true the power you have worshipped and trusted will destroy you, but you are living today and the day of your end will be determined by chance only. Until you are called to follow them into that "world of light", or it may be of darkness and oblivion, you are immortal.'

That is all.

CHAPTER I

The Bookman as Professor

'A Professor? Ugh!' Remark by a Washington politician.
'This Einstein, has he got anything real on the ball, or is it all theory?' Same source.

For forty-two years I was a teacher, of English (two years) and Comparative Literature (forty years), at Dartmouth College in Hanover, New Hampshire. It is a part of the world I love, and I would not choose to live anywhere else.

The time has come, before it may be too late, to put down some of my thoughts concerning my life work, and report on my experience.

I have seen Dartmouth change from a small college, with a handful of administrators, to a third-rate university, headed by a huge bureaucracy which now occupies several buildings.

I went through Dartmouth on less than a thousand dollars a year; it now costs four or five times as much.

I have lived to see teaching de-emphasized, and research, often of a trivial nature, glorified. I have witnessed a small liberal arts college, a fountain of wisdom as Emerson put it, where there was a friendly and intimate atmosphere, and where the professor had some regard for his students, change into a cold and ruthless place where the student all too often is merely tolerated, where he reeks with apathy and is often more unhappy than he should be.

The faculty which once had power has now become the low man on the totem pole. Favouritism is rampant. The organization man has taken over. Where there was once the fresh air of freedom of speech, there is now an atmosphere of timidity and fear. No opposition to the policies of the administration is tolerated. The college controls all dissemination of news. It might as well be selling a detergent, and for all I know it does. Truth telling and truth seeking is a hazardous occupation.

17

A few months before the poet Dylan Thomas died, I met him at a party given by the writers, Dilys and Alexander Laing, in Norwich, Vermont. Thomas, somewhat exhilarated as usual, asked Mr Laing, as an aside, who I was and what I did. Mr Laing answered, 'He's a professor of Comparative Literature.' Mr Thomas' reply in a shrill and rising inflection was quick and characteristic: 'What does he compare it with, shit?'

On the whole my life as a teacher has been a delightful and happy time (interrupted by many reasonable lengthy trips to Europe where I worked and studied in London, Paris, Berlin, and Stockholm, and a wonderful year of graduate work at Harvard under Irving Babbitt), but it has not been without its hazards, and its inevitable moments of discouragement.

Good teaching, in which the teacher makes an intense effort every day to interest the casual and apathetic undergraduate of our time, can be the most exhausting work known. The man who lectures year after year (I once did this for fourteen years without a break and ended up with a severe heart attack), who gives of himself every hour to hold the attention of his students, many of whom wouldn't be interested if the Devil himself spoke from the platform, who puts himself out to be friendly and helpful to adolescents, often lonely and bewildered young men, in time becomes one of T. S. Eliot's 'hollow men', completely exhausted nervously and physically.

The suicide rate is always higher among intellectuals, sometimes because of overwork, in other instances owing to 'the discrepancy between the material and actual world and that of their thoughts and dreams'. This gulf may cause strange and sudden acts in undergraduates as well, who need sympathetic and understanding treatment.

Good teachers, and therefore popular ones, inevitably arouse envy, jealousy and even hatred, among their less gifted colleagues, who are forced to band together and plan a curriculum that requires students to take their courses.[1] This sometimes involves

[1] In forty-two years I made but one utterance at a faculty meeting, and that was to state that the curriculum under discussion was planned for the faculty and not for the benefit of the students who would be forced to submit to it. I was, of course, snowed under, but a few stalwarts, them-

departmental politics which in cleverness and intrigue match that of the wariest ward heeler. The degree of feeling aroused in a teaching body by a popular teacher among the more frustrated members of the faculty has to be experienced to be believed. Academic life appears to breed far too often petty and mean spirits rather than broad and generous ones which may seem to be a curious phenomenon among men paid to read Plato and the Gospels.

A teacher is also subject to badgering, if not worse, by the Church and professional men of God, the American Legion, and other laudable organizations. Tremendous pressures are at times exerted by politicians on colleges that are not privately endowed, and sometimes even on those that are. Alumni sometimes throw their weight about at the wrong time.[1]

I think it is to the late President Emeritus Hopkins' eternal glory that he once allowed, in the good old days one must add, the Communist Candidate for President, William Z. Foster, to express his ideas before a Dartmouth audience. This would be unlikely to happen today.

Mr Henry Morton Robinson, writing in the November 1955 *Holiday* on the 'Superiority of Ivy League Colleges', says: 'Yet one of the tragedies of our time is the reluctance of many scholars to assert their hereditary independence of thought and speech. This timidity is understandable, perhaps, in those "denominational" schools whose faculty members are expected to sneeze in unison whenever the prebendary takes snuff. And one can almost sympathize with the plight of teachers in state-controlled institutions where county politicians "vote the school money". Caution is the watchword in such places; any departure from orthodoxy— in curriculum, teaching methods, published findings, even in personal reading matter—may cost a faculty member his job.'

selves stimulating teachers, voted with me. The present trend towards required courses is, in my opinion, deplorable, and against all experience. Even worse is the rat race of a three term system in which the students have no leisure to think or to read.

[1] This happened at Dartmouth concerning a professor who was not entirely satisfied with the conduct of the famous, or infamous, Sacco-Vanzetti trial. Needless to say, the then President Ernest Martin Hopkins stood by the professor.

He continues: 'The Ivy League scholar is happily exempt from these frightening pressures. He speaks out and fears no one. He knows, moreover, that his president and board of trustees will back him up—even though they may not agree with his opinions.'

Nevertheless, though this may still be partly true at Dartmouth, there is today far more timidity here than in the time when William Z. Foster could speak, and criticism of the Administration is severely frowned upon. Time marches on, and history and tempers with it. When Senator McCarthy was riding high in his party and scaring the pants off men who should have had more courage and played less politics, he crossed swords with President Pusey of Harvard over the Wendell H. Furry case. Mr Pusey, I am glad to note, held fast to the best traditions of his great university. He boldly announced: 'Harvard is unalterably opposed to Communism. It is dedicated to free inquiry by free men. . . . We deplore the use of the Fifth Amendment . . . but do not regard the use of this constitutional safeguard as a confession of guilt.'

Dartmouth reacted with less courage. President Dickey, on April 30, 1953, speaking at San Diego, California, is reported by *The Southern Cross* to have said: 'I have not been able to escape the conclusion that anyone who invokes the protection of that privilege must accept the fact that by doing so, he, of his own choosing, calls into question the quality of his citizenship. . . . A man who exercises this privilege either genuinely believes his words may incriminate him or he is using the privilege improperly. . . . Either way you take it, it seems to me we must say as a matter of general policy that such a person has compromised his fitness to perform the responsibilities of higher education and unless there is clear proof of peculiar circumstances in the particular instance which would make application of this policy unjust and unwise, the normal consequences of such disability must ensue.'

John R. McLane, one of the senior trustees at that time, asked to clarify Dartmouth's policy as regard the Fifth Amendment, is reported by the newspaper, *The Valley News*, of May 13, 1953, to have said that the trustees and Mr Dickey have taken the following position:

1. Dartmouth has not hired and will not retain on its faculty any person known as a Communist.

2. The Communist, by the very nature of his beliefs, is barred from admittance to the market of ideas which must be approached with a mind free from outside influence.

3. The teacher under questioning who makes use of the Fifth Amendment also forfeits his right to enter the free market of education, and places himself in the same position as the known Communist, so far as his retention on the faculty is concerned.

In other words, any teacher at Dartmouth who avails himself of his constitutional rights will be fired—a far cry from the courage of our forefathers who wrote our Constitution.

Momentarily Dartmouth panicked. Perhaps it is basically a question of an institution which suffers from no inferiority complex and is sure of itself. At any rate, Harvard stood staunchly by the Constitution and Bill of Rights, and in my opinion demonstrated its right to leadership in pointing the way that all Ivy League colleges might wisely have followed.

One rift in the dam and the way to inundation has been made.

After my last lecture at Dartmouth College on May 28, 1964, which attracted more than a thousand listeners, my remarks were broadcast the following Sunday evening over the college radio, but only after much of my criticism of the present Dartmouth administration and trustees had been deleted from the tape. When I remonstrated to one of them, an old friend of college days, that the College had dared to censor my last lecture I did not have the courtesy of a reply. The fact seems to be that the trustees, who appear to love money more than truth, do not allow any editorializing over the college owned radio. All news media is controlled by the administration, nothing is released that might destroy the 'image' of a truth-loving Ivy League school.

Incidentally neither do the trustees allow the publication of the Dartmouth salary scale. The reason for this is obvious as my own salary never reached the level of what is paid a good high school teacher in California, or New Canaan, Connecticut. However, the alumni are led to believe by the College that full professors of my standing get from $15,000 to $18,000 a year. When I retired my salary was a little more than $10,000 a year. It is the deception practised that really tarnishes the image.

Perhaps I am implying that under no circumstance must we ever jeopardize what has been known as the Dartmouth spirit.

Just what is this? Just what is the most important thing about Dartmouth? Administrations, trustees, and faculties come and go, even as do generations of students. Something, however, that which Plato called 'the one in the many', remains constant. It is a bold man who will try to define it, as, perhaps, it is indefinable: an essence, impalpable like a mysterious force, ever living, ever powerful, ever holding us up to our best and to the highest ideals of the College. Ever holding us up to our most honourable selves. It is one thing about Dartmouth that we can all venerate and love. What is this?

I once wrote to some of my students who were in the armed forces overseas during 1943: 'Dartmouth, it seems to me, is a state of mind more than a group of buildings on the Hanover plain, though they, too, through association and memory, are included in this. The intangible thing we call the Dartmouth Spirit is at bottom a spiritual thing which may be traced back to the wilderness days of 1769 when Eleazar Wheelock built the first log cabin to teach the Indian and which has grown and endured, like an ever flowing stream getting deeper and stronger as it reaches the sea, to the present time. It covers all lands, all the seas and great waters, the heavens above, and it stretches on into infinity. It is made up of the love and devotion of thousands. It is composed of the thoughts, feelings, and sacrifices of countless men, almost all of them forgotten now, but whose graves may be seen in the old and new Dartmouth cemeteries. I often walk through them and read their names: Wheelock, Emerson, Tucker, Bill, Laycock, Richardson, Poor, Adams, Stewart, and many others. Most of these men, generally poorly paid, who sought diligently for truth, who worked unceasingly and unselfishly for the good of the College, either as a teacher or administrator, are those who made what we call the Dartmouth Spirit. The strongest manifestation of this spirit is, I think, the love and loyalty for the college held by most Dartmouth men everywhere, but another even more important manifestation is its determination to seek and publish the truth no matter what the cost. When this spirit ceases to be, Dartmouth, too, will cease to exist, even though its campus may be crowded with buildings old, new, and in the process of construction. In the life of learning the spirit is the reality, and not the shadow of it.'

The late President Emeritus Ernest Martin Hopkins, '01, the creator of modern Dartmouth, said during the war: 'It would be a tragic paradox if, as a result of the war, we were to allow our system of higher education to be transformed into the type of education which has made it easy for a crowd of governmental gangsters like Hitler's crowd to commandeer a whole population.'

At Duke University the late Wendell Willkie added a footnote to this: 'The destruction of the tradition of liberal arts, at this crisis in our history, when freedom is more than ever at stake, would mean just that. It would be a crime, comparable, in my opinion, with the burning of the books by the Nazis. And it would have approximately the same results. Burn your books—or, what amounts to the same thing, neglect your books—and you will lose your freedom, as surely as if you were to invite Hitler and his henchmen to rule over you.'

It was in the spirit of these ideas that President Eisenhower made his famous 'book burning' speech at Dartmouth at the 1953 Commencement, which was not appreciably damaged by his 'backing and filling' later on, and which gave great joy to those of us who had fought against 'McCarthyism', surely the spirit of inquisitorial evil reincarnated in our time, with all the resources at our command.

Let it be said and understood at once that any parents who send their sons to a free, non-denominational liberal arts college, are taking a genuine risk. They cannot expect a son to come back with the same ideas with which he went, whether these reflect the Union League Club, Republican isolationism, McCarthyism, the Americanism of the professional patriots, the ideas of his church and Sunday school, his high school, or the home from which he came. If the education 'takes', it becomes a live and vital force which lasts until he dies. If he is well educated he has been taught to think for himself, to develop critical and creative thinking, to read for pleasure and for information, to question, and to doubt. The educated man knows how to *observe* AND to *think*. He is taught to seek the truth whatever the personal cost may be to himself, either in his state of mind (ignorance *is* bliss), or in his actual profession. Seeking truth these days can be a hazardous, costly, and unhappy business, because we are living in an age when almost any idea is suspect, and the man who has ideas becomes all too often a traitor, or a fellow-traveller, in the opinion of the all-too-many.

Henry Steele Commager, an astoundingly prolific historian, thought wisely when he wrote in 1959: 'If we establish a standard of *safe* thinking, we will end up with no thinking at all . . . we cannot . . . have thought half slave and half free. . . . A nation which, in the name of loyalty or of patriotism or of any sincere and high-sounding ideal, discourages criticism and dissent and puts a premium on acquiescence and conformity is headed for disaster.'

What is the liberally-educated man? and how successful is the American liberal arts college in turning him out?

As a basis for an answer to the first question it might be fairer to accept the conclusions of a group of educators who worked on the recent report, 'General Education in School and College', rather than to accept the definition or one person. This report defines him as follows:

'The liberally educated man . . . is articulate, both in speech and writing. He has a feel for language, a respect for clarity and directness of expression, and a knowledge of some language other than his own. He is at home in a world of quantity, and measurement. He thinks rationally, logically, objectively, and knows the difference between fact and opinion. When the occasion demands, however, his thought is imaginative and creative rather than logical. He is perceptive, sensitive to form, and affected by beauty. His mind is flexible and adaptable, curious, and independent. He knows a great deal about the world of nature and the world of man, about the culture of which he is a part, but he is never merely "well informed". He can use what he knows, with judgment and discrimination. He thinks of his business or profession, his family life, and his avocations as parts of a larger whole, parts of a purpose which he has made his own. Whether making a professional or a personal decision, he acts with maturity, balance, and perspective, which comes ultimately from his knowledge of other persons, other problems, other times and places. He has convictions, which are reasoned, although he cannot always prove them. He is tolerant about the beliefs of others because he reflects sincerity, and is not afraid of ideas. He has values, and he can communicate them to others not only by word but by example. His personal standards are high; nothing short of excellence will satisfy him. But service to his society or to his God, not personal satisfaction alone, is the purpose of his excelling. Above all, the liberally-educated man is never a type. He is always unique as a person, vivid in his distinction from other similarly educated persons, while sharing with them the traits we have mentioned.'

Now as to the question of how many college-educated men reach this ideal, I should say that it is a discouraging number and the average college man would be the first to admit it.

In one of the most interesting chapters in *The Education of Henry Adams*, in which Adams discusses his life as a professor, he says: 'The number of students whose minds were of an order above the average was, in his experience, barely one in ten; the rest could not be much stimulated by any inducements a teacher could suggest. All were respectable and, in seven years of contact, Adams never had cause to complain of one; but nine minds in ten take polish passively, like a hard surface; only the tenth sensibly reacts.'

For years I have asked students how they personally would rate themselves, and almost invariably they have answered that one in ten was a fair ratio. However, I would tend to give the present-day student a little more credit. Stimulate his interest, show him the relation of his course of studies to his own life, and his own time, and he will often show astonishing progress in the difficult task of thinking for himself. With all the will in the world he finds the cards stacked against him because all too often he is the victim of obsolete curricula, drab and dull courses he is forced to take, ill-natured and inferior teachers, administrations whose minds and attitudes at times suggest those of a juvenile. If he really begins to be educated it is often in spite of the educational institution rather than because of it. I couldn't begin to estimate the number of students who have told me that the first two years have been a complete loss, and that they only began to realize what it is all about their last year or two.

Logan Pearsall Smith, in his autobiography *Unforgotten Years*, 1938, has something interesting to say concerning the quality of the education he received. It has changed but little today, and I am not at all certain that it is as good as in Smith's time. Who with any degree of certainty could argue that the *quality* of education, the net result, today, is any better than it was in, let us say, Daniel Webster's time? Not this writer.

Mr Smith says: 'I went at the age of sixteen to the near-by Quaker college of Haverford, and began to undergo that vague, diffused kind of intellectual varnishing and plastering over which was then regarded in the United States, and is, I believe, still regarded, as an adequate collegiate education. The scheme of teaching in this small Quaker college, though rather sounder, I believe, than that in some of the larger universities, had but little influence on me: no stirring of the mind resulted from those instructions . . . I and my companions were simply enjoying our brief, irresponsible hour in the sun, before we should take up that business career to which we were destined. That every American should make money, that even those who already possessed it should devote their lives to making more, that all of them without exception should betake themselves every morning to their offices and spend all the hours of sunlight in these great business buildings—this was the universally accepted and grotesque ideal of life in the world we lived in.'[1]

And what of today? Few would so sneer at American business today, but all too often misguided parents now urge their sons to study 'practical' subjects such as economics, thinking that this will help them get into business, whereas if they majored in Latin or Greek they would get a better education, get into the best graduate schools of business, and be as great, if not a greater, financial success than if they had taken nothing but the social sciences during their college years. No doubt these courses have some reason for being, but that they should be stressed as they are today at the expense of the humanities is a dismal mistake.

[1] Robert B. Ryan, 32, the movie actor, once wrote me about his 'wasting four perfectly good years in college'.

Dr Raymond Adams, for many years President of the Thoreau Society at the University of North Carolina, said in his Phi Beta Kappa address there on May 12, 1955: 'Here's another crumb from the very same course of *The Banquet*, the very same paragraph of Dante's book:

We are not to call him a real philosopher who is a friend of wisdom for profit, as are lawyers, physicians, and almost all the members of the religious orders, who do not study in order to know, but in order to get more money or office; and if anyone would give them that which it is their purpose to acquire they would linger over their study no longer. (*Convivio*, III, xi, 102–109.)

Roll that crumb on your tongue awhile. It says that there is a mercenary kind of learning, some of it nothing more than skills, other of it real learning perverted into means toward money or office. In 1955, not in 1308, universities give hundreds of courses that are studied in order to get money or office as soon as possible after graduation; and a department or a discipline or a separate course has a hard time keeping alive in a university unless it can show that studying it will bring cash returns—and quick. In a state university the constituency, the legislators and business interests and citizenry, seldom understand anything but this dollars-and-cents language. If any of you had that motive and got high grades in order to get high salaries or high office later on, then you're in Phi Beta Kappa under false pretences, for "we are not to call him a real philosopher who is a friend of wisdom for profit". '

Dr Adams goes on to say, and I think it true also at Dartmouth, though to a lesser degree, that 'hundreds of people every year finish their courses and get diplomas . . . who never once in their four years fell in love with the thing understood, never once in college felt the ecstasy of learning. In a very real and high sense they have wasted four years . . . in classes and courses that yielded good grades and good skills and were respectably taught and respectably taken and yet never struck the least spark of what could have been a flame. College can be a pedestrian procedure with feet to earth and no wings to lift one; and too often it is just that. It can be a series of semesters with no moments, though in the ecstasy of learning there can be moments that redeem whole semesters. There can be such moments; there *should* be such; but to student after student, year after year, the moments never come. One can graduate without them; one can achieve Phi Beta Kappa without them; but without them graduation and Phi Beta Kappa will profit you nothing—nothing, that is, but money and office.'

Dr Adams' address is so good that I wish I could quote it all, but I have given enough to indicate a truth that most college professors would admit. We fail lamentably to set our students on fire. We fail to develop in them an intellectual curiosity. We fail to arouse them to the belief that truth, too, has its room, its bed, and board. We fail.

We ought to turn out more 'civilized' men than we do. Indeed do we turn out any? Clive Bell, on page 163 of his *Civilization*, says:

'The first step towards civilization is the correcting of instinct by reason; the second, the deliberate rejection of immediate satisfactions with a view to obtaining subtler. . . . From these primary qualities, Reasonableness and a Sense of Values, may spring a host of secondaries, a taste for truth and beauty, tolerance, intellectual honesty, fastidiousness, a sense of humour, good manners, curiosity, a dislike of vulgarity, brutality and over-emphasis, freedom from superstition and prudery, a fearless acceptance of the good things of life, a desire for complete self-expression and for a liberal education, a contempt for utilitarianism and philistinism, in two words: sweetness and light.'

Instead, as a college we are becoming more and more like a great industrial plant, over-organized, over-committed, with far too much centralization of power in the hands of one or two men. There is consequently less and less freedom and responsibility in the faculty, more and more bureaucratic organization in the administration. There is increasing emphasis on the social sciences (which are neither social nor scientific), and less emphasis on the heart of education, the very core of it, the study of MAN through great literatures and philosophy. We are becoming thoroughly Philistine.

Henry Steele Commager in an excellent article in the *New York Times Magazine* for January 29, 1956, writes of the contemporary American college (and he might well be describing Dartmouth): 'Another way to counterbalance the cost of numbers is to cut down substantially on administrative overheads. All too commonly the most impressive buildings on a university campus are the gymnasium and the administration building, and this architectural pre-eminence is not too misleading. The tendency of administration to take over the primary function of any institution—education, religious, economic, or political—is familiar enough. Yet English and European universities manage without an administrative bureaucracy; it is only in the United States that the administrative tail seems too often to wag the educational dog.'

At Dartmouth the number of people on the administration (not faculty) has quadrupled since I began teaching.

This situation wouldn't be so disastrous to an institution like Dartmouth if most members of the administration had had a broad and humanistic education, or were civilized and educated men in Clive Bell's sense, but when many of the top echelon are trained bureaucrats from Washington, or lawyers who yearned for higher things, or men with the souls of clerks, Philistines in fact, then, indeed, liberal education does deteriorate rapidly.

I am quite sure that when Aristotle in the *Politics* asserts that education should be valued 'not because it is necessary or useful, but because it is liberal and beautiful', he would be laughed out of court by most of the administration and trustees of today.

From a wise book that all parents should read who have sons or daughters in college, *To Teach the Senators Wisdom*, 1952, by J. C. Masterman, Provost of Worcester College, Oxford, I take the following: 'Latin may be said to be the foundation of every sound system of education. For teaching precision of thought and economy in the use of words it has no equal; nor do I believe that the profitable study of modern language or history or law, or English literature for that matter, is possible without it. Latin is the basis of our Western European civilization. Yet for all that . . . it seems to me that English can rise to the same level of dignity and beauty as Latin of the Golden Age.'

Today only a handful of students study either Latin or Greek, and never has literature fallen to a lower ebb than today, where obscurity has become a virtue, and clarity a vice.

James A. Froude once wrote: 'Virgil and Horace lived nearly two thousand years ago, and belong to a society of which the outward form and fashion have utterly perished. But Virgil and Horace do not grow old, because while society changes men continue, and we recognize in reading them that the same heart beat under the toga which we feel in our own breasts.'

During the war I had a letter from a former student, then a Captain in the United States Marine Corps in the South Pacific area, who wrote: 'From my experience, I see no value in compulsory science courses. When I think how much more beneficial the arts were, I feel very sorry for every lad that has to struggle through such junk. The majority of our technically trained men have been failures. I have seen divinity students improvise things to put captured equipment in order that have baffled our specialists. They are trained to think beyond a smug formula. I hope someday the colleges become liberal enough to allow students to pick their entire course without any hitches. To my mind, colleges have compulsory courses to keep old and unqualified men in their positions.'

I believe that the Captain was mainly correct.

Train a man to think out things for himself and he can turn to almost anything. This may be the main fault of our service academies, West Point and Annapolis, though I am aware that efforts have been made to give their men some liberal arts courses. Any naval or army officer with some imagination, or even good military sense, should have expected the attack on Pearl Harbour on December 7, 1941, but even when warned, and told that it was on its way, some of the military refused to believe it. A lot of good men lost their lives owing to this hardening of the brain arteries in the higher echelons. This has been all too true in all wars.

Many Dartmouth men had magnificent war records as commissioned officers. Their education, though far from being perfect, sometimes gave them a superiority over the technically trained professional soldier. This was especially true of those Dartmouth students who had been taught to think.

'I well remember,' writes J. C. Masterman, 'a stocking manufacturer coming to me and asking for someone to draft into his

30

business. "What sort of man do you want?" I said. "A first in Greats,"[1] he replied. "I've never been to Oxford or to any other university, but they tell me that the first in Greats is the man with the best brain. I can teach him all the technical knowledge he requires, provided he has a keen and an adaptable brain." He may have been aiming rather high, but his theory was surely right.'

John Henry Newman's confession of faith concerning education was: 'If I had to choose between a so-called University which dispensed with resident and tutorial superintendence, and gave its degrees to any person who passed an examination in a wide range of subjects, and a University which had no professors, or examinations at all, but merely brought a number of young men together for three or four years, and then sent them away . . . if I was asked which of these two methods was the better discipline of the intellect—mind I do not say which is morally the better, for it is plain that compulsory study must be good and idleness an intolerable mischief—but if I must determine which of the two courses was the more successful in training, moulding, enlarging the mind, which sent out men the more fitted for their secular duties, which produced better public men, men of the world, men whose names descend to posterity, I have no hesitation in giving the preference to that University which did nothing, over that which exacted of its members an acquaintance with every science under the sun.'

A great American jurist, Learned Hand, has written in his book *Spirit of Liberty*, 1952: *'Fais ce que voudra*. I would write that on the gates of every university; and I would shape the curriculum solely to teach and learn what these words really mean.'

If the reader is interested let him turn back once again to read Rabelais' own great book, *Gargantua and Pantagruel*, from which this phrase is taken.

One more quotation, this time from the late James Norman Hall. In his book *My Island Home* he says: 'Unless life changes

---

[1] A first in Greats means a man who has studied a classical course or a liberal arts course and done well in it. He must have a reading knowledge of Greek and Latin, some ancient history, philosophy, etc. What we call here in America: a major in the humanities.

beyond anything we have reason to expect, liberal arts colleges will never outlive the need for them, provided that they remain true to their long-range purposes . . . and that is to teach young men and women that the bird in the bush is worth two in the hand.'

And what in general terms is the situation today? Instead of colleges being places where a student learns discrimination and good judgment, to think out things for himself, to be himself instead of being the perfect conformist, to sense the difference between bad and good taste, between the important and the unimportant, they are all too often rolling mills of learning, with no co-ordination of purpose whatever between departments. In fact the purpose of education is scarcely ever defined.

The student is forced to take a smattering of this or that, which he completely forgets a few weeks after the course is over, and which makes no permanent impression on him whatever. He must read dull textbooks, most of them written solely for profit, to take even duller examinations, some of which, to make it easier for the instructor, are 'machine-corrected'. Little has happened to the young man's mind or spirit in the process. Most of them are bored to death.

The young men of today, even in the best preparatory schools like Andover and Exeter, which are competing with each other to get their boys into the best universities (generally Harvard, Yale and Princeton), and colleges, become the slaves of examinations which have become an end in themselves rather than a means to an end.

Few students on graduation are able to write a decent English sentence; few can converse or even read with facility in any foreign language, least of all an ancient one; few have developed the ability to gain knowledge of a subject on their own or have cultivated a taste for reading which is the basis of all solid intellectual advance. Fewer still have developed a critical intelligence, desperately needed in the world of today.

With the ROTC now ensconced in many liberal arts colleges, the quality of education is lower than usual. For instance, a few years ago at Dartmouth it was possible for a student in his whole four years to have not more than half-a-dozen elective courses out of the sixty required for graduation, and elective courses are the heart and soul of every curriculum. Each semester the ROTC student has to take a course in military science, universally acknowledged to be badly taught and an insult to any intelligent student; he has to complete the requirements for his major subject, usually ten courses; and in his senior year he may have no electives at all as he has to take not only his military science courses but also, *for the whole year*, a course called 'Great Issues', which not only is supposed to keep the educated senior informed about the important issues of the day, but is also supposed to teach him how to read the *New York Times*, something he should have learned to do in the eighth grade or, with a proper educational background, should be able to do himself without difficulty.

A great many courses merely funnel out information on which the student dutifully puts into his notebook and later writes again at examination time. I remember once taking a course in economic botany, and all I remember is that the state of Maine produced that year a certain number of bushels of potatoes, which fact was available to anybody who could afford a *World Almanac*. I recall nothing else whatever.

The student forgets such a course immediately, and unless his mind has been stirred to think and act for itself he has simply been wasting his and the instructor's time. It is safe to say that probably 75 per cent of his college courses are of this type, and he is lucky if it isn't 90 per cent. The second rate teacher and the second rate student, who seldom has the chance or the incentive to be a first rate one (incidentally marks have little or no connection with a first rate student), merely regurgitates what he has memorized from his textbooks and lectures. However, the first rate instructor and the first rate student may accomplish much more.

The sign of a first class man is distinction of thought: that is, one who has ideas. Genuine ability in a student shows itself in his power of discrimination, in the sorting out of the essential from the unessential, of the important from the trivial.

Examinations, instead of the memory tests they usually are, should be, instead, tests which reveal the quality of a student's thinking rather than of acquired information. It is on this basis that most of our examinations in comparative literature were made out.

Hugh MacLennan, in his book *Scotsman's Return and Other Essays*, has some intelligent things to say about education. He obviously believes in the classical disciplines. 'The purpose of education,' he writes, 'was merely to teach the student to read, to write, to learn basic mathematics, to work in a disciplined way and finally to expose him while doing this to the best minds in civilization and to let the classics become a part of him.' He continues, 'One of the losses of contemporary education "is the ancient respect for truth as something valuable and unassailable in itself, as something hard to find but precious, as something which cannot be juggled with by advertisers and politicians without regard to the final consequences, as something more important, however austere it may be, than conformity for the sake of comfort to any market place necessity of the moment".'

This is all too true in the modern college today.

I had a fairly rough time with the faculty, as, from the start, I unfortunately was a 'popular' professor, with a distinct talent for attracting students. In the winter of 1940, for instance, my electives were something more than two hundred students, while three other professors combined had only thirty-five men. This lopsided situation went on for many years, and the climax was reached in 1964 when 1,060 students elected my courses.

Instead of reaping praise for the huge amount of work, under the strain of which I once had a physical breakdown, I earned increased jealousy of many of my colleagues.

Men took our courses because, for one reason or another, they wanted to take them. Competition is good for any teacher, and we had to work hard or fold up our tent. Always out-voted by other departments, we never played politics (there were only two or three of us to vote), never had any voice (at least I never did) in educational policy, and all we could do was to mind our own business and tend to our knitting, which we did.

Certainly one of the most interesting facts about our department was that, as long as I have been connected with it, it was the subject of constant criticism from certain members of the faculty, especially those with whom we were in competition for students. I regard this as a mark of distinction. None of these critics, so far as I can remember, ever took the trouble to go to any of our lectures, and there is no doubt that this constant behind-the-back carping, familiar I might say to every college, and about every excellent teacher, originated almost entirely because of our large electives.

I know that one department in my early days used to have special meetings now and then to discuss the alchemy of my apparent appeal to students. This occurred when their electives dropped a perceptible degree, and ours went up, which happened rather too often for my own good. I had my defenders in that department, but I fear they were few and far between. I was accused of about everything from unprofessional ethics to downright dishonesty in marking. In my younger days I was at times indignant; I had my older colleague Professor Stewart correct my exams. This made no difference in my electives. I finally accepted with resignation, and even some amusement, as a part of the college scene, the envy, jealousy and even downright ill will of men whose names I did not know, and for whom I personally had nothing but good will.

Woe to the young instructor who becomes popular with the undergraduates. He will be immediately under suspicion no matter how good he is, and at the worst will be hounded and badgered, calumniated to an amazing degree, and it will take much character and will for him to weather the storm.

Gerald Warner Brace, who has taught English in several colleges, including Dartmouth, writes in his novel, *The Spire*: 'I wish you'd tell me why the teaching profession, and English teaching especially, leads to the destruction of normal integrity. Did you ever see so much assembled vanity, hypocrisy, affectation, and general masculine atrophy? I ask you candidly whether it is possible to remain decently human under such conditions.'

And another distinguished writer who ought to know about such things is the late J. Frank Dobie, of Austin, Texas, formerly on the faculty of the University of Texas, who wrote: 'With numerous exceptions, academicians the world over are a lady of Shalottish kind of people looking at the reflection of life in a looking glass instead of diving in the stream of life itself. Or if they do essay diving, they are apt to be splay.

'A majority of them distrust vitality and are "fit to live with maiden aunts and keep tame rabbits". As scholars they must concern themselves with what has been; yet they are not to be singled out as the chief maintainers of Tory strongholds. A Tory is one who is afraid of change and affects the attitude of holiness towards things as they are, because the arrangement assures special privileges for himself. The Tory's coat of arms is a sitting hen. There are always Tories everywhere. . . . They manipulate actions in all sorts of ecclesiastical and educational institutions in order to embalm their own corpses with the complexion of life. Yet, witness, I stand in bareheaded salute to all genuine scholars, of all creeds and tempers. They are the only preservers and fertilizers of civilization down the ages. . . .'

It has always appeared curious to me that men who are paid for the pleasure of reading great writers like Plato, Montaigne, Emerson, or St Beuve can become as envious and petty as frustrated old maids condemned to a perpetual frigidity. I long ago decided that I preferred the company of business men, doctors, or lawyers, than to that of many, but not all, of my profession.

A successful teacher must not only know his subject at least a little better than his students, but he must also have histrionic ability, a sense of humour, a sympathetic view towards the young (who between the ages of sixteen and twenty-two go through the most difficult period of their lives), the ability to speak clearly but without pompousness (whirling constantly a Phi Beta Kappa key), and above all he should have a *jeux d'esprit*.

As J. C. Masterman has written, and I believe it is true: 'The *jeux d'esprit* of professors will be remembered long after all their learning is forgotten. I shall always remember a bishop who dined one night in Common Room, and next whom I sat. Over the soup his conversation, in which I did not take the major part, was concerned with some philosophic niceties in the works of the early Fathers. As the evening wore on, the bishop unbent more and more. Of his early remarks I remembered nothing, but I treasure his farewell utterance—for it was a *cri de coeur*. "Ah," he said, slowly shaking his head, "had I but known that spades were trumps, I should have played the hand far otherwise!" '

Very often college administrators are men who have lamentably failed as teachers, and, frustrated and embittered, spend part of their time harassing in small and petty ways their betters on the faculty. Viewing these men in committee meetings is an education in itself, for their preciseness in the use of the slide rule, as well as their strict interpretation of college regulations, is comedy in the grand manner.

It has been my experience that most committee meetings are a grievous waste of energy, and that one good man could accomplish the same end in about one-fifth the time. There are, however, born committee men, just as there are born paper hangers, and bottle capmakers, and they have to be kept busy. They are men generally in favour with the administration, and most dutifully almost invariably carry out the administration's wishes. There are, of course, exceptions, and I was on one committee when one other man often stood out with me against all the high college brass, but he was decidedly an exception.

What some American philologs think about, and listen to at the Modern Language Association meetings, may be understood by the programme of one of the meetings of the MLA of America. The paper in question was entitled: *Epanaphora and Epanorthosis in 'Leaves of Grass'*, by a southwest professor from the Texas State College for Women. It was described soberly as follows: [Heretofore the frequency of *epanaphora* and *enaporthosis* in the 'Leaves' and their relation to Whitman's lyricism have not been noted. Initial repetition (epanaphora), involving units of even eight words, and extending to a thirty-four line sequence, characterizes 4,000 out of 10,500 lines. Repetition within lines (epanorthosis) occurs in 4,397 lines out of 10,500 governing sometimes 50 per cent of the words in a passage.]

It could be argued plausibly that teachers could spend their time in more profitable ways if they played scrabble, or roared over the unfunny antics of Martin and Lewis.

If the instructor, however, writes enough papers of this kind, promotion in most educational institutions will come to him. Certainly there can be no other valid excuse for writing them.

Comparative literature as taught at Dartmouth before I retired could be defined as the study of literature and ideas in their international relationships. We taught courses including American, English, Italian, French, and German thought. We also had a course on the Romantic Movement from 1750 to 1830 in France, England and Germany. Later on courses were added on rebel thought, modern thought, the history of literary criticism (which I studied under Irving Babbitt at Harvard),[1] the modern novel, the nature writers, a course on the great travel books, arctic, antarctic, and so on, mountain books and the classics in nature writing (called by Henry Beston a pioneer course), a course on Dante and the Middle Ages, and a course on Chinese art and literature.

The ideas and literature of Western Civilization were presented in a lively fashion as truthfully and as impartially as possible. It was hoped that those who took the courses would develop a critical acumen to appraise them for themselves. No student can pass in review before the great thinkers of the past without having his own mind tempered and geared to meet with less friction the intricate problems of our times. The rare student may even achieve the miracle of creative thought for himself.

I have always thought a statement by Marcel Proust had real validity and meaning in regard to that intangible and not easily measured process we call higher education, as elusive as quicksilver, and as delicate as a rainbow. He once wrote: 'No man can be certain that he has indeed become a wise man—so far as it is possible for any of us to be wise—unless he has passed through all the fatuous or unwholesome incarnations by which that ultimate stage must be preceded. . . . We are not provided with wisdom, we must discover it for ourselves after a journey through the wilderness which no one else can take for us, an effort which no one can spare us, for our wisdom is the point of view from which we come at last to regard the world!'

---

[1] I introduced this course as the 'History of French Criticism' as it was called at Harvard. The French Department, suspecting something, refused me permission to introduce it into the curriculum. Identically the same course was accepted when I changed the title to the 'History of Literary Criticism'.

This I subscribe to.

Our department always hoped that through its courses the wilderness may become for the student more civilized and urbane. It is hoped that this happens *during* the course, but also *long after* the course has been taken.

We have always hoped, often I realize vainly, that as the student reads and thinks about the ideas to which he is subjected, willingly, as no student is forced to elect our courses, he will become more international in his thinking, less provincial, more intellectually curious, and more aware of the significance of facts, ideas, and events than before he took the course.

We tried to stimulate the student to want to make this exciting journey for himself. We also wanted to help him make an original contribution, if possible to the variegated whole of human life, as full and as truly characteristic as his nature permitted. Through the reading of great books the department attempted to develop the student's mental and emotional resources, so that he might lead a balanced, moderate, and even joyous and reasonable existence. We were, in fact, really teaching ethics.

Through a synthesis of Western ideas we hoped that this might point toward a new society in which all men, irrespective of colour, race, or creed, may share access to the world's physical resources, and above all the resources of the human mind. Unless this occurs we believed that the world will constantly be dislocated by wars and revolutions. By devoting ourselves to a study of the great minds and great books of the past and present, we hoped to add to and enrich the individual response of the student's mind.

I personally have believed that the main purpose of our courses was to aid the student to a broader and deeper knowledge of himself and the world about him, to a keener vision of purpose, to make him *want* to read and *understand*, above all, as Joseph Conrad has said, to make him *see*. I have hoped that the more knowledge of great books and of great ideas he had, the quicker would he rid his mind of waste material picked up during his 'fatuous incarnations', and so make his mind a keener instrument (more critical in other words) to solve the problems he is sure to face in his own life.

I think that few liberal arts students tend to remember much of material in a course, but if the course has been successful and the instructor has succeeded in his purpose, something will have happened to the student along the way so that he will never be quite the same again. A mere accumulation of facts and information is not enough. The student should have more of a thirst for knowledge, he should have more awareness of life and the beauty of the world about him, and he should, if he is fortunate, be seeking from now on the *significance* of the material studied in the course. What does it all mean in the relation to his own life in these United States in his own time?

We have desired above all that our courses give breadth of knowledge and even that rare quality *understanding*: we hope our students will comprehend better the universal human spirit as represented by various races and nationalities, for without this understanding and intelligent action upon it, in a world constantly shrinking, we are utterly lost.

Considering the world conditions of the present, I believe that courses in comparative literature must inevitably help to prepare undergraduates to develop a global outlook, to try to understand the Russians and the Chinese, two great peoples we must learn to live with, from the point of view of a Russian or a Chinese, and not always from the point of view of a midwestern high tariff isolationist, a member of the American Legion, many of whom are not exactly experts of foreign affairs, or any ignoramus who happens to be in Congress who scarcely knows where Russia or China is. With the H-bomb the property of Russia, the ENEMY, we, unless we perish, must leave our provincial and isolationist thinking behind. We *must* know about all the countries of importance in the world: their ideas, their problems, their way of life, history, traditions, point of view, art, literature, and philosophy. We must know something about their people. They are far more important than their leaders, who may well be international gangsters. We must know what makes these people tick, think and act the way they do, because, whether we like it or not, we *must* live with them, and tolerate them. As Communism is here to stay for a while (though it will unquestionably change as time goes on as it has changed already) we must learn to live with it. It is quite possible that Russia and China have something to teach us.

Change in the curriculum will mean little unless the teacher himself is alert enough, and intense enough, to hold the student's attention, and to stimulate his intellectual and emotional processes along paths that will lead him somewhere: presumably to what the humanists are wont to call the good life. What is more important than the regurgitation of notes and textbook material on examinations is to give the student a better sense of values in the only world he is ever going to know, to make him see the direction in which he is heading, and to make him see the meaning of what he has been studying.

The late Dr Einstein has said: 'It is not enough to teach man a speciality though he may become a kind of useful machine, but not a harmoniously developed personality. It is essential that the student acquire an understanding of and a lively feeling for values. He must acquire a vivid sense of the beautiful and of the morally good.

'Otherwise he with his specialized knowledge more closely resembles a well-trained dog than a harmoniously developed person. He must learn to understand the motives of human beings, their illusions and their sufferings, in order to acquire a proper relationship to individual fellow men and to the community.

'These precious things are conveyed to the younger generation through personal contact with the teacher rather than through textbooks. It is this that primarily constitutes and preserves culture. This is what I have in mind when I recommend the "humanities" as important, not just dry specialized knowledge in the fields of history and philosophy.'

What Dr Einstein speaks of as 'personal contact with the teacher' is what drains his life blood if he has several hundred students each semester, as under normal conditions I always had. It is also what makes his work rewarding. His influence on young men is incalculable and in most cases, I think in fairness to teachers, dull or interesting as the case may be, it is beneficial rather than harmful.

No less a person than George Kennan, one of the most astute of our diplomats, and so knowledgeable that he had to be shelved, wrote in the May 1953 *Atlantic*:

'Whoever would understand foreign affairs, therefore, cannot and will not do it solely by understanding the intricacies of tariffs or the various classifications of treaties or the ways in which the United Nations Charter differs from the Covenant of the League of Nations, or the techniques of sampling mass opinion. International affairs are primarily a matter of the behaviour of governments. But the behaviour of governments is in turn a matter of the behaviour of individual man in a political context, and of the workings of all those basic impulses—national feeling, charity, ambition, fear, jealousy, egotism, and group attachment—which are the stuff of his behaviour in the community of other men.

'Whoever does not understand these things will never understand what is taking place in the interrelationships of nations. And he will not learn them from courses that purport to deal with international affairs alone. He will learn them, rather, from those things which have been recognized for thousands of years as the essentials of humanistic study: from history and from the more subtle and revealing expressions of man's nature that go by the name of art and literature. . . .

'It is my impression, from the recollections of my days as an undergraduate, that understanding based on a firm grasp of the humanities, and character based on an uncompromising integrity in all personal associations, are the very essence of a liberal education and represent goals to which our colleges have clung in the face of very considerable pressures. This is my idea: let those students who want to prepare themselves for work in the international field read their Bible and their Shakespeare, their Plutarch and their Gibbon, perhaps even their Latin and their Greek, and let them guard as the most precious of their possessions that concept of personal conduct which has grown up around the honour system, but of which the honour system is only a part and a symbol. Let them guard that code of behaviour which means that men learn to act towards each other with honour and truthfulness and loyalty, to bestow confidence when confidence is asked, and to build within themselves those qualities of self-discipline and self-restraint on which the integrity of a public service must be founded.'

During the Second World War, after being turned down for technical reasons in November 1942 for a commission in the Navy (I was then nearly forty-five years old), aware of the vast gulf between a world in flames and the remote classrooms of Dartmouth, I succeeded in procuring various speakers to talk to my classes on the burning issues of the day, or on some of the great events of our time. As usual I drew some criticism for this from some members of the faculty, who asked, with apparent reasonableness, what this had to do with comparative literature? My only answer was that with a world in flames it was perhaps justifiable to try to lessen the distance between the classroom and the world at large—a world at war—which was to take the lives of many of the listeners.

In spite of all criticism I persisted. Among the speakers were Major John Howland, fresh from Guadalcanal, the late General Robert C. Richardson, USA retired, who had been in command of the Mid-Pacific area, Sergeant Meryll Frost, himself a serious war casualty, who was on General Doolittle's committee to investigate the relationship between the enlisted personnel and the officers, Frank Wallace, who opened the prosecution's case at the Nurnberg trials, the writer Henry Miller, Anais Nin, who drew at least 400 students to her lecture, Albert E. Kahn, Robert Frost, Henry Beston, Mrs Stafford, Admiral Peary's daughter, Lewis Mumford, Charles Jackson, the late Robert Lincoln O'Brien, Wing-tsit Chan, Dimitri von Mohrenschildt, Vilhjalmur Stefansson, Ernest Martin Hopkins, New Hampshire Supreme Court Justice Amos Blandin, John S. Dickey, Paul Sample, Alexander Laing, various professors on the faculty, and other distinguished men.

This programme was carried out without extra cost to the college, or to anyone else, and proved highly successful so far as student interest was concerned.

During the war a course was planned on democratic thought and ideas in America to be given by about a dozen carefully selected members of the faculty. Though I had given such a course for nearly a quarter of a century, I was neither consulted in planning it, nor asked to contribute any lectures. The ironical result, which I confess gave me a little innocent merriment, was that the course drew only about ten students, while my course on American Thought drew more than ten times as many. This fact did not endear me to the good and brave men concerned. Their course soon folded up.

During the war teaching had its particular hazards. It must be remembered that Dartmouth at that time was a Navy college and its student body, predominantly Navy, but with many Marines, consisted of many men who, under ordinary conditions, would never have been able to get into a first-class Eastern College, owing to inadequate preparation and low scholastic ratings. However, I never had a more interesting group to work with, and the effect of Dartmouth on many of them was astounding. One could almost *see* their interests and horizons broaden, their intellectual curiosity quicken, their views and opinions change, including, alas, their religious views. This naturally caused pain to the Catholic Church, especially, which has a wholly understandable desire to educate its own, and to protect them from ideas inimical to the faith.

This question of the Catholic student sent to a liberal Protestant non-denominational college is not without interest to the whole system of higher education. It is one thing for the Catholic student, from a liberal or 'Commonweal' type of Catholic family, to come voluntarily to a liberal college; it is quite another when he is sent by the United States Navy, perhaps against his will, or his parent's wishes, and certainly against the wishes of his Church. Trouble was almost certain to ensue, as it did, though I have testimony to the effect that most of the Catholic students profited greatly by the liberal atmosphere of Dartmouth, by its matter-of-fact acceptance of ideas, and by the general atmosphere of intellectual freedom.

At Dartmouth and in other Ivy League colleges, together with some smaller endowed colleges such as Williams, Amherst or Bowdoin, there is less fear of ideas, nor is there any orthodox religious line. Religious thought, however, is encouraged, and in fact sincere efforts are being made at Dartmouth to bring the student back to Christianity. It must be admitted, however, that the results of these efforts have been far from overwhelming. However, the chapel ceiling has been redecorated, and this may help.

An orthodox and devout Roman Catholic is allowed to read, to see, and to believe, only what the Church permits, in matters of faith and morals, or specifically in the field of religion and philosophy. This he cannot do at Dartmouth as many of the books assigned are still on the Index, forbidden, that is, to good Catholics.

Perhaps the reader may better understand this issue if he is aware of the great many attacks by conservatives in religion and philosophy on the ideas of the democratic educator, John Dewey, one of the finest Americans of our time. Though Dewey's philosophy is read and studied, if not universally admired, in most philosophy departments in the non-denominated colleges, he is still anathema to the orthodox.

In the fall of 1939, and this kind of attack has been going on ever since, as my files indicate, a Father O'Connell charged that Dewey and three of his associates, Professors W. H. Kilpatrick, R. L. Thorndike, and Harold Rugg, all prominent in their respective fields, had, for more than three decades, 'made Teacher's College (Columbia) their point of vantage in their attempted destruction of Christian aims and ideals in American education'.

He goes on to say that John Dewy's theory of education 'ignores God, the supernatural, religion, the Ten Commandments, the eternal moral law, the soul, immortality; everything, in fact, which is above and beyond the purely empirical realm of existence'.

This good priest is quite correct, from his own rigid and authoritative point of view, in his accusation. Dewey has long made it clear in his books, *A Common Faith*, and in his more famous *The Quest for Certainty*, that the only values he can believe in are those which may be gained from experience (empiricism) itself, and that he has no faith whatever in transcendental values of religious and philosophical absolutes. We must create our own values empirically from the stuff of life itself, and not look for them, mystically, in some supernatural realm, beyond the veil or in some imaginary kingdom. The quest for certainty, according to Dewey; that we are living in a Christian universe, a teleological world inspired by some supernatural, all powerful, Christian God, who promises eternal Paradise to any believer, is gone for ever. The truths we are supposed to live by, God, free-will, and immortality, must give way to the relative values and truths of the here and now.

For Dewey the words soul and immortality are devoid of real meanings. They are 'unknowns' and we must use as our starting point 'knowns', or facts in our experience, and work pragmatically from there. Dewey is a relativist; Father O'Connell and his Church are authoritarian and absolutist. There can never be any agreement between those two schools of thought.

The Church's attitude towards Dewey is the same it took to-ward Galileo, Bruno, Copernicus, Darwin, Freud, and other important thinkers with whom their theology disagrees.

The late Dr L. J. A. Mercier, once Professor of Philosophy at Harvard, remarked before the National Catholic Alumni Federation that 'naturalism', and Dewey was a naturalist rather than a supernaturalist, 'must be defeated if Western Civilization in general and our American institutions in particular are to be saved'.

Naturalism completely ignores the Christian God and makes Nature (as Bruno and Spinoza did) self-sufficient and supreme. It also places Man in nature along with other animals without soul or transcendental significance. In other words a naturalist is one for whom, as Theophile Gautier remarked, the blood of Christ was not shed.

With this brief interlude into philosophy the sudden attack on my reputation during the war may better be understood. Without previous warning, I found myself in the September 1943 issue of the Catholics' weekly, *America*, the object of a bitter attack (though my name was not mentioned), based solely on the testimony, in the form of a letter home, of a young and intellectually immature Catholic student, whose name I never troubled to find out.

This vicious and unprovoked attack on my professional good name and character included also Dartmouth College and most of the faculty.

It can, I think, only be understood in the light of the Church's attacks on Dewey and other pragmatists, whose concepts are not in tune with Catholic teaching. It shows how bitter the Catholic educators felt about circumstances which sent their obedient and intellectually submissive sons to institutions which for centuries had enjoyed the tradition of free and liberal thinking even in matters of religion.

I had given my course on American thought (which was now under attack) to many more than 1,000 students who choose it as an elective over a period of nearly a quarter of a century. So far as I knew up to that time nobody had been 'corrupted' by it, nor had I ever had my character assailed because of it in a national weekly.

The subject that was upsetting the student, with whom I could entirely sympathize and to whom, given the opportunity, I could easily have explained the differences between Unitarianism and Roman Catholicism, was Ralph Waldo Emerson, a philosophical anarchist, who did not happen to believe in the divinity of Jesus, nor in the mysterious doctrine of the Trinity. Emerson was also America's greatest mystic who believed only what he heard directly from his voices, without any intermediary of Church or priest, from what he chose to call the Over-Soul.

The article in *America* was called 'Unconquerable Spirit', and it said in part: 'Disheartening is the story told in a letter from a former Catholic-college student. Today he is studying in the Navy V-12 Unit of a noted Eastern institution. He wonders why he and his fellow young Americans are assigned to training in an atmosphere at once fetid and lethal to our ideals.'[1]

He described my course as 'the most pagan thing you can imagine'.

Quoting, out of context, he reports me as saying: 'if you're going to sin, do it with a clear conscience. . . . There is only a thin veneer which separates man from his Simian ancestors. . . . In the eyes of God, a mythical creature, all men are equal. . . . Man is endowed by His Creator—this was before the doctors knew about hormones—with certain inalienable rights, etc.'

[1] Fetid, according to my dictionary, means 'having an offensive smell'.

The editorial went on to say with quite a few irrelevant clichés, it seemed to me, 'Nor can we see why this young man, now preparing to become an officer, to lead others into the shadow of death and perhaps to die for his country, should be exposed to such a faculty. Hitler himself could not better prepare him to betray his oath to his flag, to refuse obedience to orders, to throw overboard every duty and abandon the American people.

'It is time that someone looked into the quality of information pawned off as "American Thought" in an institution of this kind.'

Some did in the persons of the late Honourable Senator David I. Walsh of the Sovereign State of Massachusetts, and the Honourable John W. McCormack of the House from the same State.

The whole attack, based on no evidence whatever except a young boy's letter, blandly assumes that no one, not even a man who spent his life in reading and study, has the right to speak publicly on philosophic or religious matters unless he agrees *in toto* with Catholic teaching, and assumes their tone.

If this episode has any real significance, save a personal one, it is to show the vast gulf that lies between the point of view of a liberal arts college and a Roman Catholic institution of higher learning, though it is, of course, quite possible that the magazine spoke only for itself, but I very much doubt this.

The article finally came into the hands of the two members of Congress mentioned above who protested to the Navy Department. I believe that the late Senator Walsh was at the time Chairman of the Naval Relations Committee and had considerable influence. The Navy Bureau of Personnel in a letter, a copy of which I later saw, pointed out to these distinguished statesmen that the course was not required of anybody, that it was taken at the student's own option, and went on to say: 'It is not believed, however, that the Navy Department should take action which would imply censorship of the content of elective courses in American colleges and universities.' And that, so far as I know, was that.

Throughout those weeks I maintained a dignified silence, a cordial relationship as it had always been with the local Catholic priest, but did feel it necessary at the beginning of every course thereafter to warn the students, navy and marine, concerning the kind of course it was: that it dealt with ideas, that ideas were unsettling, and if they distrusted ideas they had better drop the course. As a matter of record hundreds of Catholic students took my courses and one wrote me, most astonishingly, that 'he had learned more good Catholicism from me than from all the priests he had ever had'. I assume that he meant that he now knew the distinction between the simple Christianity of Jesus, and the complex theology and dogma of the institutionalized Church. Dante had known this long before.

I might say that I have never been able to get a Catholic priest to speak to my classes to explain the Catholic position, in contradistinction, let us say, to Unitarianism. I have assumed that they have not been allowed to do this. I can see why, for from their point of view there is no question as to where the truth lies: wholly in the Catholic position.

This attitude of a powerful and great Christian Church in its intolerance towards ideas with which it disagrees has been carried on with increasing intensity by demagogic politicians owing to the astonishing rise in strength and power of Communistic Russia, a totalitarian power which is a constant threat to us, and which gives demagogues a wonderful excuse to throw their weight about, disparaging anybody or any idea with which they disapprove. Russia's rise to that of a great power has been used cleverly by unscrupulous men and professional patriots as an excuse for an all out attack on ideas and books which do not fit their own narrow concepts of Americanism.

It is indeed unfortunate for the Roman Church, it seems to me, that Senator McCarthy, a Roman Catholic, should have injected, perhaps inadvertently, the issue of Protestantism in his attacks on the clergy with all the fervour and venom of an early Spanish inquisitor. It is bad enough to cause books to be burned, but it is even worse to start a Holy War, and to inject into the bloodstream of the body politic the idea that Protestantism is somehow, by the nature of things, connected with Communism. Here he started something that brought about his eclipse.

Educators have been alarmed for some time by the growing censorship of school and college textbooks in this country. Anyone who does not concur with the isolationist, reactionary, America-First views, becomes *ipso facto* subversive—a Communist or, even worse, a pinko or fellow-traveller; their books have been attacked and school boards, feeling the pressure often of illiterate members on a school board, have removed them from the classroom.

It was dangerous during McCarthy's heyday to read and to think, but I then took the stand, boldly and without any equivocation whatever, that, personally as an American scholar of excellent repute, I would read what I wished and think as I pleased and would continue to speak out against what I considered un-American tactics wherever and whenever I saw them. I refused to be one of the sheep-like pedagogues who write sheep-like textbooks which try to please every professional patriot in the land, provincial and ignorant school boards, and try to become all things to all men.

In many instances librarians have been persuaded to remove textbooks, or not to order material or books that might create a controversy. Self-appointed committees were organized in some areas to 'screen' the books used by colleges or by the general population. Thus books that have been in use for years suddenly become suspect when an unfavourable review appears in print, or when the author is credited with a decent liberal idea. This sounds more like Ireland, Spain or Mexico than it does America.

Book burning, such as took place in Sapulpa, Oklahoma, and in various information centres abroad, does not often occur, but the end result is the same if books are removed from library shelves either here or abroad. If we do not protest against this 'poisoning of America's historic spirit of freedom', we shall suddenly awake to find ourwelves living in a totalitarian and authoritarian land, under *whatever* name we give it. In fact, these zealots, ignorant and unscrupulous as some of them are, in their hatred and fear of communism, are destroying the very thing they are ostensibly trying to protect: the American spirit of freedom and liberty.

The *New York Times* summarized the situation in May 1953, based on a nation-wide report:

1. There is underway a concerted campaign to censor school and college textbooks, reading material and other visual aids.

2. Voluntary groups are being formed in nearly every State to screen books for 'subversive' or un-American statements. These organizations, not accountable to any legal body, are sometimes doing great harm in their communities.

3. Librarians are being intimidated by outside pressures in their choice of books and other materials. Unwilling to risk a public controversy, they weakly accept the results of the self-appointed censorship groups.

4. Several textbooks and other materials have already been re-moved from school or college libraries and are effectively on the 'blacklist'.

5. The attacks on the 'subversive' school textbooks appear to be a part of a general campaign against public schools and other edu-cational institutions.

Even greater assaults on the principles and traditions of Ameri-can democracy may be anticipated.

That these attacks are all part of a great fear, hatred, and suspicion of intellectual matters, and that they are made by the most ignorant members of our population, makes it an even greater threat, for the ignorant are always in the majority.

As for myself I can see little difference between these attacks and the one made on me by the magazine *America* in 1943. They are all part of the same spirit of intolerance which confuses the free exchange of ideas, a commonplace practice in free educational institutions, with indoctrination, and is all too ready to con-demn anybody as subversive and dangerous who fails to endorse certain narrow conceptions of democracy or religion.

Copying the Nazis or the Communists in thought control tech-niques in education is not the way to meet our problems. Free inquiry is the very cornerstone of American education. Without this, our greatest institutions of learning will perish, and this is what a mass of ignorant and reactionary people would like to see happen.

I have never forgotten my experience at Harvard, when I was rowing on the Charles. The 'townies' would on occasion spit on the rower from above as he passed underneath the bridges, to show their disgust, envy and hatred for something they didn't and never would understand. Close to the surface in every man is a fearful spirit of hatred and intolerance ever ready to manifest itself in lynchings, race riots, book burnings, and the destruction of libraries and universities as has occurred throughout history. Let us not fool ourselves that this couldn't happen again. It should surprise nobody that this spirit of witch burning still exists. This intolerance has been merely slumbering, and we, as Americans, can never relax our vigilance or we shall be given over to the fascists or Communists, two sides of the same coin of totalitarianism.

Dr Luther H. Evans, former Librarian of Congress, is well aware of the dangers. He argues that we must refuse to yield one inch of the hard-won ground of freedom. 'The experts in vituperation,' he writes, 'the sadists of freedom, are abroad in the land, and they are having a heyday of it. We must learn not to fear them. We must show them up for what they really are. They are really cowards who are unwilling to live the American dream.'

This is putting it mildly, and I would go Dr Evans one better. I think that most of these enemies of freedom are scoundrels, demagogues, and ignorant zealots, who know very well what they are doing. They enjoy their power, and having studied the techniques of Goebbels and Vishinsky with telling and dangerous effect, they are getting away with murder. Never underestimate them. They use the technique of the big lie, the American psychology of salesmanship, and their coffers are well filled by the same reactionary groups who forced Frank Dobie out of Texas University. They are the oil millionaires, among others, who invited McCarthy for weekend conferences. They differ only with the Communists in that they are capitalists, but their methods and ends are the same. They destroy whatever there is in the world of truth and of beauty which they do not understand. They are the eternal Philistines whose ideals never go above and beyond the cash register, and they are as much a part of the American scene as termites, grasshoppers, Japanese beetles, tornadoes, woodrot, mildew, or any other natural destructive force. I personally fear them as much, if not more, as I do the Communists, who are mostly imbeciles.

Imagine a headline in a great American newspaper in the late summer of the year of our Lord 1953: *Lawyers Uphold Free-*

dom to Read. It seemed incredible, especially to our European allies and friends (or now enemies) that more than 2,000 years after the death of Socrates, three or four centuries after the burning of people like Bruno and Servetus and 177 years after the Declaration of Independence, that the American Bar Association should have to adopt, in this enlightened and free country, a resolution upholding the freedom to read as a corollary of the constitutional freedom of the Press!

As for me, I have been brought up too long in the ancient English tradition of liberty as exemplified by John Stuart Mill to change now. Each year I have my students read Mill's great essay on *Liberty* in which he says:

'First: The opinion which it is attempted to suppress by authority may possibly be true. . . . All silencing of discussion is an assumption of infallibility. . . . To call any proposition certain, while there is anyone who would deny its certainty if permitted, but who is not permitted, is to assume that we ourselves, and those who agree with us, are the judges of certainty, and judges without hearing the other side. . . . But, indeed, the dictum that truth always triumphs over persecution is one of those pleasant falsehoods which men repeat after one another till they pass into commonplace, but which all experience refutes. History teems with instances of truth put down by persecution. . . . The real advantage which truth has consists in this, that when an opinion is true, it may be extinguished once, twice, or many times, but in the course of ages there will generally be found persons to rediscover it, until some one of its reappearances falls on a time when from favourable circumstances it escapes persecution until it has made such head as to withstand all subsequent attempts to suppress it. It can do truth no service to blink the fact, known to all who have the most ordinary acquaintance with literary history, that a large portion of the noblest and most valuable moral teaching has been the work not only of men who did not know, but of men who knew and rejected the Christian faith.'

To sum up the gist of Mill's wonderful essay, one of the really great landmarks in the long flight for human freedom, allows me to quote once more:

'First, if any opinion is compelled to silence, that opinion may, for ought we can certainly know, be true. To deny this is to assume our own infallibility.

'Secondly, though the silenced opinion be an error, it may, and very commonly does, contain a portion of truth; and since the general or prevailing opinion on any subject is rarely or never the whole truth, it is only by the collision of adverse opinions that the remainder of the truth has any chance of being supplied.

'Thirdly, even if the received opinion be not only true, but the whole truth; unless it is suffered to be, and actually is, vigorously and earnestly contested, it will, by most of those who receive it, be held in the manner of a prejudice, with little comprehension or feeling of its rational grounds. And not only this, but fourthly, the meaning of the doctrine itself will be in danger of being lost, or enfeebled, and deprived of its vital effect on the character and conduct: the dogma becoming a mere formal profession, in-efficacious for good, but cumbering the ground, and preventing the growth of any real and heartfelt conviction, from reason or personal experience.'

If teachers everywhere have the courage to defend with their blood, if necessary, their right of free inquiry against both Church and State, if these would deprive them of their ancient privilege, the present inquisition will retreat in disorder, but yield an inch and it will advance a foot—it is a devilish and in-exorable pressure, and I for one have felt its power.

The London *Times* of August 6, 1955, had a succinct paragraph or two: 'It may be that the menace of "McCarthyism" to free speech and thought is prone to exaggeration, just as the fear of domestic Communism on which it feeds has no defined substance; that both are manifestations of a mass neurosis often depicted an inevitable phase of the great American tradition. The stage has not been reached by the great Hearst Press and its allies where almost any resistance to the Senator's privileged attacks is seen to be tarred with Communist brush.'

It is greatly to Dartmouth's credit that so far as I know no teacher in it, nor any course, has ever changed its wind or its sails to please anybody. Therein lies its greatness. The Comparative Literature Department, through the very nature of its course, has always been in the vanguard in the College in spreading the great English tradition of liberty.

Every year with the exception of the war years, when mathematics and the sciences were emphasized by the Navy, the Comparative Literature Department, for the service rendered to the College, was, I am reasonably sure, the most economical the College ever had. Despite our great number of students, despite a vast personal correspondence carried on with Dartmouth men during the war years in connection with two columns I wrote in the *Dartmouth Alumni Magazine*, called 'Round the Girdled Earth', and 'Laurelled Sons of Dartmouth', I never had secretarial help, unless I paid for it myself, nor did the department.

And what about the most important thing at Dartmouth, the student himself? The public often thinks there is a stereotype Dartmouth man, as there is supposedly a stereotype Princeton, Harvard, Yale or Brown man. As we are an outdoor college set in a magnificent natural setting, with a great tradition since 1909 in winter sports, the Dartmouth man, commonly known as a 'chubber', is one who dresses in mackinaws, sweat shirts, drinks heavily, deliberately 'roughs' the tender Princeton boys on the gridiron, and is mighty dangerous to the gentle, timid, shy females who venture within striking distance.

Actually the Dartmouth undergraduates as I have known them have invariably been decent, *conforming*, well-meaning young men, reasonably bright, and eager for a course which would stimulate their thinking and broaden their knowledge. They have been entirely worthy of the warmest friendship a teacher can offer them. Some are intellectually gullible, but others develop critical minds, and when they get their degrees are just beginning to get a glimmer of what truth, learning and the intellectual life is about. Some graduate as ignorant, if not more so, than when they entered, for they think they know something, whereas they know little, have seldom if ever had an original idea, and have avoided all courses which might unsettle them, or strain their intelligence.

All in all I have enjoyed greatly my association with them. I believe in them, and many have become life-long friends.

During the last few years of my teaching career there appeared to be more and more student apathy toward his studies. I am not at all certain that this is entirely his fault.

It may be partly owing to the pressure put on him by the three-term system, which is primarily an economic measure, the pressure of having to get high grades (which are the bane of education) in order to get into graduate school, and the fact that he has very little leisure to think or to read for pleasure. In the modern system there is always the threat of a 'quiz', or hour exam, or paper hanging over him, in which he seldom may express his own ideas, but must throw back what the textbook or the instructor has given him to memorize. Furthermore, it may well be the fault of the professor who more and more finds that the student is a hindrance to his professional advancement. He 'must publish or perish'; he must write for the 'learned' journals articles often badly written, full of special knowledge that has little value. His office hours for students may be as little as half an hour a week. If he wants advancement he must do 'research'. Teaching has little value any more in the modern college.

Robert Frost would have been a great teacher but anyone practising his methods would not last long in any American college today. Mr Frost believed that education was for life and living, and that it should also indicate the fundamental values of character and conscience. One time, the story goes, he was lecturing to a class of teachers, and read them Mark Twain's story of the jumping frog which failed in a jumping contest because someone had filled it with quail shot so that it couldn't get off the ground.

The teachers characteristically couldn't see the point of this story in a course on education. Frost explained that the story was about teachers; the kind that fill you with so much quail shot that you can't move, and the kind that just give you a little prod behind and you jump to the skies.

One of the most difficult of the administrative jobs is that of Director of Admissions, who has to select a freshman class of around eight hundred from around several thousand qualified applicants. He has to try to please everybody, obviously an impossible task, soften the blow to parents and alumni whose sons may fail to meet the competitive requirements, and no one envies him his job, which he and his assistants do remarkably well, considering today's emphasis on grades.

Only a highly selected few get into Dartmouth or any Ivy League school these days. Exactly how men are selected is known only to God. If the applicant is from Texas, he appears to have a better chance to get into Dartmouth than if he is from New Jersey, as Texas applications are fewer, and Texas is a preferred area. If he is a star football player he will probably end up at a high-pressure football school. If he has those qualities which have made him a 'best camper' or 'an all around boy', he will probably not be admitted. If he can play chess blindfold, or compete mathematically with a computer, he is sure to be admitted.

Once in a while the unusual individualistic type is accepted but he very seldom stays for long. Colleges today, more than ever, want conformists, not non-conformists, in spite of Emerson's wise dictum that all real men *must* be non-conformists.[1]

Admitting a man to college is, as I have said, a mysterious procedure to an outsider, probably involving percentages and, for all I know, a slide rule as well. It also involves something of the Calvinistic doctrine of the perseverance of the saints:

> We are the chosen few,
> All others will be damned.
> There is no room in Heaven for you,
> We can't have Heaven crammed.

I can honestly say that I have never really disliked any Dartmouth undergraduate I have known, so, as far as I am concerned, he is a pretty fine fellow, who has proven himself in every major war crisis the country faced since Dartmouth began about 197 years ago. He deserves the best and very often the College doesn't measure up to *him*.

[1] See a most interesting article by Howard Mumford Jones in the October *Atlantic*: 'Undergraduates on Apron Strings'. This is a general plea for free electives, and for the undergraduates' untrammelled right to make mistakes. Dartmouth today is a long way from this ideal—and, in fact—detests it. A student now at Dartmouth is 'guided' by advisers from the time he enters until he graduates. He is not allowed to mature, make mistakes, and scream defiance at the College's silly rules. He conforms or he is fired.

During the last war the college man did a marvellous job as officer or enlisted man in the army, navy, and air force. I had a tremendous respect for his achievements and was in a position to know how initiative, and the process of free education at its best, made the American fighting man so potent a force in defeating the rampant Germans and Japanese.

I wrote a letter to the soldiers, as I was editing two military columns for the *Dartmouth Alumni Magazine* throughout the war, but a member of the administration wouldn't have it printed, as it seemed to imply a slight criticism of the College.

Here is part of my letter:

You are the men who have seen things and have had visions under the conditions which produce desperation, boredom and fear. *We* have been sheltered, but nonetheless I hope our vision will somehow approximate yours.

I hope we are spiritually prepared to meet your challenge when you come back whether as undergraduates or as alumni. We must realize your maturity and the experiences which you have had which have made you men. We must sense, too, your impatience with high school standards and high school discipline. [This statement was questioned but the whole new curriculum at this time reflected this point of view.] We must treat you not as school boys fresh from high school, but as men fresh from vital scenes of action and vital jobs. I hope we may prove worthy of you. I am not always sure that we will. [This last statement, altogether true when I look over the faculty and administration of that time, was also questioned.]

Humility and wisdom are always needed and are always rare, and if we do not have it in abundance I hope we have it in part.

Frankly, I hope we may never go back to the 'old' Dartmouth. I hope we may go on to the 'new' Dartmouth. A thing is dead, as Emerson says, which seeks rest. We must move on with the times—we want to be restless—to be vital—above all, to be alive. If our curriculum needs a shot in the arm I hope it gets a million c.c.'s, not once but many times. Let the dead things be buried and let the elan vital fill our veins. If we are smug and provincial [changed by the administrator to 'if we have any tendency to be'], may help us to be humble and international in our outlook.

May God give us the wisdom we need after the war.

In college circles critics are few and far between, as most

faculty and administrative members find an acquiescent attitude the safer and more diplomatic course.

Fear of criticism, fear of taking bold stands, reveals weakness, whereas a strong organization need fear nothing except a small town provincialism, self-satisfaction and smugness.

I might as well boldly go on record as saying that I am beginning to question the wisdom of turning over a college as old and fine as Dartmouth to a handful of lawyers and bureaucrats. When, in God's name, were lawyers supposed to know anything about education?

And whereas I may be willing under pressure to admit that what is good for General Motors is good for the United States, I am not so sure that what works well at R. H. Macy's will work as well at Dartmouth.

All too often at alumni gatherings there is far too little self-analysis, far too little honest self-criticism. The fact is that in many ways we are improving. Many of the things that have happened in the last decade are forward looking, indeed inevitable in our time. Too many, however, are of an astringent and restrictive nature. Dartmouth is in danger of being departmentalized and organized to death. If I should desire even to change the number of one of my courses I would have had to go through one committee if not more. I would probably have been refused. So I asked for nothing. There are almost as many committees at work here as in the Pentagon. It is really becoming ridiculous.

Dartmouth alumni are the most loyal in the country. They love the Hanover Plain with a consuming passion. They donate beyond all normal limits of generosity to the alumni fund which started with a goal of $100,000 and is now a million and a half. I think that most of them would agree, however, that too many leave most of their reading and thinking to their wives, that not enough carry on the living processes of education much beyond graduation, that, in fact, their education didn't 'take' as well as it might have, in spite of the four years spent in a traditional liberal arts college.

This situation the present faculty and administration, as I have hinted, heavily tinged with lawyers (the president, vice-president and treasurer, and even the librarian are lawyers), are trying to remedy in a somewhat hit-or-miss fashion. Though their purpose is often laudable, the execution is poor.

It is quite possible that the kind of liberal arts college I would desire, with the emphasis on the humanities and classical studies, is too much of a luxury in an inflationary and atomic age. It is also quite possible that the culture I believe in is out of fashion now and will be for a long time to come. If so, I think it a pity, but as I believe that half a loaf is better than no bread at all, I intend to stand by and use whatever influence I possess, which is little in present-day Dartmouth, to keep the humanities here a living force.

Mr Gerald Warner Brace's amusing novel of New England college life contains the following: 'No college president can retain his integrity. . . . He promises, he pacifies, he flatters and bribes, he plays both ends against the middle, he acts as God's personal representative—and as sure as sin he turns out to be a stuffed shirt.'

I intend to leave out personalities in this book. One thing, however, I have noticed. Surrounding themselves with mediocrities seems to be an occupational disease of college presidents. Perhaps it gives them a feeling of security and superiority.

I myself have never been a member of the administrative 'team'. I have always regarded myself as a member of the loyal opposition: loyal, that is, to the principles I have come to believe that Dartmouth should stand for: an unequivocal respect for truth, an impartial dispensing of justice in the disciplinary field, a sturdy defence of academic freedom, and always an objective seeking of the truth whether political, religious, or philosophical.

I have found myself more often than not opposed to the utterances and policies of power-happy administrators, and I have noticed that a little power is apt to corrupt.

These are tendencies I can but deplore: a centralization of power in the hands of a few, occasionally legal double-talk which uses a lot of words and says practically nothing, an over-expansion of personnel in the administration (first it was the faculty room which was broken up for offices, and then Crosby Hall was taken over, and both are now bulging at the seams, with new buildings being erected by the minute), an air of omnipotence, and an unusual demand for conformity.

Teaching has been exciting and exhausting. Confounding my enemies (and I have made many) and my critics has become a sport I enjoy more and more. I have finally come to the conclusion that when the attacks cease, I shall know I am slipping. Since my heart attack in 1947, these matters seem less and less important. I would be untruthful, however, if I intimated that they had failed to leave a mark, which must be evident here.

For myself I have proved that doubt and scepticism can lead to a happy way of life. I am certain that in maintaining an intellectual and spiritual integrity, in never professing a belief one does not share, gives one a strength, power, and contentment that is truly remarkable. This I believe I have found, and so life is interesting, ever exciting, and never more so than when battling with authority that has seemingly gotten out of hand.

The teacher's real reward comes from the satisfaction he gains from stirring up the minds of young men, in making them think for themselves, in helping them to find a balanced and rational philosophy of life. Once in a while the teacher is rewarded with such a note as this one I got during the war from Jack Daniels, '37. He wrote: 'I have just been reading the very moving words of Toyokiko Kagawa, the Japanese "Saint of Shinkawa". He sees life with such a clear vision that he has gained the power to disturb the souls of others and to make them grope for the truth which he has already found. I am writing you at this moment, because I know that you have some of the power to stir up the souls of young men, which spurs them on in search for a truth. At least I found this to be so in my case. And because of this fact I figured that you would read whatever I have to say with understanding.'

And a few years ago I received, unexpectedly, the novel *Waterfront*, by Bud Schulberg, '36, with the following inscription: 'For my good friend Herb West, who has always managed to be his own man, and who, as a sort of one-man department of literature, has kept alive a true love of books at Dartmouth.'

After my final lecture at Dartmouth another student wrote me: 'I hope to follow in your footsteps as an instructor of youth. If I can someday sit back after forty years of teaching, and realize that my efforts have resulted in just one student seeing that Truth is all important, then I may count my life a success; on this basis your career has been extraordinarily successful.'

I hope he is right.

At any rate, with my retirement the Department of Comparative Literature as known for forty-five years is no more. This is no doubt the Will of Allah. It is well.

CHAPTER II

The Bookman as Collector

Much have I travell'd in the realms of gold.
John Keats

As I look back after nearly fifty years as a collector there are several conclusions about collecting that might be drawn. What were the rewards?

I was always the 'impecunious amateur'. Never, until in recent years as a rare book dealer, could I buy a book that was costly. This restricted me to a certain kind of collecting. I could not afford the real rarities: Caxtons, Kelmscott, Doves, or Ashendene Press books, or the rare incunabula, i.e. books printed before 1500. I was forced by economics and, to be candid, interest, to collect the books I could afford: that is to say, modern first editions both English and American.

Through the years I made many friends through collecting; authors, dealers, and collectors; corresponded with many writers; wrote the first life of R. B. Cunninghame Graham, and the first monograph on Henry Williamson; wrote three books on book collecting and reading; enriched my forty-two years of college lecturing on literature with my knowledge of modern writers: and gave to the Dartmouth College Library books, manuscripts and letters of incalculable value. Lastly I had a lot of fun. All this was accomplished on the small salary of a college teacher.

Let me reminisce for a moment. One summer just forty-two years ago I was staying in Princes Risborough in Buckinghamshire within walking distance of the Pink and Lily, a pub Rupert Brooke used to visit. Over a glass of ale my friend, the late Thomas Lloyd Humberstone, asked me if I have ever read any books by Cunninghame Graham. My answer was in the negative but on our return to the University Country Club where we were staying,

63

he loaned me a copy of *A Hatchment*, and there began for me the rewarding experience of finding a writer exactly to my taste.

About three weeks later I stood quietly and unknown by the open grave in Canterbury of Joseph Conrad while the priest droned the impressive Latin phrases of the Roman Catholic burial service. Half an hour later I entered the great cathedral with a friend with whom I had driven down from London. We were alone there except for a dapper gentleman (a combination in looks of Buffalo Bill and Don Quixote), slim and slight, of fine carriage though betraying that he was a horseman by his stance, finely chiselled features, pointed beard and handsome head.[1] I recognized him at once as Robert Bontine Cunninghame Graham who, after the funeral of his old friend, had come for a few brief moments of quiet, as we had, in this lovely cathedral. No words were spoken between us but soon I began seriously to collect his books. My enthusiasm grew as I read his travel book *Mogreb-El-Acksa*, 1898, and his volume *Success*, 1902, and his other books which contain autobiographical reminiscences of South America, Texas, Scotland and England, as well as the distillation of his keen and ironic turn of mind in his magnificent sketches.

In the summer of 1929 we met and began a friendship and a correspondence which lasted until his death at eighty-four in 1936.

The ultimate result of our friendship was the first life of Cunninghame Graham, *A Modern Conquistador: The Life of Robert Bontine Cunninghame Graham*, London, 1932, now a reasonably 'scarce' book, a definitive collection of his books, prefaces, 666 pages of his letters now in the Dartmouth College Library, which has attracted scholars from the British Isles, Europe and the United States.

The curious reader may want to refer to Chapter V, 'How One Thing Leads to Another in Collecting', from *Modern Book Collecting for the Impecunious Amateur*, 1936, to see how collecting one author has a chain reaction which never ends. From Cunninghame Graham, I turned to his friends, W. H. Hudson, Joseph Conrad, Wilfrid Scawen Blunt, an absolutely fascinating and partly neglected writer, and this led to the great writers on

[1] See the Epstein bust of Cunninghame Graham.

Arabia: Gertude Bell, C. M. Doughty, T. E. Lawrence, Freya Stark, Bertram Thomas, H. St John Philby and now Ernest Thesiger.

Collecting books has influenced my life as it has that of thousands of other collectors.

When did my reading and collecting begin? As far back, almost, as I can remember. I became a rapid and voracious reader as a child in Amesbury, Massachusetts. One of the reasons for this, perhaps, was that children in the early part of this century had few mechanical diversions: no movies, no radio, no television. A few families possessed Edison 'talking machines', but more common were stereopticon views of Niagara Falls, Old Faithful, and other natural wonders, and occasionally we saw 'magic lantern' pictures at a Sunday school party.

Most of us had nothing except our own resources and these seldom failed us. I had a most happy childhood living a life somewhat similar to that of Huck Finn or Tom Sawyer. Judge Shute's books on his childhood in Exeter, New Hampshire, reflected my own early life. Our house was near the old Quaker Meeting House and only a few doors from Whittier's house on Main Street. The old swimming hole was not far away.

One thing I learned early in life was that I could always learn more on my own, outside the school room, than inside, and this conviction stayed with me through college and university. After a lifetime of teaching at Dartmouth I believe it even more now.

Edward Everett Hale wrote in his *A New England Boyhood*, 1893: 'That it would be easy to pass the Harvard Greek entrance examination in four months of interested study.' Many years are wasted in school, the pace being much too slow except for the dullest, especially in grammar and high school days.

Katherine Anne Porter has written: 'Childhood is the fiery furnace in which we are melted down to essentials and that essential shaped for good.'[1]

This could be so and I like to think it is true. One of my own essentials, which has been one of the most valuable assets of my life, is an insatiable and incessant love of books, and I read at an early age everything I could find.

[1] From an article on Willa Cather in *Mademoiselle* for July 1952.

My imagination, too, was most active in my childhood, and Davy Crockett, Colonel James Bowie, Masterman Ready, Robinson Crusoe, General George Armstrong Custer, and David Livingstone became as real, or more so, than people I actually knew. The story of the Alamo I knew by heart, as I did later the story of Custer at the Little Big Horn, and naturally my versions were more romantic than historic.

As my childhood years rolled on, faster and faster as each year went by, I read Andrew Lang's Fairy Books, the Green, the Yellow, the Blue, the Red, and all the rest. I read all I could find of the enormous output of Edward S. Ellis, with sheer ecstasy his Deerfoot stories: *Hunters of the Ozark, Camp in the Mountains,* and *The Last War Trail,* in which book Deerfoot is killed. His death proved as much of a shock to me as a boy as did that of Sherlock Holmes at the Reichenbach Falls later when I was a little older. Ellis, as Conan Doyle revived Holmes, brought back Deerfoot years later, at least to the extent of writing another series of books about him under different surroundings.

I read all I could find of Harry Castlemon (Charles Austin Fosdick, 1842–1915), including the Gunboat Series: *Frank on a Gun Boat, Frank before Vicksburg, Frank on the Lower Mississippi;* The Rocking Horse Series, the Rocky Mountain Series, the Boy Trapper Series, including *Buried Treasure, Boy Trapper,* and *Mail Carrier;* The Rod and Gun Series, the Forest and Stream Series, the War Series, the Hunter Series, and many others. All in all, Castlemon's output was enormous and I read all I could get my hands on. Even so, his output was less than that of Horatio Alger, Oliver Optic, or Ellis.[1]

I read all of Horatio Alger together with Kirk Munroe whose *With Crockett and Bowie, In Pacific Waters, The Flamingo Feather, Through Swamp and Glade, At War with Pontiac,* and *The White Conquerors* were favourites. I liked the books by Otis,

---

[1] The late James E. Knott of New London, Connecticut, had a magnificent Castlemon collection and had more than sixty titles among his books, which now rest in the Dartmouth College Library. See also: *A Critical History of Children's Literature* by Cornelia Meigs, Anne Eaton, Elizabeth Nesbitt, Ruth Hill Viguers, New York, The Macmillan Company, 1953.

Tomlinson, Stratemeyer (Captain Ralph Bonehill was another pseudonym), and Joseph Altsheler. Judge Shute's stories of Exeter were devoured. Trowbridge's *Cudjo's Cave* was also a favourite as was R. M. Ballantyne's *The Coral Island.*

Nor were the books of G. A. Henry overlooked. I certainly missed some of the hundred or more he wrote, but I recall *Hold Fast for England, St Bartholomew's Eve, Lion of St Mark, True to the Old Flag, With Kitchener in the Sudan, With Clive in India, Beric the Briton, At Agincourt, The Tiger of Mysore, St George for England, By Pike and Dyke,* and many others.

Horatio Alger inculcated into his books characteristics such as honesty, industry and truthfulness which I feel sure hurt none of us. Though these books seem naïve today, nevertheless they gave pleasure to millions of boys and helped mould their characters. Psychiatrists were unknown in my childhood, nor was there as much juvenile delinquency as there is today.

As I grew up I also read many nickel novels such as those featuring 'Young Wild West' and Aretta: Old King Brady, Sexton Blake, Nick Carter, and many others. I can here report, truthfully I think, that none of them did me any harm.

These were counterbalanced with *Tom Sawyer, Huck Finn, The Prince and the Pauper, Roughing It,* and other works of the great Mark Twain, who died when I was twelve.

All books that I found interesting were grist for my mill, and I read thousands then, as I have since. I progressed naturally and inevitably from the trivial to the best in writing: from Robert Service to Frost, from Conan Doyle to the Odyssey, from Sexton Blake to Joseph Conrad.

I suspect the better comics do not cause as much harm as many people believe. My son outgrew them and though he may still look at Peanuts and Pogo, as I do, his immediate passion at seventeen was Joseph Conrad and T. S. Eliot.

The acquisitive instinct is one of the strongest (greed is the most intense) in the human psyche. Collectors have it sometimes in an exaggerated form. All of us, if we can, collect cash, bonds, mortgages, stocks, real estate, and diamonds. Others collect Lincoln 1909 pennies, stamps, empty bottles, Sandwich glass, silhouettes, tea caddies, ship models, etchings, engravings, beds which Queen Elizabeth and/or George Washington slept in, wax flowers, postcards, cigar bands, theatre programmes, old copies of the *National Geographic*, cartridge cases, horseshoes, guns, Colonial hinges, bottle caps, stuffed animals, stuffed shirts, candlesticks, pewter, Wedgwood, first editions, incunabula, chapbooks, press-books, dime novels, horse-chestnuts, trademarks, iron crosses, double crosses, Shakespeare folios, and I actually knew a man who had a fine collection of Kreugeriana. Some even collect castles, stone by stone, and then add a five car garage. Our feeling for the tangible is very strong.

Some collectors obviously are not quite 'all there', nonetheless most of them could be invited to one's home without any inner trepidation.

I knew one book collector, now gone to the happy-hunting grounds, who bought books completely without discrimination. His house, garage, and even a rented barn completely bulged with books. Occasionally out of the spate of books he acquired, there would be one worth acquiring. I once, when young and hard-up, refused from him a first issue of Robert Frost's *A Boy's Will* for $75. I offered it to Earl Bernheimer, with whom I was then corresponding, who of course bought it from him. (Later I paid $350 for the same book.) Whatever the case this man kept buying and buying and when he died there were carloads of useless and useful books for his heirs. Their ultimate fate I never learned.

Being myself a specimen of a peculiarly harmless sort, I wish to justify, if possible, the gentle mania of collecting books. Why, you may ask, does one collect books? The obvious answer is, I suppose, that public libraries being what they are, one collects books that one desires to read and so attain the pleasant anodyne that reading books supplies. But this answer does not explain the collecting of 'first editions', nor does it explain the amassing of 'signed-limited', 'association copies', or fine 'press books'. Many collectors search with an eye for profit, which is a very human and natural thing to do. As a matter of fact, shrewd judgment in book buying has reaped for the astute professional great and glorious profits, as witness recent auction sale records.

I am speaking here for the amateur who collects for the sheer love of collecting and who has no desire, save in the case of sheer necessity, to sell or to part with his collection, although he may intend to leave it eventually to a grateful alma mater. I myself confess a feeling akin to reverence for the memory of the collector who has died whenever I see a particularly well chosen group of books, as, for example, the collection of my friend, the late Irving Kerlan's books at the University of Minnesota.

Collecting, it must be admitted, is a mild sort of madness. It cannot be explained any more than can love, or the ideas of Barry Goldwater. Like Topsy it just is, and to carry the simile one step further, it grows. Collectors all know the symptoms, but there are no cures save the final one; take away his money and the genuine collector will start searching for four-leafed clovers.

William McFee once wrote on the subject. I quote the following passage from the excellent McFee bibliography compiled by Mr James T. Babb, where the curious reader may find it for himself in an amusing introduction. 'It is impossible,' says McFee, 'to be a collected author and remain innocent of irony. The materials confront one on every hand. The scorn and contempt for a collected author like myself, who makes very little money, cherished by the big fellows who make six-figure incomes from serials and novels but whose work is considered as garbage by collectors, is one of the joys of my life. The wistful desire to be reckoned "important" by critics who earn less than their own chauffeurs saves many a successful writer from haughtiness. I confess I share, sometimes, their bewilderment. At other times, when I am reading their works, I fancy I understand. I seem to have read it all somewhere else, long ago, in other best sellers. Perhaps collectors are a cannier lot than we authors give them credit for being. If somebody did not preserve the beginnings of literature, they would be irretrievably lost. Think of the librarian who discovered Chatterton manuscripts being used to wrap up fried fish! Think of the well-to-do novelists of Chatterton's time who have no value in a collector's estimation at all, but who have turned to dust! Collectors, in short, in these days of manipulated reputations, money prizes, and book clubs are the repositories of integrity in our profession. Theirs is a noble madness. It behooves us never to betray their confidence.'

Thus, among other things, collecting may be said to develop literary taste and to sharpen critical judgment, so that the collector, after an honest apprenticeship, during which he will make many mistakes, will eventually be able to recognize good from bad literature. He will pick up less and less trash. He will discover new authors who, because they write honestly of life as they find it, or because they write to please themselves, can never become popular, though they are certain to be collected by a few. I would like to remind my readers that two of the finest English prose writers of modern times wrote for two-thirds or more of their writing lives with no recognition at all save for a small literary one. They kept on writing because the desire to create was stronger than the discouragement and apathy they encountered, and the publishers kept on printing their books because a few astute readers and collectors bought them. Thus it may be said that a small group of collectors kept alive the writing careers of Joseph Conrad and W. H. Hudson. Conrad's *Almayer's Folly* appeared in 1896. His first real popular success came about twenty years later. W. H. Hudson was successful, so far as sales go, only a short time before his death at the age of eighty-two. Very few authors can keep on punishing themselves by just writing manuscripts. They need the catharsis of the printed page. Intelligent collectors make this possible long before a larger reading public steps into line.

The first edition of that remarkable book, *The Sea and the Jungle*, by H. M. Tomlinson, was five hundred copies. Several hundred literary sleuths bought it, read it, and delighted in its prose. They found classical descriptive passages. The smell of the hot oil which permeated the tramp steamer, winding its way through the South American jungle, got into their nostrils. These early readers found authenticity and a great talent for writing with continual evidence of what Pascal called *l'esprit de finesse*.

H. M. Tomlinson is not at the moment over popular with collectors, but he will be back as he is an excellent craftsman with something to say.

Taste, as Professor Irving Babbitt has said, is one of the real needs of our time. Owing to the brash impetus of modern art, the

radio, television, Crime Club novels, Sunday newspapers, Holly-
wood Homers, taste can hardly raise its delicate head without
being knocked down by a democratic brickbat in the form of a
majority. I have never met a genuine book collector who did not
have taste. Obviously I am not labouring under the delusion that
they monopolize that commodity, I aver only that it is one of their
characteristics. Neither would I decry those who collect, and later
send to Aunt Hannah, the works of Ayn Rand, or Norman Vin-
cent Peale. To these authors belong the joys of 100,000 copies in a
first printing, and the approval of 'a large body of delighted readers'.

What pleasure the ardent collector derives from unexpectedly
meeting a fellow bibliophile! Speaking out of my own experience,
I find that interests shared in common immediately break down
shyness and reticence, more quickly even and more successfully
than does the cup that cheers. Many years ago I happened to be
speaking at the Elizabethan Club at Yale, and met several men
who were enthusiastic collectors of certain authors in whom I myself am interested; the *camaraderie* which sprung up among us
bore little resemblance to the back-slapping and hand-shaking
that goes on at a Legion convention. That is undoubtedly good in
its place (all are brothers), but the amenities of book collectors
assume subtler forms, such as pleasant conversation. One of the
group was a young professor, Archer Gee, now deceased, who had
a fine H. M. Tomlinson collection. Not that he did not have all
the necessary books of his profession as a teacher of English
literature; his cases were full of them. I could not with any degree
of veracity say that he deprecated these books, but certainly they
provoked not the fire, the shy almost quivering enthusiasm which
he displayed when showing me an early letter which H. M.
Tomlinson had written to a literary agent, asking rather humbly
about some articles he had sent in. I find it a little difficult to
analyse this feeling of sudden, close intimacy which rapidly
develops among collectors. I know only that the impulse which
makes a man love, with a fine passion, letters and first editions of
a certain author has for me an instant appeal. It is an emotion
untainted by any of the devices of the market place or of our
legislative halls.

Though the collector may or may not write himself, he does

create vicariously by reacting to all the nuances of his favourite author. He finds life there, and the solace to be had from contact with a comprehending mind. He finds experience assimilated by the alembic of a sensitive and observing spirit. He finds beauty and truth. What more can one expect of a printed page? But you still ask why first editions? I can only say that most people prefer a diamond to a piece of glass, although both so closely resemble each other that only an expert can tell them apart.

Collectors sense each other with an instinct which they alone understand. I remember finding in Cambridge, England, many years ago, a gentleman by the name of Sidney Cockerell, curator of the Fitzwilliam Museum, and later knighted. Meeting primarily on a matter of literary investigation in the life of Wilfrid Scawen Blunt, whose secretary he had once been, we went to his house for tea, where he showed me with due reverence a copy of Lucretius with the signature of Ben Jonson on the title page, the original manuscript of *John Bull's Other Island*, several Hardy manuscripts, and three volumes of autographed letters from the poet Wilfrid Scawen Blunt. These various books led to a discussion in which were revealed to me many interesting facts gathered by Sir Sidney during a lifetime of close contacts with the great literary men of the past century. It was a most pleasant afternoon.

Collecting leads to many stimulating and valued friendships. Another perceptive and generous man I got to know in London was the author and critic, Edward Garnett (1868–1937). At his flat in Chelsea, in Southwestern London, he was literally surrounded by and immersed in books and manuscripts. He was a publisher's reader at that time for Jonathan Cape, and always had several manuscripts at hand for his decision. His tables and chairs were filled with books as were the cases which lined his walls. Most valuable items were crammed in every available space.[1]

[1] All too often I have noticed in buying books from various English dealers that those which came from author's libraries were almost invariably in terrible condition. At Harry Pratley's in Tunbridge Wells some years ago I bought some books from the library of William Scawen Blunt. There were books by W. H. Hudson and R. B. Cunninghame Graham, but most of them were dampstained, faded, and in generally disreputable condition so they were bought for five shillings instead of £5 or £10.

When he leaned forward, ashes from his herbal cigarettes scattered over his vest, and as he peered over his glasses, an enlightening remark almost invariably came. It might have concerned the present state of Irish literature as represented by Sean O'Faolain, or some anecdote about Joseph Conrad, whom Garnett knew for thirty years, or something about the always enigmatic Hudson.

Edward Garnett helped scores of writers get into print from Charles Montagu Doughty, John Galsworthy, Joseph Conrad, and W. H. Hudson to H. E. Bates, Liam O'Flaherty and W. B. Drayton Henderson, author of a forgotten epic poem *The New Argonautica*.

He was one of the most generous men in the world. Having been in the centre of literary activities in London for almost four decades, he had scores of priceless books. I will mention a few that I saw one afternoon, volumes calculated to whet any bookish appetite. One of his prize possessions was a manuscript written by Aircraftsman Shaw, which describes in delicious detail the goings-on of the British Air Force in Karachi, Pakistan. It has since been published as *The Mint*.

Those who believe that T. E. Lawrence was no more than a lucky adventurer will in this manuscript find much evidence to the contrary. I recall seeing a letter he had written on the work of Henry Handel Richardson; it was a shrewd appraisal and revealed a critical mind of the first order. Mr Garnett also possessed one of the rare early copies of the justly famous *Seven Pillars of Wisdom*.

Mr Garnett, who seems to have known everybody, had also in his collection a pile of unpublished D. H. Lawrence poems. There was a first edition, inscribed, of Doughty's magnificent *Arabia Deserta*, presentation books from Conrad, and scores of other rare volumes. The majority of collectors get the same pleasure out of viewing a fine, discriminating library, that a music lover does in hearing the Ninth Symphony of Beethoven; I was always filled with a deep satisfaction after visiting Mr Garnett.

It was through Cunninghame Graham that I met Mr Garnett. His first letter to me was dated July 25, 1930, and less than a month later on August 18 he wrote:

'I shall be delighted to read your book on Cunninghame Graham. I am most anxious to see it and if I think a short Preface from me would assist it I will gladly add one. Also I shall be happy to add some of R.C.G.'s letters to me that are most characteristic and touch on his view of Conrad, etc. It must have been a difficult book to write. I will mark the MS. and make any suggestion for revision should I think such necessary.'

About a month later I had his verdict: 'I have now read your MSS. R.B.C.G. and must congratulate you on the result. Considering the very great difficulties involved in the subject I think you have done very well and that the volume is a valuable one.'[1]

During the period I knew Mr Garnett we often dined at the Comercio Café, at the top of Frith Street, in Soho, and I recall meeting E. M. Forster there, and other literary men who frequented this café. We met also at the Anglo-Russian Café on 50 Harrington Road, not far from South Kensington Underground station, and there was also a memorable weekend at the Cearne, in Kent, where he spent weekends with his wife, Constance Garnett, who was still doing Russian translations even though her eyesight was bad. The Russian was read to her, and then she did the translation.

Later when I had finished my *Modern Book Collecting for the Impecunious Amateur* he read the manuscript, which was published in 1936 by Little, Brown & Company. He wrote: 'Your book is so American both in its strength and weakness that I can hardly envisage an English edition. It, indeed, is excellent in portions, candid in tone, and valuable in its information. Chapter VIII for example is a most comprehensive and valuable guide to the books on the Great War and Chapter IX brings together a most interesting collection of items showing your catholicity of spirit.'

When he died suddenly on February 9, 1937, the world lost a great, simple, and generous man.

Jonathan Cape wrote well of him: 'His influence on literature during the past forty years was very considerable, but it was

[1] In one of T. E. Lawrence's letters the verdict is not as flattering: 'It is a disappointing book. Anything about the old Don should have been written with swagger . . . a wonderful old man.'

74

mainly a hidden, a self-effacing influence. In the thousands of reports which he submitted as a publisher's reader, there are to be found wisdom, wit, and many flashes of sardonic humour; his reports were often marked with constructive criticism.'

In one of his letters to me, now in Dartmouth College collection, he mentioned *William Plomer*. This was written more than thirty years ago: 'Add William Plomer's eight books (prose and poetry) published by the Hogarth Press. Plomer is about the most original of the younger English authors.'

Today there is a real flurry in collecting all the Hogarth Press books, and William Plomer is still a desired author.

Each summer when in London I always wander down to where 19 Pond Place stood. It is only a few stops from Fulham Road, but now one sees a block of flats as Garnett's rooms were destroyed in the blitz. Still his image is very vivid and as long as I live I will always revere his memory and his kindness to a total stranger. I was only one of the many beneficiaries of his excellent taste, judgment, advice and knowledge, freely given.

As we are a wealthy nation we probably have more great collectors than any country in the world. Thomas W. Streeter of Morristown, New Jersey, is one, and I have enjoyed hours with him in his library well equipped with a fire-proof vault. C. Waller Barrett's library at the University of Virginia is a great monument to his genius as a collector. I could spend days there, months even, without exhausting my wonder at the great books he has: Thoreau's mother's copy of *Walden*, Robert Frost's unique volume *Twilight*, and thousands of others, some of which, I am glad to say, he acquired from me.

But I also recall other, less affluent collectors. One was a Chinese student of mine, I think his name was M. C. Sun, I once knew at Dartmouth. He was a shy and lonely alien in a strange foreign country. He used to eat on a few dimes a day so that he might purchase books by the English poets. When I first got to know him he was purchasing on the instalment plan an expensive edition of Shelley in ten volumes, issued, as I recall, by Scribners. The youthful and expansive idealism of Shelley at that time appealed to him. Perhaps now he is collecting Gerard Manley Hopkins. Somehow I shall always remember this

Chinese boy, but there is no moral to his tale. Where he is now I do not know. China, which might have been our friend, is now our enemy. A real pity.

Collectors may be found most easily in old bookshops. They are to be recognized by stooping shoulders acquired through long years of searching every nook and corner for a lost letter to Harriet or, perhaps, a first edition of *The Love Sonnets of Proteus*. The avid collector is always hoping to stumble upon some exceptional rarity. On one of the quais of Paris some years ago now some prowler among musty tomes found a volume heavily annotated, from Montaigne's famous tower; it had once belonged to Stephen de la Boetie before coming into the possession of Montaigne. Such an experience is the dream of every collector.

London, it seems to me, is the book collector's paradise. The city teems with bookshops, and most of the booksellers that I know there are friendly, knowledgeable, sometimes witty, and always willing to help.

You will probably find no high-, or even low-powered, salesmanship. You may enter a shop and the door rings a bell somewhere in the rear. Perhaps it is Thomas Cutbitt who comes swaying through the maze of books which fill his shop in the King's Road. If you look blatantly American he will tell you in a wheezy voice that Queen Alexandra used to come there. He bids you welcome. There are thousands of volumes piled everywhere. Occasionally one finds a long-lost book he has been seeking, buys it after a pleasant chat, and is on his way. Mr Cutbitt has his idiosyncrasies. He has been known to order people angrily from his place when they stooped to barter. He is a little crazy, perhaps, but so are many men who frequent such dens of delight.

Mr Cutbitt lives with ghosts; Thomas Carlyle used to come into King's Road quite often, enter the shop, and depart with a copy of Schiller or Novalis. In fact, it may be said that thousands of ghosts line Mr Cutbitt's shelves, and in the twilight when his door is shut they emerge from their dusty coffins and converse gently with him. What they say I know not, but Mr Cutbitt knows, for he has told me. This may account for his weird appearance, which struck me as being a cross between Scrooge and Lord Macauley. Mr Cutbitt sees visions and, like William Blake, converses on occasions with the great that have passed. He is peculiarly fond of Hazlitt. In the day time, however, he sits at a desk in the rear with a pot of tea near him. Man wants but little here below, and I imagine Mr Cutbitt is satisfied with what he has. He is now in Valhalla.

Years ago, the Lantern Bookshop at 103 Fulham Road was owned by another genial philosopher of quite a different sort. Mr Peacock used to be in the British Navy, a lieutenant I believe, and he also was a ranchman in South America. His thousands of books were in great disarray, but this only added zest to the hunt. I have found there early Cunningham Grahame prefaces, books of W. H. Hudson, George Gissing, Conrad, and a copy of Dr Munthe's *Red Cross and Iron Cross*. Mr Peacock used to share his tea and buns with me. He regaled me with tales of the pampas. We became good friends and remained so until his death a few years ago in Kent, where he had moved before the war.

I recall introducing Edward Garnett to him and they saw quite a good deal of each other thereafter.

After leaving Fulham Road, I used to take a bus to Great Russell Street, No. 61, where the late Mr Ashley Gibson ran the Java Head Bookshop. He was the author of a fine war book, *Postscript to Adventure*, and of several books about Ceylon, one with the charming title, *Cinnamon and Frangipanni*. Let Mr H. M. Tomlinson introduce him: 'Ashley Gibson was inside. . . . He was smoking a pipe, examining a first edition of Forrest's *Voyage to New Guinea and the Moluccas* (beside it was a Batak book of runes, printed on bark), waiting to sell us such stuff, while the Chancellor of the Exchequer elsewhere, at that very hour, was taking our money from us and praising our dumb supineness as heroic. What about Gibson's heroism? We had the shop to ourselves. I found there, for the first time, the *Pagan Races of the Malay Peninsula*, and more of Ceylon than I knew existed. You'll have to go. Gibson did not talk business. He rated me because of my preference for Ternate, and tried to prove that Amboyna is the best island in the Moluccas. It isn't. But anyhow, we ought to spread the news of this isolated outpost of the archipelago, and maintain it in London as long as we can.' Alas, both are now among the shades.

London bookshops are often like this. Walking further down Great Russell Street I found Jake Schwartz, who at that time looked like the Biblical Holofernes. Dr Schwartz was then known 'among the trade' for his own bibliography of first editions, and for his small volumes written by A. E. Coppard, Havelock Ellis, and H. H. Richardson.

I met Jake first in a big bookshop on Piccadilly as I was asking about a book by C. M. Doughty. After receiving a negative answer, I was turning away, when suddenly I was accosted by a bareheaded, heavily bearded man of handsome proportions, who informed me with a gleam in his eye that he had a rare Doughty pamphlet that was cheap at £2. I promised to come to his shop, but told him that if I could not, I would send him a wire that afternoon. I sent him the wire. Two years later I entered his place and met him for the second time. 'Here,' he said, 'is that Doughty pamphlet. You can have it for ten shillings!'

Fashions change in collecting as they do in everything else. Old authors drop out of sight, new ones emerge into the lime-light, and then, too, fade out. Finally after a long time only the really important ones come back into favour.

Each summer I made every effort to call on that remarkably keen and brilliant gentleman, John Hayward, at his flat in Carlyle Mansions in Chelsea overlooking the Thames. In June 1963 he casually remarked, 'Don't you think that T. S. Eliot is sagging a bit and that Robert Graves is coming up?' Certainly as a book dealer I had begun to feel this myself. Still, Eliot is a great poet, one who has influenced the course of English literature, and I suspect that he will always have his place. Robert Graves, too, is too big a figure to fade too far from the centre of the picture.

By the very nature of things dealers have to be sensitive to the demands of the market and not load up too heavily on writers who have no collector's interest. As a collector-dealer I do not always follow this precept and find myself buying Tomlinson, Montague, Galsworthy, and others, who at the moment are not in demand. Their day will return.

I remember years ago when Mr James T. Babb of Yale had done a sumptuous bibliography of his friend William McFee. At the time McFee was not as neglected as he is today, but the author of *Casuals of the Sea*, and several other really fine books, will not be forgotten and I am sure that William McFee again will have his moment of truth.

In 1936 the *Forsyte Saga* (1922), by John Galsworthy, even though it was an edition of 10,000 copies, was bringing $25 to $100 in the market. Today it brings much less. And then I read one of Mr Gilbert Fabe's books, in which he described the first issue wrapper of Mr Galsworthy's novel, *The Silver Spoon*. He said that the author didn't like the first wrapper so most were destroyed although several books did appear with it. Two other wrappers were then designed for the book and issued. Mr Fabe suggested then, and this was in the late 'twenties, that for the first edition 'with the first issue wrapper' £25 was a fair price, while with a plain or coloured wrapper the book was worth only £5. Today I think you could get the book for £1 or so, with or without the proper wrapper. Even Mr Galsworthy is now being underrated and is not collected as much as he used to be. I have a feeling that he will not completely vanish from the literary scene as his Forsyte stories were really first-class pictures of a vanished society.

A much neglected author today is C. E. Montague, author of the famous war book, *Disenchantment*, and some marvellous short stories on war and mountain climbing. *Action* is a fine book. Surely he will come once again into his own.

How long will the current fashion in Laurence Durrel hold up? Some of his more esoteric items are now bringing high prices but I have a feeling that his boom will bust. It is not entirely improbable that his brother Gerald's books on nature and animals may endure longer than his.

Still the really good writers, even if their charm dims for a while, are not eclipsed for long, and it seems to me that the books of W. H. Hudson, Joseph Conrad, Wilfrid Scawen Blunt, and Cunninghame Graham, will always have an appeal for the discriminating collector and especially for the one who reads the books he collects.

It has always been my contention that a collector should read the books he buys and that he should collect not necessarily the writer now in fashion but the writers he enjoys reading. He will find that reading develops his critical faculty and what Pascal called the *esprit de finesse* (good taste and judgment) more rapidly than any other interest. These are qualities which we in America do not possess in any overwhelming abundance. It is not long before the persistent reader and lover of books learns to differentiate between the quality of one writer as compared with another. He also may develop catholic tastes so that he can enjoy the writings of Rudyard Kipling as well as the magnificent poetry of Chaucer or Donne.

I have heard from many graduate schools and also from many industries that they prefer a person, especially in executive positions, who has a wide background of interests and knowledge and is not a narrow specialist in a small field.

Some years ago I spoke at the College of Physicians in Philadelphia on 'Rabelais, Sterne and Osler, Companions in Wit' and I tried, in the course of the talk, to show not only what a great doctor Sir William Osler was, but also that he was great as a humanistic scholar; and that although one could emphasize his significant contributions to the history of medicine, one should also emphasize his humanistic attitude and his idea that the medical profession would be wise if it pursued literary and humanistic studies along with its interest in medicine. Because of his reading and studying Osler became a true citizen of the world. 'What I inveigh against,' said Osler, 'is the current spirit of intolerance, conceived in distrust and bred in ignorance, that makes the mental attitude perennially antagonistic, even bitterly antagonistic to everything foreign, that subordinates everywhere the race to the nation, forgetting the higher claim of brotherhood.' He quoted from the *Religio Medici*: 'I feel not in myself those common antipathies that I can discover in others; those national repugnances do not touch me, nor do I behold with prejudice the French, Italian, Spaniard or Dutch; but where I find their actions in balance with my countrymen's, I honour, love and embrace them in the same degree. . . . Full knowledge, which alone disperses the mists of ignorance, can only be obtained by travel or by a thorough acquaintance with the literature of the different countries. . . . The great minds, the great works, of literature transcend all limitations of time, or language or of race.'

I was glad to read also, being then a member of the teaching profession, that Dr Osler held that the function of a university is to teach men to think. Original thinking and outspokenness are sometimes risky business in our time, but those who have the courage to think for themselves and to write what they think are those who are contributing greatly in preserving the fundamental freedoms necessary in a democracy. With Dr Osler, I can again but agree that a teacher should have not only a full personal knowledge of the branch he teaches, but also enthusiasm and a sense of obligation to his students. Dr Osler did value the idealist, many of whom are teachers. He once said, 'They alone furnish the Geist that finally animates the entire body and makes possible reforms and even revolutions.' Note the calm use of the word 'even'.

At one time Sir William Osler was Walt Whitman's physician and he quotes once with approbation these lines of Whitman: 'Ah, the glory of the day's work, whether with hand or brain! I have tried to exalt the present and the real, to teach the average man the glory of his daily work or trade.' With Whitman, Osler would quote, 'Join the whole creation of animate things and a deep heartfelt joy that you are alive, that you are the sun, that you are in this glorious earth which nature has made so beautiful, and which is yours to conquer and enjoy.'

I had a similar feeling about life in 1947 when I was recovering from a severe heart attack. In *The Coronary Club*, a small booklet I wrote concerning this, I said: 'Thus illness brought me to a quickened realization that life is good, insecure as it may be, and in spite of the overwhelming evidence of the greed, and stupidity of men on every side. It also brought a sense of humility, a feeling of thankfulness to whatever gods there be, to Nature herself, the Mother of us all, for the manifold blessings one has in this life— the beauty of the sky at night, pines against an evening sky, white birches bending in a breeze, a deer browsing alertly on a Vermont hillside, a rippling trout stream, the majestic sea crashing on our Eastern and Western coasts, white sails against a blue sky at Marblehead or Boothbay Harbour, geese flying south in the fall against a turquoise grey sky—the New York skyline, San Francisco from Sausilito.

81

Sea-winds, blown from east and west
Blown from the eastern sea, and blown from
the western sea,
till there on the prairie meeting.

Osler, as I have already indicated, believed that everybody should collect a library of books. He was, with all his Puckish humour, a man of deep faith. 'One should,' he said, 'begin the day with Christ and his prayer.' He also believed thoroughly in knowing and reading the Bible. 'At the end of the day, from your bedside library, one should spend the last half-hour in communion with the saints of humanity.' Great lessons are to be learned, and perhaps even more necessary in our nuclear age, from Job, David, Isaiah, St Paul, Shakespeare, the Stoics Epictetus and Marcus Aurelius, and from Jowett's great translation of Plato.

Alumni tell me constantly their sense of loss and regret that after leaving college they do not read any more. If they had been fortunate in college to develop the habit of building up a personal library they would not feel this as acutely as many of them do. It is certainly pathetic indeed to see the great number of men and women who appear to have no inner resources whatever, who are afraid to be alone, who play bridge hour after hour and golf with an almost sinister desperation, and who pursue themselves in circles in their effort to 'kill time'. They make a lot of psychiatrists rich.

My friend George Matthew Adams' life was made infinitely richer because of his love for books and he was one who read the books he collected. He wrote me once:

For many years I have been a modest collector of first editions of books that have specially interested me. There was a time when I smiled at first edition collectors. I do it no more. I crave their association. I learn something new from them all. I wrote to an old friend of mine and told her of my beautiful collection of first editions and asked her to come to see them. Her reply was: 'I thought books were to be read.' Well, great books *are* to be read, and should be, but when they are great books, they are also to be loved.

Adams then goes on to say that Hilaire Belloc, a highly civilized writer, once said that after he had read a great book in its first edition, all other editions were spoiled for him.

I can understand; a first edition, especially of a really good book, represents so much of the dreams, the struggles, and the anticipation of the author. Often it has meant his hunger in its creation . . . George Gissing had to borrow money to get his first book, *The Workers in the Dawn*, into print as no publisher would assume the risk. Stephen Crane had to do the same when he had his *Maggie: A Girl of the Streets* published. And so few people were interested that only a few hundred copies of each were ever sold. Today a first edition of either is costly and *Maggie* once brought $3,700 at a sale. There is something of the soul of an author in the first edition of his books, and especially in the first edition of his first book.

Collecting, I repeat, is a gentle madness which can do no possible harm; if taken too seriously, it naturally forfeits some of its appeal. As most students unfortunately lose interest in books after leaving college, collecting is one way of keeping this interest alive. Poets are filled with *furor poeticus*, but the book collector is urged on by *furor biblicus*, a passion which will enrich his life. We can only wish him God-speed and good luck.

Book collecting has given me (1) loads of fun; (2) a valuable asset in my estate (far better, I think, than stocks or bonds would have); (3) many real and rare friendships with such diverse writers as Henry Williamson, R. B. Cunninghame Graham, Richard Curle, Edward Garnett, Kenneth Roberts, Ben Ames Williams, Robert Frost, Henry L. Mencken, Henry Miller, and Henry Beston, to name a few; such booksellers as Bertram Rota, a friend for more than forty years; Harding-Edgar, Heywood Hill, and Dusty Miller, and in this country the Drakes, John van E. Kohn in New York; in California, Maxwell Hunley, David Magee, John Chanalis, and Warren Howell; such bookmen as Tom Streeter and Waller Barrett, and I could not omit Kenneth Hobson, engraver and designer extraordinary for Sangorski and Sutcliffe; (4) a pleasant and enlightening lifetime reading the books I collected, and (5) an opportunity to go into the rare book business in my later years, which is both great fun, and at times even profitable.

Reasons enough.

83

CHAPTER III

The Bookman and a few American Writers

Talent alone cannot make a writer.
There must be a man behind the book.
Ralph Waldo Emerson

Of the writers I have known in America perhaps the one who will have the most lasting fame is Robert Frost.

He thoroughly understood New England: its idiom, institutions, quirks, transitions, people, and countryside. Even though he was born in San Francisco in 1874, he lived in New England most of his life, and I can think of nobody who better typifies the best that *is* New England.

One of the great things about him, which helped make him a great poet, is the fact that by the age of seventeen Frost realized his calling in life to be poetry and, indeed, throughout his life, he kept his eye steadily on becoming a poet, allowing nothing whatever to lead him astray.

'The best thing I ever did,' Frost remarked once, 'was to write poetry. I guess so, anyway. That's the thing I get most out of. I've written it for about sixty years—I didn't make much work out of it, though. I didn't complain about the work. I can't say I'm a serious artist.'

From Shakespeare he learned early that one should observe faithfully the observance of natural speech rhythms. 'We don't get tones enough into our poetry,' he said once. 'All poetry is a reproduction of the tones of actual speech. The fun's in *how* you say a thing, and the chance it gives you for *tones* of voice.'

To the late Robert S. Newdick he wrote: 'I have three characters speaking in one poem, and I was not satisfied until I got them to speak so true to their characters that no mistake could be made as to who was speaking. I would never put the names of the speakers in front of what they were saying.

'The test is when you've worried a poem out. Then you should know whether you've got anything really new—we won't say original, but we can say a fresh thought. For instance, follow what you get out of a man like Matthew Arnold, who was confident and authoritative in prose and a lost soul in poetry. You get that lostness in phrase after phrase in his poetry. (It's by phrases that you know a man.) Arnold has explained the academic world to me.'

Mr Frost went on: 'A plain where ignorant armies clash by night. There is in the line the idea that the world is meaningless, is corrupt and impure. Arnold says—I don't remember exactly—"let the long contention cease. Geese are swans and swans are geese". It's the despair from sitting out instead of sitting in. Arnold is asking too much. We all who are literary feel a little of that. But there is difference and harshness and difficulty and that's all right. *You have to be blinded by something*. There has to be a blinding light. Love has to be blinding to make things right.'

During an interview with Frost some time ago Harvey Breit, of the *New York Times*, recalled an aphorism of Blaise Pascal, French divine and Jansenist: 'The heart has reasons of which the reason knows nothing.'

Frost nodded: 'Yes,' he said, 'Pascal's is a great kind of mind that has to be in poetry. If those things that Pascal knew are not in poetry, then you're just fastidiating along, wantoning along.'

All of Frost's friends have heard the old bard think out loud in this fashion. It is a pity that he didn't have a Boswell, though many have recorded his conversations, as I have myself in a daily journal. Lawrence Thompson comes as close as anybody to this title. Frost's own statement in 'The Figure A Poem Makes' in his *Complete* (Incomplete!!) *Poems*, 1949, explains quite well his own point of view.

The story is now fairly well known of how he sold his first poem, 'My Butterfly', when he was living in Lawrence, Massachusetts, to William Hayes Ward, of *The New York Independent* in 1894. It is also well known that in 1892 he came to Dartmouth for a couple of months, but here the education didn't *take* (no fault of Frost's), and he went off. He was 'a great fellow for poking fun, but that's about all he did at Dartmouth', one contemporary reported. He lasted two years at Harvard, a superior institution if there is one in this country, but even there he didn't like their 'busy work', and so he became a farmer.

These Derry days of Frost have been recalled to me many times by his (and mine) old and dear friend, a fellow teacher with Frost at Pinkerton Academy, Miss Sylvia Clark, of Derry Village, New Hampshire, who died in January 1964.

In 1900, the *Derry Evening News* had a slight item: 'R. Frost has moved up in the Magoon place which he purchased recently. He has a flock of nearly 300 Wyandotte hens.'[1]

For some eight years Frost farmed thirty acres of land on the Derry-Salem road and lived in a small white house that sits back from the highway a few feet. It is now called Frosty Acres and I used to pass it often on my way to Beverly when visiting my parents.[2]

West-Running Brook was between his farm and Derry Village.

A neighbour remembered: 'When lunch time came out there in the fields Rob used to wander off into the woods, and sometimes he had to be called to come back for the haying, and sometimes he just forgot to come back. Rob was like that.'

Not long ago when revisiting Derry Village, Frost reminisced: 'I was a bona fide farmer but a bad one. I milked the cows twelve hours apart, as it should be, but the milking hours on my farm were noon and midnight.'

Up to his death he was able to recall clearly former neighbours, the Websters, the Lowes, and Mr Berry, who changed 'works' with him at haying and other tasks.

There were many circumstances involved in Frost's moving to Derry. Briefly they were these: Robert Frost's mother, Isabel Moodie, came from Scotland when she was only fifteen. Miss Susan Nash, of Lawrence, Massachusetts, the sister-in-law of an old friend of mine, Walter H. Wright of Somerville, Massa-

---

[1] During the summer visit I made to Frost on August 6, 1953, at Ripton he told me that he paid $1,750 for the farm; taxes were $30 a year for ten years, and then when he sold it for $1,900 his ten years' living there had cost him practically nothing; if these figures were remembered correctly actually: $150 or $15 a year.

[2] It is now, unromantically, an ugly car dump, about to be cleared up.

chusetts, remembered Mrs Frost as 'a delightful woman, a charming personality, and a great favourite of the children in the neighbourhood'. She was very fond of young people and enjoyed reading to them and telling them stories, some of them about her girlhood in Scotland. Robert Frost's father, William Prescott Frost, Jr., was born in Kingston, New Hampshire, a small village of about a thousand inhabitants, near Exeter, and he was the ninth generation of his family to be born in New England. Frost was born in San Francisco on March 26, 1874, but remained there only until his tenth year when his father, a newspaper man, died of tuberculosis. Since most of Frost's relatives lived in New England, his mother brought him back to Lawrence, Massachusetts, where they lived with his grandfather. He went to Lawrence High School and was co-valedictorian with Elinor Miriam White whom he married on December 28, 1895. After his two attempts at formal college education, his grandfather bought him the Derry farm with the provision that he work the farm and live there ten years, after which it would become his property.

Frost stated in 1952 that *A Boy's Will* and *North of Boston* are almost completely made up of Derry-written poems. He termed the poetry: 'The good luck of my rather hard years here.'

His Derry period did prove immensely important in his development as a poet. 'West-Running Brook', one of his best poems, is about this brook in Derry which runs through the village, north of his farm, and on whose banks the first settlers built their homes in 1719. 'To the Thawing Wind', 'Now Close the Windows', 'Home Burial', 'Blueberries', 'After Apple-Picking', 'The Code' and 'The Wood-Pile' were all written about this time.

And Frost has identified the birches in one of his most famous poems as a Derry product and observed that the birch trees described are those of Southern New Hampshire and not the great White Mountain trees.

Some of his inspiration for his earlier poems came from his walks in the woods around Derry. After taking a walk with Edward Pettee, through the woods in back of Dr Clark's house, Frost wrote 'Rose Pogonias'. It is clear that in the poem 'Flower Gathering' Robert Frost's wife is the figure mentioned, and a clear picture of his farm is given in his poems 'Storm Fear',

'Wind and Window Flower', 'Tree at My Window' and 'Mending Wall'.

The poem 'Mending Wall' concerns two neighbours who made a ritual of rebuilding a stone wall between their properties each spring though the need for any fence had long since passed. The two neighbours were Robert Frost and a French Canadian, a Mr Guay, who occupied a farm next to Frost's. Frost reminisced not long before he died: 'Mr Guay was a very first class neighbour. He made beautiful axe-handles and I have helped him sand them. He was also sceptical of education. He didn't want to send his children to school. He moved often and someone said he was ducking the truant officer. His little girl said once she didn't want to see no arithmetic coming at her.'

'Mr Guay was sometimes too thrifty to be a good farmer,' Frost said, as he told of his neighbour's experience with a crop of apples. When the apples were packed in a barrel for shipment, Guay tried to put the windfalls in with them. But when the apples were taken to the station the 'cider in the air' caused the buyer to reject them. When the apples were re-sorted, the neighbour was still too thrifty to throw out all the poor ones and finally all the crop was lost.

Frost knew the farmers north of Boston very well as he has worked with them for a lifetime. He liked them. They are close to the soil, realistic, suspicious of change and new-fangled gadgets (though many now have tractors), hard-working for the most part, thrifty, tough and honest according to their own lights, and they face the elemental facts of life without fear.

To the Rev Charles Merriam and John C. Chase goes the credit, says Frost, with 'squeezing me into Pinkerton. . . .'[1] Before I was given the job,' he went on, 'I was asked by them if I would read a poem written for the occasion at the Men's League banquet in town.'

This was a poem called 'The Tuft of Flowers', later printed in *A Boy's Will*. Frost refused to read it himself, being terribly shy, but the poem was well-received, and he got the job on a part-time basis. This teaching job at Pinkerton was a life-saver at

[1] Pinkerton Academy in Derry, New Hampshire.

that time as Frost desperately needed to supplement the wholly inadequate income he got from the farm.

Of this first two year period Frost has said: 'I taught harder two years at Pinkerton than I've ever done since.' One of the years he taught thirty-five periods a week!

For the first two years he worked his farm and taught, too, but he finally had to give up his farm and give full time to teaching when he moved his family into Derry. During his last three years Frost taught English and also Latin, history and geometry. He maintained all his life a genuine interest in reading Latin, and loved the classics both in Greek and Latin.

Like Thoreau he was an innovator in teaching. He used to tell his students to 'Keep from knowing more than they know how to think with'. 'All truth,' he said, 'was dialogue.' He believed thoroughly in the Socratic method of coming to truth through question and answer.

Miss Sylvia Clark, who lived in Derry Village in her old homestead until her death and who was teaching at Pinkerton at the same time as Frost, was one of his best friends and remained so. She once wrote to me:

'The first time that Mr Frost became known in his special field to the people of Derry was when he read several of his poems at a meeting of the Derry Village Men's Club. Little did we think then that the modest young man who read to us in such a pleasing manner would be heralded as one of the country's greatest poets before many years had elapsed! Soon after this he became one of the teaching staff at Pinkerton Academy—and it was then that I came to know him well. His original method of presenting the subject of English was most interesting to his pupils, so far was it from the usual manner in which the subject was quite universally taught. His manner in the classroom was most informal and foretold the seminars which have made his college work so unique.

'One late afternoon I saw a most wonderful sunset as I looked from the chapel window at school. Anxious to have someone share the beauty before me, I called Mr Frost and our librarian to enjoy the gorgeous display. I thought that my fellow workers did not show the proper amount of enthusiasm and I told them so quite emphatically. [An understatement.] The next morning, as I

sat at my desk, Mr Frost dropped before me the following lines
written in pencil upon a sheet of yellow school paper:

An A No. 1 Sundown
(written by request)
Miss Clark gave a small party
At a western window in Chapel,
And because our delight wasn't hearty,
Or we couldn't find words to grapple
With the ravishing skyscape before us,
Miss Clark got as mad as a taurus.
She appealed to the innate calf in us
If the gold wasn't here diaphanous,
There hard and metallic and glittering.
The maddened still more by tittering
At her words diaphanous, metallic,
She called us dolichocephalic
And everything awful but feminine;
Said she wouldn't have nobody run down,
Or in anyway squeeze a lemon in,
Her beautiful A One Sundown.'

John Bartlett, one of Frost's favourite students, gave this view
of Robert: 'Robert Frost's English classes were always easy classes.
He had none of the taskmaster's attitude, yet his classes did a great
deal of work and covered fully as much ground as an ordinary
class. Any feeling for literature displayed by a student was cultivated; any talent for writing was nursed along. A few in each
class were gradually developed who could always be counted on
for lively discussion.'

Robert Frost, like many good teachers before and after him,
was shocked by the evident lack of ideas in the pupils, and he tried
to teach them to put two and two together and reason out problems for themselves. He believed that students should not be
compelled to do things, but that they had value only if they were
done on the student's initiative. He taught his students that the
importance of reading books was not just to study books by famous
men but to read for pleasure, for experience, and for the ideas one
might pick up. He was friendly to everyone and never acted like a

stuffed shirt. His class used no textbooks but instead he read poems or stories. His methods were successful but few teachers or school systems have ever adopted them.

Besides his regular teaching duties Frost also directed five plays successfully: *The Importance of Being Earnest, The School for Scandal, The Land of Heart's Desire, Comus,* and *Cathleen Ni Houlihan.*

Frost was so promising a teacher that he was invited to be Principal but the idea of losing his freedom by accepting a higher position frightened him away. It is a blessing that it did, but turning it down when he so badly needed more money is still another indication of his character, and of his tremendous desire to become a poet.

At the age of thirty-five Frost had held on to the farm at Derry for ten years and, according to his grandfather's terms, he now owned the place and could do with it as he willed. He sold it for $1,900, and with his savings from teaching at Pinkerton and the State Normal School at Plymouth for two years, he left Derry for good and sailed from Boston in August 1912 for England. Living was cheap there and in the summer of 1953 he told me that after he moved from Beaconsfield to Leadington, North of Dymock, in Gloucester, he got a house for $50 a year! In England he thought he might find himself and receive the recognition so far denied him as a poet. Derry, as he has said, had been 'a hard time', except for the poetry.

He made many English friends: Walter de la Mare, Edward Thomas, A. E. (George Russell), W. B. Yeats, W. H. Davies, and 'that young squire T. E. Hulme',[1] whose guest he was in London. With a talent for making friends, he bound all these men to him, and when his two books were issued by David Nutt, some of them wrote the reviews which made him famous, though the road ahead was still long and hard.

I have never found Frost wholly happy in his reminiscences

---

[1] T. E. Hulme (1883–1917) was an English philosopher and poet, who was killed in action in the First World War along with another English friend, Edward Thomas. Hulme also translated Bergson, and the syndicalist Sorel, as well as writing books: *Lecture on Modern Poetry, Speculations,* etc.

about England, though his time there has been called his golden summer, with walks through the lovely hills and valleys of Gloucestershire and Herefordshire, and all night talks at the Old Nailship, where Wilfrid Gibson lived, or at the Gallows, where Lascelles Abercrombie was staying. Frost has always been a stimulating talker, and he would go

> on and on and on
> In his slow New England fashion for our delight,
> Holding us with shrewd turns and racy quips,
> And the rare twinkle of his grave blue eyes.
> Again Frost's ripe and rich philosophy
> That had the body and tang of good draught cider
> And poured as clear as a stream.

The older Frost grew, the more American he became, and the more his English memories faded into the background. Perhaps he resented it a little those later years that England was the first to recognize and publish him.

The limit of his ambition he once declared was 'to lodge a few pebbles where they will be hard to get rid of'. This he has done as no American poet, I think, has ever done before.

In appearance, he was a man of granite. He had a large and stately head covered with a shock of white hair, a face deeply lined, but with glints of humour ever flashing in his blue eyes and playing around his lips like a never-ceasing flame. He carried himself with the pride that only great integrity can give a man. He is one who came up the hard way, knew poverty, disillusionment, exhausting days on the farm, constant advice to be 'practical', though never from his wife who followed his star gladly and happily, but owing to an ingrained trust in his own destiny, and to an ambition to write poetry that proved invulnerable to all the shallow lures of life, he finally triumphed, and his world-wide reputation as poet and sage is secure.[1]

Though a New Englander who writes about New England, Frost is *not* a regional poet, for his writing possesses universal appeal.

'I am not a regionalist,' Frost stated once, 'I am a realmist. I

[1] There has been a recent German edition of his poetry.

write about realms of democracy and realms of the spirit. The land is always in my bones. Someone once asked me if I was for democracy or against it and I could only say that I am so much of it that I didn't know. I have a touchiness about the subject of democracy of America. It amounts to touchiness. I know how much difficulty there is about democracy, and how much fun it is, too.'

Frost knows life and human nature as Socrates and Montaigne knew them, as many an inarticulate farmer who has lived close to the soil all his life knows them, but Frost has been endowed with the divine gift of poetry, and so has become another great writer in the humanistic tradition.

My old friend Edward Garnett did not fail in regard to Frost. As soon as he had read *North of Boston* as far back as 1915, he recognized a new voice:

'So complex may be the interlacing strains that blend in a writer's literary ancestry and determine his style, that the question first to ask seems to me whether a given author is a fresh creative force, an original voice in literature. Such an authentic original force to me speaks from *North of Boston*. Surely a genuine New England voice, whatever be its literary debt to old-world English ancestry. Originality, the point is there, for we may note that originality of tone and vision is always the stumbling block to the common taste when the latter is invited to readjust its accepted standards.

'Mr Frost possesses a keen feeling for situation. And his fine, sure touch in clarifying our obscure instincts and clashing impulses, and in crystallizing them in sharp, precise images, for that we cannot be too grateful.

'But is Mr Frost then a humorist? The reader may inquire, seeing a gleam of light. Humour has its place in his work: that is to say, our author's moods take their rise from his contemplative scrutiny of *character* in men and nature, and he responds equally to a tragic episode or a humorous situation.'

All of these remarks, and others the reader may find in Edward Garnett's *Friday Nights*, New York, 1922, are as astute and pertinent today as they were over forty years ago. As Frost's career progressed his subtle, almost pawky sense of humour appeared again and again in his poetry.

When I was in his company we both laughed a great deal at life and at people, but the laughter was never malicious. One of our pet subjects we laughed about was the possessive attitude that some of his friends took toward him. It was sometimes difficult to combat.

I trust the reader has already noted the 'comic spirit' in Frost's *A Masque of Reason* and *A Masque of Mercy*. Someday someone will write a chapter on 'The Comic Spirit in Frost'.

I think Mr Herman Wouk makes a good point in the following, and though he didn't have Frost in view when he wrote it, he might well have had: 'The ability to laugh and to make others laugh at the wretched predicament of mankind, poor spirits trapped in muddy cranky doomed bodies, is beyond the powers of all but the most brilliant and mature minds; minds, moreover, steeped in the melancholy knowledge of the inescapable blackness in life. It is not for the young fresh folks who rightly love the world and see it as green and good.'

I think Frost saw it as green and good, but he also saw and knew some of the ever present shadows.

He was, in spite of personal losses in his family, able to maintain a salty, humorous, and almost 'above the battle' attitude. He had courage and wisdom. He was also a kindly man but one afternoon in the summer of 1953 he said to me while driving to Ripton from Middlebury, 'Never use the word compassion in connection with me. To Hell with so and so, this and that.' He conveyed the idea that he was not a softy. . . . That he admired the Tory type which is realistic and without the mushy sentimentalism which he felt Henry Wallace showed before he dropped out of public life. He was somewhat of an isolationist in that he thought we should stop trying to prove to everybody how good, generous, and nice we are. This earns only contempt and hatred for us everywhere in the world. There was a great deal of sense in everything Frost said, though I did not always agree with him. He was stimulating, and generally left one with a few new and original slants on life and people.

On August 6, 1953, I drove with a Texas friend, Gentry L. Rowsey of San Antonio, to Ripton, took Robert out for lunch beyond Middlebury at the Dog Team Dining Place, and then we came back to sit in his new pine-panelled study in the farm-house to chat a while. I was happy to see a large watercolour of mine there. He was in excellent form, extremely friendly and genial, and looked hale and hearty. I asked him if he wanted to rest after lunch. 'No,' he said, 'I never rest, I'm too restless.' He was somewhat incensed by what he considered a deliberate slight on the part of the nearby *Rutland Herald* which had recently mentioned him as 'R. Frost, a Ripton poet'. As Frost is internationally known this had hurt his feelings, which were, I might say, highly sensitive to criticism. He felt that Vermont loved to 'take him down a peg'. He told me that this is the reason he never read reviews of his books. He couldn't sleep for twenty-four hours if he read something unkind or bad about his work. I told him that I was writing on him and that I was emphasizing his humour. He told me that once at Amherst the president meant to introduce him with one line from his poetry, but later in the excitement had failed to do so. The line was:

The way to understand is partly mirth.

We then looked up the poem from which this line came, 'Not Quite Social', and I asked Robert to say it to us which he did in his familiar form and then, after he had finished, he remarked, with pride, 'That's a good poem.'

The stanza in question goes like this:

You may taunt me with not being able to flee the earth.
You have me there, but loosely as I would be held.
The way of understanding is partly mirth
I would not be taken as ever having rebelled.

He was reading my *Rebel Thought*, bits at a time, spoke especially of how interested he had been in the Bruno chapter, and then growled imprecation, using dignified but strong language against the iniquities of the church, which he figured had inveigled Bruno back to Italy to kill him. He is not strongly religious in *any* churchy sense. He spoke of our Carlos Baker's book on Hemingway, which he thought had been a little too insistent on stressing Hemingway's religious tendencies. He said, with somewhat Rabelaisian turn of phrase, that the book should have

95

been called *Bulls, Balls, and Beatitudes*. We roared with laughter, and then he went on to explain to Rowsey about the Danakil country (which he had read in Nesbitt's book) and of the strange customs there having to do with the testicles of the conquered. This from *Desert and Forest* which I have already mentioned, and which we both had always admired.

Robert had a little house of his own at the top of the hill above the Ripton 'Homer Noble' farm, and he told us both how he had to live alone. He *had* to feel free and independent. There was a living-room in the cabin, with a fireplace, a bedroom, and a lot of books along the wall, on the floor, and on chairs and tables. They indicated a varied taste: poetry, philosophy, Latin poetry, travel, Well's on the Catholic Church (very anti), history, but little fiction. There was a blanket on the chair where Frost had been sitting that morning, as it had been cold, reading. Mornings he took for himself, though he was willing to be sociable in the afternoon and evenings with friends. And he knew *everybody*. He liked Robert Taft, who was forthright, and who a few weeks before Taft died had said bluntly to Frost, on being asked how Eisenhower was doing: 'He's learning.'

Frost defined war as 'acute and bloody politics' which comes pretty close to hitting the nail on the head.

We got discussing nudism and Frost averred that he would rather be a Communist than a nudist.

Gentry, himself a budding poet, told me later that Frost spoke poetry in almost everything he said; instinctively he spoke in pleasing rhythms. We had been discussing Ireland, and how her good writers have to live away owing to the medieval attitudes still prevailing at home. Frost said:

> At night
> The priests went, with a club
> Among the hedges,
> And found the boys and girls,
> And married them
> On the spot

This he had heard from some Irish writer.

Once in New York at a gathering Frost saw Auden and another

poet talking to a priest. Frost nodded without speaking to the poets, one a strong Anglo-Catholic, and said to the priest, 'Are you a convert?'

The priest looked piously horrified and replied, 'Goodness, no!'

Frost said, offering his hand, 'Shake on it, neither am I,' and walked off.

A young American, Philip Booth, has written well of Frost as a poet. I would like him to have a word here on Frost, which he wrote on the occasion of Frost's seventy-ninth birthday: 'Now he is an old hand at both seed and harvest, but the roots of his words have gone deep. That his lesser poems seem stunted in the shade of his great ones is natural; his deep woods lyrics grow further above the forest each year. Such poems as "To Earthward", "Directive", and "The Gift Outright" generate a delight that is more than laughter and are themselves wisdom as whole as love. Working tight joined words together, Robert Frost celebrates a world with which (as he says) he has no more than "a lover's quarrel". It is a world about which he has the courage to say, "Let what will be, be". And he himself has stood as a constant symbol of the poetry in it. What that poetry is, nobody knows better. "Poetry", his whole life tells, is "words that have become deeds".'

In this age of irrationalism, dishonesty, and political stupidity, Frost was indeed a man of great sanity. His talk, and most of his poetry, cut cleanly through the muddled thinking of our time, like one of Mr Guay's sharp axes. He is indeed not far from being the embodiment in wisdom and sound humour of George Meredith's 'comic spirit'. It is always a benign humour but it has a sharp cutting edge, and as time goes on, and as I read more and more of Frost, it appears to me to grow richer and wiser with the years.

For the collector Frost will offer real difficulty as there is much ephemeral material, dear to the true collector, which is almost impossible to procure. Furthermore, there is only one copy of *Twilight,* and that is now in Waller Barrett's collection in the University of Virginia.

Two other writers who were also close friends of mine were the late Ben Ames Williams and Kenneth Roberts.

It is so easy for the pedagogue, especially the teacher of English, to sneer at popular writers—writers who become rich through serial and movie rights, and royalties on the books themselves. Few of them can sell anything and too often forget Samuel Johnson's realistic remark, quite without cant and containing a lot of truth and good sense: 'No man but a blockhead ever wrote except for money.' Furthermore, successful does not always mean inferior work. Many of the great novelists in the past have been great financial successes, as witness Dickens, Thackeray, Galsworthy and, toward the end of his life, Conrad.

Ben Ames Williams was the most business-like of any writer I have ever known. When he died suddenly in February 1953, he left behind records of his writing life which must be unique in the history of American fiction writing, and which will offer some future literary historian a literal gold mine of fascinating information.

When Williams left his Boston newspaper job to become a writer he kept an account of the number of words he wrote each day, of when each story was sold, and how much he got for it; later he did the same with his books. His account could be no more complete had he been in business selling soap or woollens. Furthermore, he kept it up right up to the day of his death.

Ben Ames Williams radiated energy and worked as hard as any businessman I know. He was a man's man, a hunter, fisherman, and gun collector; an indefatigable traveller, tireless as a worker, most unassuming and unusually modest about his success, and courageous in facing difficulties. He was also the kind of a father who entirely won the love, pride and devotion of his family.

He learned his craft by hard work. He worked first as a practising newspaperman in Boston for four years, and every night during that time he wrote short stories. The four years were up before he sold his first story, but by then he was beginning to know his business. Nothing deterred him, and he came to have ambitions to be a writer of importance. From then until his death at sixty-three his output was enormous.

His novels run from the 205 page *All the Brothers Were Valiant*, 1919, to *House Divided*, 1947, which runs to 1,500 pages.

One of his happiest books is called *The Happy End*, published by the Derrydale Press. It consists of autobiographical sketches and tells about his Maine friend and mentor, Bert McCorrison, a farmer who, thinly disguised if at all, is the Chet McAusland in his short stories about Fraternity (Searsmont, Maine), issued in 1949 as *Fraternity Village*.

According to his own statement, meeting McCorrison one day in the summer of 1918 was the most important event in his literary life. McCorrison lived in Searsmont, and when he died in 1931 he left Williams his farm, over which, by his request, Williams' ashes were scattered after he died. Ben wrote: 'Bert had an abiding love for the out-of-doors, a timeless memory, and a strong instinct which led him to remember most vividly those incidents in which dwelt the elements of dream. Through him and with him, I began to know the countryside around his farm, and some of the things that in his memory had happened there.'

These 'Fraternity' stories were written from 1919 to 1940, and seem to me to represent the best writing Williams did, giving us, as they do, an authentic picture of a part of the real American scene. They lack the finesse and artistry found in Sarah Orne Jewett, but they compensate for this in their masculinity and vividness.

As Williams' writing years progressed, as he became more and more and more the master of his craft, his ambitions and stature grew. He wrote a trilogy *Thread of Scarlet*, 1939, *Come Spring*, 1940, and the best known, *The Strange Woman*, 1941. This was an enormous success but what impresses me most is Williams' amazing industry—three long novels in successive years, all requiring intensive research. *Come Spring* alone runs to 900 pages.

His *House Divided* seemed to me to be a major work of American fiction, and one of the best American novels on the Civil War that I am aware of. At least twenty years of research went into it, and four and a half years of writing.

Ben Ames Williams was born in Mississippi, and he knew the South well. Though he sympathized with her, he never lost his faith in the Northern cause. He once wrote: 'The South today boasts not so often of its "cavalier"; it has learned to hold a just pride in its men of humble ways. The war saved the Union, but it did much more; it proved, once and for all, the valour and virtue of the common man.'

In *Owen Glen*, 1950, Williams again drew from his own memories of Ohio where he had lived as a youth, of his father, and his Americanism, and wrote a novel about a great labour leader in which he shows his sympathies, always realistic and never sentimental, for the common man. Though not a success as far as sales go, it shows Ben's love and wider understanding of these United States.

The last time I saw Ben we drove from Hanover over the mountains to North Woodstock, New Hampshire, to see a rather eccentric old man who advertised himself as 'Schiff the Gunman' whom Ben knew well. His shack, built off the road in the deep woods, was deceptive, for, though it looked like an old junk shop, it contained many valuable guns, some of which were worth a thousand dollars or more. Though Mr Schiff looked as if he didn't possess the price of a cup of coffee, Ben told me that he would be able to pay two or three thousand in cash for a gun if he wanted it badly enough, and knew that he would find a ready collector for it. Old Schiff, who must have been ninety that summer of '52, was an ardent Republican, and kept repeating himself about 'Delerium Trumans', in tones of disgust, but he knew his guns and their value. He was deaf, yet he could always hear what he wanted to hear, Ben told me. If you offered him $20 for a gun, he wouldn't hear you, but if you had said $60 he would have heard you across the shop. He was a shrewd trader, but Ben was shrewder, and knew Colts probably better than Old Schiff. Ben bought a couple of revolutionary war powder horns, one for his friend Ken Roberts and one for himself, but he saw no guns, no model of a Colt that he didn't already possess. He drove an old Plymouth roadster, and drove it fast, and more than once I had to grasp the side of the car to keep from being thrown about. It was a pleasant day, and I regret that there will be no more like it, for both Ben and Old Schiff are now discussing the relative merits of this or that Colt in a world unknown.

Kenneth Roberts was a man of great probity, irascibility and charm. His wide experiences as a soldier, correspondent for the *Saturday Evening Post*, and almost professional state of Mainer, fitted him perfectly for writing the chronicles of Arundel. He

100

wrote at his best with the gusto and vitality of genius, and in depicting epic marching, hardships of the pioneer trails, battles on land or water, he has had few, if any, equals in American historical fiction. What he lacked, it has always seemed to me, was the power of selection and discrimination in order to create an artistic whole. Seeking to find the truth about a character, such as Robert Rogers, he insisted on telling the whole story of his life, instead of a segment which had unity, or a beginning, middle and an end. In *Northwest Passage*, for instance, the best part of the book, and in fact a masterpiece of historical writing, is Book I, in which Roberts describes most graphically Rogers' trip back from the attack on St Francis, down the Ammonoosuc and Connecticut Rivers to Old Number 4, in Charlestown, New Hampshire. The latter part about Rogers in London, and his subsequent decline, is well done, but it detracts from the artistic whole which Roberts achieved in the first part of the book.

Referring to Metro-Goldwyn-Mayer's film, *Northwest Passage*, Roberts wrote me, 'Those b——s did a worse job of massacring on the book than Rogers ever did at St Francis.'

The fact that Kenneth Roberts became passionately concerned about America's water supply and of the supersensory powers of Henry Gross may make one forget his early and extraordinary powers as a novelist. His last two books were written with the zeal of a fanatical crusader, and with a little too much readiness to damn with an irascible kind of petulance anybody who couldn't accept the mysterious powers of Mr Gross. It is meet and right, it seems to me, for science and scientists to be most sceptical of any signs of the miraculous, especially from one in mufti. Miracles are the rightful property of the Holy Church, and even there they are beginning to wear a little thin.

For years I have been collecting his books, but only, I think, his historical novels have permanent significance.

As I felt back in 1936 that Roberts' painstaking research in writing his novels marked an important step ahead in the writing of American historical fiction I got him to write out a statement which would throw light on the way he went about his work. As the book which reproduced this letter has long been out of print, and will probably remain so, I again reproduce his words here:

I have a theory that history can be most effectively told in the form of fiction, because only in the writing of fiction that stands the test of truth do falsities come to the surface. Historians of the Northern Army have either ignored the most enlightening details of the campaigns or have failed to dig up the detail which they should have possessed, or have refused to point out the misrepresentations and downright lies for which diarists, journalists and so on were responsible. They have, for example, failed to reveal the singular literary knaveries of Gen. James Wilkinson; the construction and rig of Arnold's fleet; who was Burgoyne's mistress, who were the male and female spies that Burgoyne used; what were the 'underhanded attempts' made in Congress and by outside enemies to undermine and destroy the reputation of 'the brave General Arnold'; what Western Indians fought for Burgoyne, where they came from and how; what was the true character of Hazen, Gates, Arnold, Wilkinson, Brown, Easton, Sullivan—especially Sullivan—Wooster and others; why St Clair testified there was a full moon on the night of the retreat from Ticonderoga when the British would have destroyed the American army if there had been a full moon, and so on and so on. . . . The constant gauge of a conscientious novelist must be, 'Is this true: is this the way it happened?' That gauge is applied to everything—conversation, characters, action. The historian isn't bothered by that gauge. He can accept a statement made by a reliable man. If St Clair says in his court martial that the moon was full on July 5, 1776, Hoffman Nickerson naturally feels free to accept it. When I come to writing the action on the night of July 5, however, I find that the night was clear with a hot wind blowing: that the Americans retreated beneath the screen of darkness and smoke, and that it wasn't until Fermoy's cabin burned that the British caught sight of the retreat. When I say to myself, 'Is this true: is this the way it happened?' I am at once made uncomfortable by the illumination that a full moon would have caused. By consulting a calendar for 1776, I find that St Clair was mistaken. The moon on July 5, 1776, was a new moon. It went down shortly after sundown. There wasn't any moon at all during the retreat.

If I trust Arnold's biographers, I must believe he was a small man physically and mentally—a cheap trader: a 'horse jockey'; a person without property, perception or good taste. Most biographers, however, seem to lack the mental qualifications necessary to understand the men they write about. Independent investigation shows that Arnold was the same height and build as Theodore Roosevelt, Sr.; that he was wealthy—generous—one of the first contributors to Dartmouth College; that at the age of thirty he built a beautiful home and furnished it with rare judgment. Among the furnishings were a Goddard block-front secretary-desk and a Goddard block-front high-boy; pieces which, 160 years later, were among the most highly-prized specimens of one of America's foremost collectors—George H. Lorimer of Philadelphia. It takes brains, foresight and the best of taste to invest in such furnishings. Few millionaires and even fewer historians, at any age, display the taste and perception that Arnold showed at thirty. . . . The conscientious novelist, applying his gauge of 'is this the way it happened' to most histories, finds himself continually disgusted at the untruths or half-truths he uncovers. Tolstoy, when he wrote *War and Peace*, was in a perpetual rage at the incompetence of French historians, and didn't hesitate to say so.

However, most of that is beside the point. What I wanted to do, in writing *Arundel* and *Rabble in Arms*, was to tell the full and truthful story of the Northern Army in such a way that any person, in a couple of days of reading, could understand what it had taken me three years to understand, and almost as long a time to put clearly on paper. I had an open mind on Arnold. I still have. But I feel free to say that no honest person can study and understand the full story of the Northern Army without giving Arnold exactly the same break that I did. The person who won't do so is either incapable of understanding motives or character, or is a moral coward, or is one who has allowed his judgment of a fact to be coloured by his knowledge of what happened later. I can show these things to you clearly in all books on Arnold. Again and again, in these books, brave, brilliant, and unselfish acts are freely condemned because Arnold *later* turned traitor. The biographies of Arnold are among the most ludicrous things in literature because of the grim determination of their authors *not* to see the truth, and their eagerness to accept any hearsay evidence.

I can give you an example of how dangerous it is to accept hearsay evidence on Arnold. I had hunted hard to find examples, outside of his final treachery, of underhanded acts on Arnold's part. I couldn't on the evidence make him out to be anything but a man of the greatest generosity, unselfishness, bravery, and good taste. In Portsmouth, five years ago, I got wind of an Arnold letter: one, my informant said, that showed Arnold, long before he turned traitor, to be a crook for ever in need of money: a spendthrift; a man who'd cheat his best friend. Since such a letter would establish, as a fact, something that I had only been able to find as hearsay evidence, I felt I must have it. Its owner, a Portsmouth man, had moved to Florida, and I was two years getting it. It had been written at Quebec, and thanked Hector MacNeil (builder of the fireship) for his offer of financial assistance to the struggling colonies. It was as kind, generous, straightforward dignified letter as any man could write. The person who told me about it had seen it; but he, like so many biographers and historians, was an 'after-the-fact' boy. Arnold was a traitor; therefore, everything he had ever done must necessarily have been bad.

People insist in thinking that in *Arundel* and *Rabble* I was writing Arnold's story. I wasn't at all. I was writing the story of the Northern Army. I wrote Arnold as I found him . . . as I tried to write everyone connected with that army.

Since this was written Roberts wrote *Northwest Passage*, but *Lydia Bailey*, I thought, though individual parts were vigorous and even brilliant, had too much in it, and was not up to the standards of most of his other historical fiction.

No writer could be more unlike Williams or Roberts than Henry Miller.

I first met Henry Miller on April 1, 1940, when I had invited him and Ranald P. Hobbs, a publishing executive, to come to lunch with me at the Dartmouth Club in New York. Miller arrived at noon, a most inoffensive chap, a leprechaun in a yellow coat and an old hat, indifferent to everything but life itself, and at the moment, a good meal. Miller told me that I looked just like somebody he knew in Paris; that I looked just as he thought I would look. 'I love to eat,' he said. He ordered a cocktail, a glass of wine, and thoroughly enjoyed himself. I was called away during lunch and can recall little of the conversation, but I do have the impression of an *individual*, an eccentric and honest one, searching for a patron who would give him food, clothing, and shelter and let him create as he will. He was anxious to come to Dartmouth as, he said, I was the first American critic to recognize him with my article about his work in the *Dartmouth Alumni Magazine* in 1938.

Shortly after he wrote me (April 10), 'I hope to be able to pay you a visit some weekend maybe next month. Am working myself to the bone now. My old man is slowly dying of cancer, and I am put to it to raise dough to pay doctor's bills and so forth. But I find that I have many friends here and that alone sustains me. I am glad you call yourself my friend—the feeling is mutual. I think you are the first American critic to speak about my work here— something I will never forget.'

Sometimes his emotional excesses and his almost complete lack of self-criticism has vitiated some of his work for me. It has been his misfortune, as it was Walt Whitman's, to believe in all the silly stuff that has been written about him by his most ardent admirers. He is the most conspicuous and violent anti-intellectual I know, and as I believe in reason and in the intellectual and intelligent approach as the only hope of correcting the excesses of our time, I have lost some faith in his thought and ideas. But he is a great individualist and at his best a great writer.

In his autobiographical books such as *Black Spring*, *Tropic of Cancer*, *Tropic of Capricorn*, and *The Rosy Crucifixion*, Miller explodes an amazing scenario about himself, in which it is most difficult to tell fact from fancy. He omits nothing, and uses four letter words excessively, and often unnecessarily, but the effect is often most convincing and at times overwhelming.[1]

It is unfortunate, it seems to me, that among the younger people I know he is read almost entirely for what they consider his pornography. Of this Herbert Read has written: 'Miller is probably, in this technical sense, the most obscene writer in the history of literature. At least he exceeds the considerable efforts of writers like Catullus, Petronious, Boccaccio and Rabelais. But he is never obscene for obscenity's sake—there is no "effort" about his obscenity—it is all part of the process of realization, a natural consequence of his devastating honesty, and also of his vitality, his *joie de vivre*.'

I can go along with most of this, but having read *The Rosy Crucifixion* in manuscript, I am not sure that this book, at least, wasn't written deliberately to be sensational.

Miller is devastatingly honest and individualistic and with these qualities I am in complete sympathy. He cannot be bought, and his integrity as a writer is clearly established.

He is a primitivist who can, once in a while, write like an angel. He is an anarchist more dangerous than Emerson or Thoreau, be-

[1] See my chapter 'The Strange Case of Henry Miller', in *The Mind on the Wing*, New York, 1947.

105

cause in them there was a hard core of rationalism which is missing in Miller. He is the mighty I AM in literature, an elemental force who can at times write the most utter nonsense, and who is capable of believing in the most metaphysical bilge one can think of, as, for instance, the Gospel of Sri Rama Krishna.

However, when it comes to some of his shorter pieces, such as 'Reunion in Brooklyn' to be found in his *Sunday After the War*, 1944, I can agree, with certain reservations, with the English enthusiast Herbert Read who has written: 'In this genre of realistic narrative Miller can stand comparison with the greatest writers of the past—Balzac, Dickens, Zola, Flaubert—and on all counts except that of sustained productivity, I think he beats the lot.'

This goes, perhaps, further than I would go, but it indicates Miller's once high standing with the best of critics and, for all I know, these critics may still hold Miller in extravagant esteem.

In 1939 my *The Nature Writers* appeared, with a foreword by Henry Beston, the most poetic in spirit of any of our living nature writers.

This little book originated in a course of mine at Dartmouth which I have called *The Nature Writers*. Its purpose was to bring before as many students as possible great books on nature, which they might read and collect through college, and, it was hoped, after college as well; though for most graduates reading often ends with their degree. Nearly all of us today, city or country dwellers, love the countryside, the rivers, brooks, forests, hills, mountains, and all the changing and ever wonderful aspect of the face of God's green earth. Nature writing has produced some of the finest literature in our language, and with the use of our imaginations, and with these books as a guide, we can enrich our lives by travelling to all the corners of the earth, we can learn even though in a desultory fashion, some of the mysteries and marvels of nature. The man who, for the first time, reads Fabre's *Social Life in the Insect World*, will undergo an experience he will never forget, and always thereafter, when he hears at night the chirping of crickets or scores of noises audible on a clear summer evening, will be wiser for being aware of the interminable warfare which goes on incessantly, as indeed it does among humans, everywhere about him. He will recognize Nature for what it is: inexorable, indifferent, beautiful, manifold, and inscrutable, and he may, as did Fabre himself, derive therefrom a saner and truer philosophy of life.

Nature writing as we know it today is a comparatively new thing. Our modern feeling for nature, which at times, as in the case of Henry Beston, assumes a half-mystical aspect, is less than 200 years old. One remembers Samuel Johnson's remark as late as the middle of the eighteenth century, when Boswell mentioned the sublimity and beauty of a Scottish hill, that it was merely 'a considerable protuberance'.

Our contemporary feeling for nature goes back to the Copernican Revolution which destroyed the ancient concepts of Ptolemy, and along with these much of the framework of Christian theology. This astronomical revolution, together with the revival of learning which we call the Renaissance, led to Spinoza's pantheism, ultimately to a faith in democracy, and finally to the displacement of an absolute and anthropomorphic God by a New Creator, or the old Creator under a new aspect, called Nature.

The eighteenth century saw the first great outburst of nature writing, and by this I mean literature which was predominantly interested in natural phenomena—birds, insects, animals, green fields, mountains, hedgerows, plains, oceans, the stars and the heavens: the natural green world in which we live.[1]

The Romantic Movement ushered in the view via Wordsworth and others that God was now revealed in a running brook, in the pines against the evening sky, and sunsets and moonrises aroused in the onlooker a feeling of religious awe. There were sermons in rocks and in evening primroses, Man had become a part of nature, not above it, and his transcendental self disappeared.

Most Protestants today, if they are not out and out disbelievers in the Christian God, are pantheists, and nature writing is now one of the most prolific of the literary genres, especially in

[1] For a fuller discussion of this development of nature writing and its implications see Chapter 1, 'The Modern Dilemma', in my book, *Rebel Thought*, Boston, 1953.

England. Here, too, nature books by Donald Culross Peattie, Edwin Way Teale, Henry Beston, Sally Carrighar, and others enjoy a great popularity, and often a wide sale.

So far as I know there was no course like it in the American college, and I was pleased when Henry Beston, an old friend of many years' standing, wrote to me on June 24, 1949, on the occasion of his receiving an honorary Phi Beta Kappa key in the Harvard chapter, 'I told the Harvard group that you had devised the most original and valuable single course in modern university history.'

For years I have had Henry Beston end the course with a lecture on the relationship of man to nature and he has never failed to stimulate and stir the class as few lecturers have been able to do.

He expressed his point of view some years ago in his little classic of nature writing, *The Outermost House*, the manuscript of which he presented, at my request, to Dartmouth. He wrote:

Whatever attitude to human existence you fashion for yourself, know that it is valid only if it be the shadow of an attitude to Nature. A human life, so often likened to a spectacle upon a stage, is more justly a ritual. The ancient values of dignity, beauty, and poetry which sustain it are of Nature's inspiration; they are born of the mystery and beauty of the world. Do no dishonour to the earth lest you dishonour the spirit of man. Hold your hands out over the earth as over a flame. To all who love her, who open to her the doors of their veins, she gives her strength, sustaining them with her own measureless tremor of dark life. Touch the earth, love the earth, honour the earth, her plains, her valleys, her hills, and her seas; rest your spirit in her solitary places. For the gifts of life are the earth's and they are given to all, and they are the songs of birds at daybreak, Orion and the Bear, and dawn seen over ocean from the beach.

Henry is a man of imposing bulk and height ('Do I look older, Herbert?'), with piercing, dark brown eyes; he stoops slightly, and has a good voice. He has great nervous energy and vitality. He wears picturesque clothes in daring colours; there is a flair about him. His speech flows in ordered cadence; he chooses his words carefully and if the effect is particularly good he is apt to repeat it, savouring the words and their meaning, and waiting, like an actor, for the effect they will have on his hearer. If one didn't know him well one would suspect him of being somewhat of a 'poseur' but he is entirely sincere; a man of feeling with an excellent sense of humour. He uses such words as 'life', 'vital', 'youth', with the suggestion that these words in themselves contain the meaning of life.

Henry Beston was born in Quincy, Massachusetts, June 1, 1888. He went to Harvard, graduating a year before T. S. Eliot, and with whom, I suspect, he has little in common. He lived in France, and learned the language so well that it is a second tongue for him. During the First World War he was first with the American Field Service attached to the French Army, and wrote a book about it called *A Volunteer Poilu*, which appeared in 1916. I think this was his first book, and one he chooses to forget. Subsequently he has written, besides the *Outermost House*, 1928, *Herbs and the Earth*, 1935, *Northern Farm*, 1948, *Henry Beston's Fairy Tales*, 1952, as well as two anthologies, *American Memory*, 1937, and *White Pine and Blue Water*, 1950. All of his books are of the American soil, richly, creatively American.

Though Beston is serious about man and his relation to nature he always has a twinkle in his eye, and he possesses a good sense of the ridiculous as is witnessed by a letter I received from him in 1939 from Pasadena after he had visited the Henry E. Huntington Library (which *is* magnificent) and Art Gallery, in San Marino. The estate also contains a palm collection, a desert plant collection, a cycad collection, an Oriental garden, and the impressive tomb which contains the tycoon's remains. Beston wrote: 'I suppose what finished me was a longish afternoon at the Huntington Museum in Pasadena [actually it is in San Marino]. The largest and most important public collection of eighteenth-century portraits in the world is shown there to a distressed public. There are acres, no less, of Gainsboroughs, Romneys, Reynolds, and Hoppners, all of 'em "cleaned" and revarnished as bright as so many California automobiles. Why do the museum people commit such barbarities? We wandered from room to room, past beauty after beauty, the dress and hands smudged on, the pretty worldly aristocratic faces studied with care, spending the afternoon among pinks and blues, and pretty hands leaning on

Georgian balustrades. When I came out I felt as if I'd been to Rumpelmayer's...two Hogarths were the best things in the house.'

Beston is fundamentally a lonely man, for he knows, as we all do, that the achievement of intellectual maturity has always included a certain loneliness, and the creative, and especially poetic, spirits of today, forced to live in a plastic and atomic civilization appear to be particularly solitary in these vexed and over-clouded times. Frost revolted in *Why Wait for Science?*

> Sarcastic Science she would like to know
> In her complacent ministry of fear,
> How we propose to get away from here
> When she has made things so we have to go
> Or be wiped out. Will she be asked to show
> Us how by rocket we may hope to steer
> To some star off there say a half-light year
> Through temperature of absolute zero?
> Why wait for Science to supply the how
> When any amateur can tell it now?
> The way to go away should be the same
> As fifty million years ago we came
> If anyone remembers how that was.
> I have a theory, but it hardly does.

Beston recently wrote me characteristically: 'Man as a poet lives as man, as a collector and user of facts, he dies as a Devil, his horrible, "de-poetized"—forgive a fearsome word—culture trembling in iron, sharp glass, plastic and blood down on his sterile and cruel bones.' Later along the same lines he wrote: 'And I liked the *Letter to a Threatened World* [a poem by Dilys Laing] and am glad to see some evidence of a power to feel still moving in the world whose characteristic disease is a separation of thought and emotion.'

Beston believes that we should, as he so often puts it, be on the side of life; on the side of the great creative forces of existence, and not on the side of death and destruction, which is to him represented by the atomic bomb, and by modern war which is a gigantic swindle, and a crime against humanity. The galaxies and constellations are outside us, but are aesthetically ours, and man must retain a cosmic perspective of the universe.

Beston is always aware of the beauty of the heavens, and some of his best passages are descriptive of the magic and mystery of the night. He knows his planets and the stars. A note will arrive: 'Tell your son to look for Mercury in the West, perpendicularly above the sun's place of setting in the darkening twilight. Visible for about three or four days more.' He likes youth and wants youth to have the right to enjoy its rightful heritage of wonder and reverence for nature. He thinks Thoreau had too celibate a mind, that he is too dry, too moral, and that in his books he misses the daemonic quality of nature. There is a gusto in Nature that one must not overlook. Nature is full of high spirits and possesses, as well, a genuine nightmare quality, as in the cartoonist Addams. This, Beston thinks, Thoreau misses. What man needs to re-capture, or regain, is a reverent awareness of life, and he should consider *himself* a part of this great adventure of living. Many must never lose his ancient sense, which the American Indians had to a great degree, of pietas, a feeling of reverence for nature and its mighty manifestations, or to revel in the pure adventure of being a human being. We must live with nature and as a *part of it*.

I have cultivated for many years the books of one for whom I have had great admiration, and whose point of view is closer to my own than any man I know. This is Henry L. Mencken of Baltimore, who, after a long and cruel illness, died mercifully in his sleep on January 29, 1956.

I suspect that the sale of his posthumous *Minority Report*, 1956, proves that he still has many readers. The publications of Mencken's *Chrestomathy* in 1949 revealed also that his writings are astonishingly little dated. What he wrote about politicos, for instance, remains for ever true.

In May 1953 I visited in Los Altos, California, Mr George T. Keating, who had a fine collection of inscribed Mencken books which he turned over, with characteristic generosity, to my college library. With the great collection we already had, we now possess one of the two or three great Mencken collections in the country. We shared a real affection for Mencken, and a sincere respect for his talents and his many books, of which probably the most lasting are his scholarly volumes on the American language, and his three volumes of autobiography.

111

In the 'twenties and early 'thirties Mr Mencken was un-questionably a force, and a symbol of revolt among the agile-minded against the incredible Prohibitionists, who nearly ruined America; against Comstockery, which made us a laughing stock among the literate nations; against science baiters like the late sainted William Jennings Bryan, once Secretary of State under Woodrow Wilson; against the incredibly low and vulgar standards, if indeed they could be said to have any, of the great American *Booberai* (to use his own word); against the Fundamentalists who thought that God dictated the Bible word for word to an earthly amanuensis, and who inhabited what Mencken was prone to call the Bible Belt; and, in fact, against all the shoddy ideas and forces which made the country he loved often ridiculous in the eyes of honest men.

During the 'twenties he, for a short time with George Jean Nathan, made the *American Mercury* the most amusing maga-zine in America.

I turn to a copy picked up at random (it happens to be the issue of October 1928) and find the following:

On the anti-saloon league:

Has the world ever seen another so impudent, so unconscionable, so profoundly immoral, an organization, or another so ingenuous, so all fired amusing? None such reveals itself in the chronicles. The human race had to wait for nineteen centuries after the death of Paul before the marvel could be achieved. It took that long for the mysterious laws of Mendel, operating through sixty generations, to produce Christians of the high voltage of [Wayne B.] Wheeler and his gang. And it took a thousand generations, beginning far back in Aurignacian times, to produce a sufficiency of morons to give them their perfect opportunity, and so make them great.'

On democracy:

The story of the Anti-Saloon League, in truth, is largely the story of democracy in latter-day America. It shows the extent to which mob rule, going on unfettered for years, can debauch and degrade govern-ment. First the mob fills all the principal public offices with heroes to its taste, i.e. cowards, ignoramuses, and scoundrels, and then bold and unprincipled pressure groups, operating upon these vermin, reduced the whole process of law-making to imbecility. . . . The eighteenth amendment was put into the constitution by the votes of less than 3,000 legislators. How many were actual prohibitionists? Probably 500. The rest were simply scoundrels selling out their honour for their jobs. The anti-Saloon League had shown them how, by manipulating the balance of power, it could punish recalcitrants. So they leaped to the crack of its whip—and the country was plunged into an orgy of corruption that has filled its legislatures, State and Federal, with rogues, polluted and disgraced its courts, and made it a practical impossibility for a frank and honest man to hold public office. Such are the charms and benefits of democracy! . . .

It is appalling to think that there are men to whom such appalling swinishness is not only disgusting, but actually laudable—that fully half of the professing Christians of the United States wallow in it and glory in it.

Mencken's book reviews and editorials were always full of sound observations. They are a joy to read even now, and their good sense is as pertinent as it ever was. In our local, state, and federal government we are, with some notable exceptions, still governed by ignoramuses, rogues, and scoundrels, and it is a mystery to me why Nemesis has not overtaken us long before this. Our persistence in honouring and rewarding scoundrels and mediocrity, in the end, I fear, will spell our doom.

Mencken's column 'Americana' in his magazine was looked forward to with a joy equalled only by that of some stuffed shirt, who has succeeded in making money, or in buying some office and exploiting it, who has just learned that he is to get an honorary degree. This was the first thing we read in the old *Mercury* with the familiar green cover. Let me give a few choice examples:

New York: The Hon. Charles M. Schwab, LL.D.:
Idealism rather than dollar-chasing is the motivating force behind big business in the United States.

New York: The Hon. A. P. Waxman, director of publicity, advertising and exploitation for Warner Brothers' Pictures, writing in the eminent *American Hebrew*:
Let me point out, with all respect, that Jesus Christ used a press agent to exploit his campaign.

New York: From an address by Dr J. H. Hawkins, at Oceanside, L.I.:

113

The way you can tell a Klansman is by looking at a clean upright man who does not live with another man's wife.

Mississippi: From an address to the Kiwanis Club of Columbus, a rising town on the Tombigbee River, by the Rev. W. F. Powell, a gifted exhorter of these parts:
God was the first Kiwanian.

This bit of wisdom is matched in humility with an even better known dictum that 'Jesus Christ was the first Boy Scout', or a remark attributed to the Hon John L. Reilly of Schenectady, 'That Lincoln was a born Rotarian.'

I think that these examples of modern American thought might possibly be matched in the Australian, New Zealand, or Canadian bush, but in no other civilized country in the world.

Such nonsense as this added joy to our lives and I, for one, will always be grateful to H. L. Mencken for his robust humour and uncommon good sense.

He once wrote me in the following fashion concerning the late Dr Raymond Pearl, Dartmouth '99: 'Dr Raymond Pearl is the very reverse of a metaphysician—in fact, he hates them violently, and has carved up dozens in his dissecting room. I have always had a suspicion that Pearl will go to hell when he dies, but on this earth he is certainly a charming and enlightened fellow.'

A characteristic note from Mencken written in the spring of 1940 reads: 'The tulips here are already six feet high, and I am hoping to harvest my first crop of potatoes next week. The temperature is now no more than 75, but in a little while it will be up to 100, and I'll feel normal again. I can never work save with the sweat running from me like beer from a keg. I begin to suspect that I must have some coloured blood. '

'I only hope you make it plain in the *Alumni Magazine* that I am a baptized man and a life-long lover of the flag.'

'I hear on all sides that Jim Farley is actually a Christian Scientist. Keep this to yourself.'

This is the playful kind of exaggerated humour Mencken was pleased to put in his letters.

Mencken, in 1931, wrote out a simple credo: 'I believe that it is better to tell the truth than to lie. I believe that it is better to be free than be a slave, and I believe that it is better to *know* than to be ignorant.'

I am inclined to believe that during his whole life, and with due consideration to what I consider his misguided pro-Germanism at times, he has been one of the most forthright men of letters we have ever had—a man who with wit and with a pure and clear style unsurpassed in our time wrote fearlessly and uproariously the truth as he saw it about these United States: its laws, its 'fraternal organizations (too often a mask for selling each other soap or insurance), its language, its writers, and its standards. He wrote always with an urbane, civilized, and cosmopolitan point of view, and his sole object was to expose American quackery and humbug, whether he found it in our politicians (where it abounds), in our education (which does a very poor job on the whole), in our churches, or in our writers and critics.

For him life was a gaudy extravagant show which he thoroughly exploited and enjoyed—and he was smart enough to get well paid for this to boot.

Irreligious in any orthodox sense, but a man of truth, honour, and decency, he is credited with the conviction, as related by the late Benjamin Casseres: 'To Mencken, God is merely the Irving Babbitt of Heaven: a stuffed shirt.' Of Rotary, a great American organization devoted to 'service', Mencken has written: 'Rotary is as old as Christianity. The first Rotarian was the first man to call John the Baptist, Jack.'

By training and inclination Mencken was a newspaper man, one trained to respect the fact, who was always congenitally suspicious of the bounders who in great part govern us, and who, with his pen, could, and did, make them squirm. He was a thorough going empiricist, pragmatist, and hedonist.

I, for one, regret that a benevolent and all-loving Creator has forced him from the scene, and I miss his letters, and conversation, more than I can say.

J. Frank Dobie, of Austin, Texas, before he recently died, was as much a phenomenon of the Southwest as is the mesquite, the lonesome howl of the coyote, or the 'Llano Estacado'. He was the one great voice audible above the fabulous roar of Texas oil gushers, and the astounding gossip concerning her billionaires. He was the most articulate voice in Texas for Civil Rights. He was the one great writer, known nationally, in the whole state, and I was delighted that he recently was awarded one of the Freedom Medals, just before his death in September 1964. He was the best-known liberal in Texas who towered like a rock proclaiming the real virtues of the Southwest, the rights of the Mexicans and the Negroes, the external verities of that amazing country: its beauty, strangeness, and charm. He loved the Southwest because it nurtured him, interested him, and warmed his emotions.

He was born and reared in the brush country toward the border below San Antonio, Texas, where the Mexicans are still more numerous than people of English-speaking ancestry. His father was a stockman who had driven horses along the trail to Kansas with Mexican vaqueros, and who later turned to cattle raising. So Dobie knew the Mexicans as well as he knew his native Texans. He himself was an old ranchman, having worked as ranch manager after the First World War, in which he served two years as a First Lieutenant in Field Artillery, on the ranch of his uncle, J. M. Dobie, on the Nueces River, in the brush country in Southwest Texas.

His teaching career had been interrupted often by one thing or another—either writing books—or spending a year in Cambridge, England, as he did in 1943–4, as visiting professor of history (see *A Texan in England*, 1945), or in battling with the Regents of the University of Texas.

Of his year abroad he wrote: 'The war had been my war since it began in 1939. On a September day, four years after the Germans began the murder of humanity, I left Austin, Texas, feeling that even though I was too old to fight it was something to be going in the direction of fighting men. . . . The one chemical blend that America can make with other nations is with the English-speaking ones, and the decencies and amenities of civilization in general and of our own civilization in particular depend upon that blend.'

He also taught two years in Southwest University (1911–13) in Georgetown, Texas, from which he himself was graduated in

116

1910, at the University of Texas from 1914 on and off until 1947, and with an interval at Oklahoma A. & M., in 1923–5. So it might be said that Dobie had been a soldier, ranchman, traveller, writer, and college professor.

I suppose his most famous course was the one which was first offered at the University of Texas, called 'Life and Literature of the Southwest'. Concerning this he issued a guide in 1943 which is a most revealing and interesting brochure. This is Dobie when he writes: 'Its emphases vary according to my own indifferences and ignorance as well as according to my own sympathetic knowledge. It is strong on the character and ways of life of the early settlers on the growth of the soil, and on everything pertaining to the range; it is weak on information concerning politicians and on citations to studies, which, in the manner of orthodox PhD theses, *merely transfer bones from one graveyard to another.*'

Dobie defined an educated person as one who 'can view with interest and intelligence the phenomena of life about him. . . . Intelligence cannot be acquired, but interest can; and data for interest and intelligence to act upon are entirely acquirable.'

A forthright Texan speaks out when he wrote: 'The Southwest has a distinct cultural inheritance full of life and drama though sheep-like makers of textbooks and sheep-like pedagogues of American literature have until recently, either wilfully or ignorantly, denied that right to the Southwest.

'To hell with the endless pages of Cotton Mather, Increase Mather, Jonathan Edwards, Anne Bradstreet, and other dreary creatures of Colonial New England, who are utterly foreign to the genius of the Southwest.

'If nothing in written form had been written about the Southwest (and lots has), it would be more profitable for an inhabitant to go out and listen to the coyotes singing at night in the prickly pear than to tolerate the Increase Mather sort of thing. It is very profitable to listen to coyotes anyhow.'

He was a great reader and has written with charm and insight on his favourite books and reading. Let him speak for himself and if this doesn't strike a responsive note for most collectors I shall be really surprised:

'I once thought that, so far as reading goes, I could live for ever on the supernal beauty of Shelley's *The Cloud* and his soaring lines, *To a Skylark*, on the rich melancholy of Keats' *Ode to a Nightingale*, on Cyrano de Bergerac's ideal of a free man, on Wordsworth's philosophy of nature—a philosophy that has illuminated for me the mesquite flats and oak-studded hills of Texas—on the adventures of Robert Louis Stevenson, the flavour and wit of Lamb's essays, the eloquent wisdom of Hazlitt, the dark mysteries of Conrad, the gaieties of Barrie, the melody of Sir Thomas Browne, the urbanity of Addison, the dash in Kipling, the mobility, the mightiness, the lightness, the humour, the humanity, the everything of Shakespeare, and a world of other delicious, high, beautiful and inspiriting things that English literature has bestowed upon us, that literature is still the richest of heritages; but literature is not enough.

'Here I am living on a soil that my people have been living and working and dying on for more than a hundred years—the soil, as it happens, of Texas. My roots go down into this soil as deep as mesquite roots go. This soil has nourished me as the banks of the lovely Guadalupe River nourish cypress trees, as the Brazos bottoms nourish the wild peach, as the gentle slopes of East Texas nourish the sweet-smelling pines, as the barren, rocky ridges along the Pecos nourish the daggered lechuguilla. I am at home here, and I want not only to know about my homeland, I want to live intelligently on it. I want certain data that will enable me to accommodate myself to it. Knowledge helps sympathy to achieve harmony. I am made more resolute by Arthur Hugh Clough's picture of the dripping sailor on the reeling mast.

'On stormy nights when wild northwesters rave, but the winds that have bit into me have been blue Texas northers; and fantastic yarns about them, along with a cowboy's story of a herd of Longhorns drifting to death in front of one of them, come home to me and illuminate those northers like forked lightning playing along the top of black clouds in the night.'

Dobie was a great reader of books. He tells of his favourites: 'Comparatively few books can be favourite to anyone as are to me Hudson's *Far Away and Long Ago*, George Borrow's *Lavengro*, the essays of Hazlitt, Lamb, and Montaigne, De Quincey's *Confessions*, Chaucer's *Prologue* and *Pardoner's Tale* and also the

118

tale of *Chaunticleer and Pertelote, Hamlet, Romeo and Juliet,* and *Twelfth Night,* various seventeenth-century lyrics, Rostand's *Cyrano de Bergerac, Deidre* by James Stephens, *Alice in Wonderland,* Dostoevski's *The Brothers Karamazov, Moby Dick,* Housman's *Shropshire Lad,* Conrad's *Youth,* Stevenson's *Letters,* Marlowe's *Dr Faustus,* the conclusion of Sir Walter Raleigh's *History of the World,* the poetry (selected) of Wordsworth, Shelley, and Keats. I cannot leave out the old ballads, Emerson's wisdom, Omar's hedonism, Pepys' urbanity, George Frederick Ruxton's zest for the wilderness, Tennyson's dream life, Barrie's charm, Carlyle's volcanic energy, Arnold's intellectual emancipation, Sir Thomas Browne's grandeur, Addison's serenity, Macaulay's pictured page, the love songs and realism of Burns, Coleridge's *The Ancient Mariner,* the Knight of the Tristful Visage, Mirabeau's "art of daring", Thomas Jefferson, the Rosalind "born under a star to dance. . . ." '

There speaks an old-fashioned reader.

He goes on: 'I will vote three times a day and all night for John C. Duval's *Adventures of Bigfoot Wallace,* Charlie Siringo's *Riata and Spurs,* James B. Gillett's *Six Years with the Texas Rangers,* and dozens of other straightaway chronicles of the southwest in preference to "The Culprit Fay" and much other watery "literature" with which anthologies representing the earlier types of American writing are padded. Ike Fridge's unprocurable pamphlet story of his riding for John Chisum, chief provider of cattle for Billy the Kid to steal, has more of the price of reality in it, and, therefore, more of literary virtue than some of James Fenimore Cooper's novels, and than all of James Russell Lowell's odes.

'And if I had as many children as the old woman who lived in a shoe had—blessing upon her!—I'd give them broth and put them to bed. And, at Christmas time, as long as they lived, I'd give every one of them, big and little, boy and girl, man and woman, a book full of wonderful people, wonderful animals, and wonderful words and pictures and deeds to make the world more wonderful for ever.'

Dobie's list of books runs well over a dozen titles. Some of them are not only difficult to find in first editions but bring prices of $100 and more.

E   119

In his first well-known book (it was a book club selection), *Coronado's Children*, he tells of all the lost mine stories and legends of the Southwest. He attempted 'an interpretation of the traditions of lost mines and buried treasures in America'. 'I care much more,' he said, 'about the drama, the flavourable characters, like the old Indian who said, "Senor, isn't God good! He gives us the nights to sleep in and the days to rest in," the vast lands in which the riches lie hidden, the "pictures and conversations" that Alice in Wonderland so approved of, than I care about interpretations. . . .'

In his best known books such as *Tongues of the Monte*, 1935, in some ways 'the strangest book that has ever been published about Mexico', and with more quality of strangeness and imagination than in his other books, as *Apache Gold and Yaqui Silver*, 1939, *The Longhorns*, 1941, *The Voice of the Coyote*, 1949, and *The Mustangs*, 1952, Dobie reveals himself as painstaking historian, and as a nature writer of imagination, great humaneness, and sensitiveness.

Like W. H. Hudson, whom Dobie admired, he liked snakes. 'I won't kill a harmless snake,' he writes, 'any more than I will kill a wren. Rattlesnakes, though not harmless, are the most interesting of all snakes in North America. I hate to think of the day when there won't be any. They make the country more interesting and more natural. After all these generations of civilized man's association with them, there are several things about them that not even the most scientific naturalists know.' For instance, 'Do rattlesnakes swallow their young?' After investigation Dobie's phrase in my copy of his pamphlet with that title is still, 'Quien sabe?'

He reveals his own philosophy in pleasant passages throughout his books. In *Apache Gold and Yaqui Silver*, he wrote, 'These people had nothing but hope. They were rich in it. As I grow older, I wonder if any other form of wealth is more enriching to lives. At the same time, I grow stronger against blindfolds. Damned if I know what to believe, but always I believe in fairies. And I hope we'll always have hope.'

When I was writing a rather controversial book called *Rebel Thought*, Dobie wrote to me: 'If I were prepared and had the

120

time, I would write a book on Emancipators. It would be on the emancipators of human minds—Voltaire, Tom Paine, Emerson, etc. I shan't ever get to it though, I guess. I have just shipped to Little Brown & Company my manuscript on *The Mustangs*. Writing it was an interminable job, and the last month of it nearly killed me.'

On the mustangs he had written eloquently: 'The true conceiver of the mustang must be a true lover of freedom—a person who yearns to extend freedom to all life. No man who in his heart limits freedom to those who think as he thinks is a true lover of freedom. No man who conceives the mustang as only a potential servant to his own bridle reins and will or values him merely by what he will bring in money apprehends the animal. The aesthetic value of the mustang topped all other values. The sight of the wild horses streaming across the prairies made even the most hardened of the mustangers regret putting an end to their liberty.'

In 1952 Dobie wrote me: 'If you're going to collect the first editions of Frank Dobie's books, I'll send you one. I didn't think you'd be interested in reading it. Its title is *John C. Duval, First Texas Man of Letters*. I don't even have a first edition of *Coronado's Children* myself. There were de luxe editions of *The Longhorns* and *Apache Gold and Yaqui Silver*. I'm looking for a de luxe edition of *Apache* for myself. You shouldn't have too hard a time getting firsts of most of the books. It will probably be harder to get a first of *A Vaquero of the Brush Country* since the printing was limited to one or two thousand copies. *Tales of the Mustangs*, 1936, will be costly as there were only 300 copies, published as an example of fine printing and selling at $10 in the beginning.'

I know from experience that the collector of Frank Dobie will have a lot of fun, and a lot of trouble.

Another writer friend, who used to be a neighbour in Orford, New Hampshire,[1] is Charles Jackson, who wrote one good book, *The Lost Weekend*, but who has since not been able to equal it in spite of the fact that he has written some really first class short stories. At my request he gave to the Dartmouth Library the manuscript

[1] He now lives in New Jersey.

121

of his famous book on an alcoholic which is certainly a fine start on a collection of this most interesting man. I think I'm giving away no secret when I say that *The Lost Weekend* is almost completely autobiographical and, through an almost pathological honesty, the realistic story of Don Birnam makes an indelible impression, and it seems to me to represent a real landmark in American fiction.

CHAPTER IV

The Bookman and a few English Writers

O goodly is our heritage!
Kipling

I had first met Henry Williamson in America in the winter of 1931 when we went ski-ing together in New Hampshire, and I accepted at that time an invitation to spend a week with him in his cottage, Shallowford, in Filleigh, in North Devonshire, where he then lived.

Henry Williamson has written many books since *Tarka the Otter* and *Salar the Salmon*. As a writer he has lost some public favour, but may gain it again sometime, as he is a talented man. When I knew him first he was exceedingly restless, extremely sensitive, and quick to take offence at a slight, imaginary or real: one of the victims of post-war neuroticism, though he was born with a most sensitive temperament and imagination. Readers of *The Flax of Dream*, composed of four early novels, of which *The Pathway* was the best known in this country, will know quite a lot about the early Williamson for these novels are but thinly disguised autobiography. Williamson was Maddison and Maddison was a dreamer, a lover of natural beauty, of birds and animals, a complete sentimentalist, and a Utopian, longing for the time (which will never come) when Christ's simple tenets would govern the world. His mind, turned too long upon itself, revelling a little too luxuriously in the inner landscapes of the soul, the prey to imaginary fears, soaring to a belief in an impossible and unearthly love, had woven for itself a body of ideals which inevitably clashed with the compromises the world of experience forces upon all men. So he was often unhappy and at times indulged in a nauseous kind of self-pity. Edmund Blunden's magnificent line, 'Something stood between me and the sun', made a big impression on Williamson and his yearning for a world of pure sunshine without shadows of any kind led him into emotional excesses which for a while threatened to overwhelm him. That he passed successfully through this stage is attested by another series of novels which are still appearing. He is a rapid writer, sometimes averaging 10,000 words a day, and he has been most prolific. Whether he has measured up to his early promise is perhaps questionable but as a nature writer he is superb and has known few, if any, equals in our time.

He will be best known, I think, for his Devon books, notably *The Pathway*, *The Labouring Life*, *The Old Stag*, *Tarka the Otter*, *The Village Book*, and *Salar the Salmon*.

When I found him one March day in Taunton where he met my train I wanted to see the Torridge, the Taw, the estuary formed by these two rivers, the villages of Saunton, Georgeham, and Croyde, and I hoped to see a stag hunt.

Shallowford, where Williamson lived with his wife, Gipsy, a lovely young woman, and their children, was a long-thatched Elizabethan cottage with walls made of mud and straw called cob, two-foot thick, and built to endure. Once it had been three labourers' cottages, separated only by a thick wall between each section. There were many fireplaces in the house for North Devon is cold and windy many months of the year. At one end of the house was a kitchen large enough to prepare the food necessary to feed hungry guests, for the Devon air breeds lusty appetites. Next to the kitchen was a dining-room with a long oak refectory table, solid as the men who many years ago hewed out its planks by hand. It was highly polished, and recently had absorbed, so I was informed, two gallons of linseed oil. At one end of the table was a hand-carved Elizabethan press. The living-room, separated from the dining-room by the entrance hall, contained books, a gramophone, tables and chairs.

Upstairs were bedrooms and Williamson's study. This room contained an old three-legged round-top walnut table, a fireplace, a radio, and many cases full of books. I noticed that Williamson had most of the books of Richard Jefferies with whom as a naturalist, and even as a man, he has most in common. There were many of W. H. Hudson's superb nature studies, several books by Conrad, Galsworthy, Arnold Bennett, who had encouraged the young and aspiring author, H. M. Tomlinson, Edmund Blunden, T. E. Lawrence, Siegfried Sassoon, Frederick Manning, Wilfred Owen, Rupert Brooke, Robert Graves, Gilbert White, and many others.

Near Shallowford, and running through a deer park, wanders the river Bray, two miles of which Williamson had the exclusive fishing rights. Around noon, dressed in rubber boots and Burberrys to keep out the driving rain, we walked through the deer park to the river where Williamson had built several small dams which he hoped would form better trout pools. With crowbar and pick axe, wading up to our knees in the swift running water, we swung 500-pound sacks of gravel-concrete into the stream. Then we tipped buckets of gravel at their bases. The water was rising fairly rapidly, owing to the rain on Exmoor, for the Bray is fed by water running down the Exmoor slopes. At two o'clock we came back to the cottage for a hearty meal washed down with a generous supply of brown Burton ale.

One afternoon we followed the Bray about half a mile down to the large weir at Stag's Head, watching every pool for trout as we walked. We saw many trout, but no salmon, owing to the low water for they could not come up from the sea over the weirs until there should come a flood. When the trout saw our shadows they would dart like arrows, faster almost than the eye could follow, to some secure retreat beneath a rock or underneath the bank. Months of this sort of observation prepared Williamson to write his *Salar the Salmon,* which he first thought of calling *The Water Dreamer.* We continued up the river for a couple of miles, picking out likely looking pools, to see if we could find any big trout. In the morning we had fed them, and in one fine pool, at a bend in the river, we had seen a large one swiftly and gracefully turn to snap the food. They were too thin in March to take on a fly, but they fatten up when the flies begin to hatch. In April or May, Williamson begins his fishing, and he was quite proud of his skill in handling a dry fly. The Bray winds up the valley, and we followed it, our feet sinking in the mushy bogs by the riverside, and so on under the viaduct of the Great Western Railroad to the Brayley Bridge, where his fishing rights end. Poaching goes on constantly as it has before and since the legendary days of Robin Hood.

Williamson, when I knew him first, was slim and fairly tall, and had flashing brown eyes. His small head and face were deceptive, for he looked very thin; actually his body was wiry and muscular, like that of the long distance runner he used to be at school. His dark hair was slightly tinged with grey around the temples. He was quick and nervous in his movements, and walked with rapid strides. He was often impetuous, quick to anger, and acted very often on sudden impulse. At times he behaved like a spoiled child but, as this is generally accepted as the prerogative of creative writers, his wife always carried on with great understanding and forbearance.

Exmoor is the stag hunting country and Williamson's books on stags compare favourably with Sir John Fortescue's *The Red Deer*, a book which is now accepted as a kind of classic. It is not generally known that stags owe their very existence in modern times only to the hunters who pay for the damage the stags do to crops and fences. In his little book *The Wild Red Deer of Exmoor*, Williamson wrote: 'The deer owed their survival, in this present time, to their swiftness and shyness developed and maintained during the thousands of years they have been hunted pitilessly by animals of prey, and men of prey, and because for hundreds of years they have been hunted—but only when mature —by staghounds, and protected by the stag hunters. . . . It will be historically true that for a great many years the hunts practically befriended the wild red deer of Exmoor. I, for one, a mere imaginative friend of the deer, shall always be grateful for this practical benevolence.'

With clear weather the day arrived when Williamson was to show me some of the landmarks in his books. Driving between Bideford and Barnstaple, we skirted the River Torridge. Here Tarka lived, and Williamson pointed out to me the place where he was killed. For years Williamson had followed the otter hounds, had watched patiently for days and weeks, the movements of the otters. He knew every square yard of the estuary formed by the Torridge and Taw Rivers, where Tarka lived his joyful water life. Williamson's book is more than simply the

126

result of his observations, for these are strained delicately through the rich tapestry of his creative imagination in a warm and glowing style. Williamson became Tarka but escaped the pit of the nature writers who endow their animals with human thoughts and feelings. Tarka is an otter and behaves like one. If Williamson had written nothing else he would have created one of the finer nature books of our time. Had he allowed Tarka to live it might have been a work of genius.

My last day with the Williamsons on this particular visit (I used to see him on and off in London) was spent on a trip to Georgeham (the village of Ham in *The Village Book*), where I met some of his characters. On the way he pointed out Sharshook, an island in the estuary, invisible at high tide, between Appledore and the Braunton Burrows. This is the gravel ridge where Maddison drowned, owing to Mrs Ogilvie's fatal oversight. The Burrows had been used by Blackmore in his *Maid of Sker*, and to a lesser degree in Barbellion's most interesting *Journal of a Disappointed Man*. Williamson's nature descriptions in *The Pathway* are faithful and sensitive recreations of this part of North Devon.

As a teacher without private means and financially able to buy few, if any, of the well-known 'high spots', I have happily been forced to collect certain authors whose books never reached terrifically high price levels but which nevertheless have generally proved themselves through the years as literary works of high calibre.

My collecting Robert Bontine Cunninghame Graham led to a warm friendship and a fruitful association which ended only with his death in Buenos Aires on March 20, 1936, and led, in fact, to the first biography of him already mentioned, which was published in London in 1932.

Hugh Macdiarmid, Scottish poet and nationalist, wrote on the event of Cunninghame Graham's centenary:[1] 'It is in keeping with the apathy and indifference, and often petty jealousy and spite, of Scotland in such matters that the finest collection of Cunninghame Graham's books, autographed letters, manu-

[1] *Cunninghame Graham: A Centenary Study*, by Hugh Macdiarmid. Glasgow: Caledonian Press, 1952.

scripts, and corrected proof and other material is to be found, not in Scotland, but in the United States of America. This is the Herbert Faulkner West collection, which Professor West presented in memory of his friend to the Dartmouth College Library, Hanover, New Hampshire.'

In the collection are several hundred items[1] including his first extant letter written to his mother from St Epsom in Patagonia on June 1, 1870, when Cunninghame Graham was seventeen years old, and his last letter to me (received several days after he was dead), dated Buenos Aires (Plaza Hotel), March 1, 1936.

I wrote at his death: After nearly eighty-four years of active life Don Roberto has at last entered Trapalanda. Once again he swings over the grassy plains, silent on ghostly hoofs, on his beloved Pampa, his black Argentine, whom he rode for twenty years without a fall. If there is another heaven, and in his more recent letters and books Trapalanda was frequently mentioned— 'the mysterious country where Gauchos and their horses rode, their horses never tiring, sustained by never-failing grass and water, the nectar and ambrosia of the equine race, their riders never ageing, and I suppose their saddlery never wearing out' —then Don Roberto is there riding like a centaur.

Indifferent to the things that most men hold dearest, Don Roberto steered a Quixotic course through life, as do all *born* gentlemen, ever tilting his lance at a world he found full of sham and hypocrisy. Born to the purple, he never sought its privileges, but preferred simple things like horses, friends such as Conrad, Blunt, Hudson, Galsworthy, and Edward Garnett, Scottish peasants who greeted him as 'laird', qualities such as decency, justice, honour, and fair play. He was born, as Joseph Conrad suggested, fifty years ahead of his time or, it may be truer to say, 300 years too late, for there was something of the Elizabethan cavalier in his gallant manner, in his distinguished appearance,

[1] See the bibliography printed in 1937: The Herbert Faulkner West collection of R. B. Cunninghame Graham, Hanover, New Hampshire. This collection has been greatly added to. In 1955 Cunninghame Graham's letters to A. F. Tschiffley were purchased, as were all of Joseph Conrad's letters to Cunninghame Graham and Mrs Bontine. It is now attracting international scholars. In the summer of 1956 Wilfrid Blunt's letters to Cunninghame Graham were added.

128

in his fastidious but simple style, and in his disdain for the market place and all its vulgar values. His like will not be seen again; he was the last of the hidalgos.

His career had been that of traveller, author, horseman, Member of Parliament on the Socialist ticket, and, at the end, he was fighting for another lost cause (though it is conceivable that it may ultimately triumph), Scottish Nationalism. In 1935, as president of the Scottish National Party, he declared in a glowing speech: 'I here and now rededicate myself to the cause of Scotland's freedom. So long as my strength lasts I shall continue to advocate an independent Scotland.'

Don Roberto, as I knew him, was a humanist in the grand manner, centring his interest more in man than in nature. He was essentially a lover of tradition (superficially understood he has been labelled a Romantic), knowing and loving the value of things that are old, and the literary artistic and political fads of our own time made little favourable impression on him. Our modernism, often wearing false hair across its manly chest, a kind of twentieth-century cult of sensibility, touched him not. His irony was that of a cultured and experienced man of the world, gentle but nonetheless piercing. He was a cosmopolitan, who had travelled far and wide his whole life long, who knew the vices and virtues of men of all nationalities but particularly those of the Arabs, Mexicans, and Spanish, both in Spain and Spanish America, Scots, and the English. Essentially he was a man of the strictest honour, who fought with spirit, and with no ulterior motive, for lost and unpopular causes. More to the point he was an amateur writer of genius, as Frank Harris called him, though not, perhaps, of the first rank. He has yet to win a wide audience.

After living sixteen years in South America, he returned on the death of his father to take over the ancestral acres of Gartmore in Menteith, some fifteen miles from Stirling. Overloaded with debt with which he and his lovely Chilean wife struggled in vain, Gartmore had to be sold in 1900, and Don Roberto moved to Ardoch Cottage (in Cardross, near Dumbarton on the Clyde), a house built during the eighteenth century by 'Doughty Deeds' Graham in the Jamaican style.

129

I shall long remember a week I spent at Ardoch with Don Roberto in the summer of 1929 while I was seeking material for his life. He reminisced about his past, and soon made it emphatic that no biographer would ever get dates in his life from him, as he never wished his past investigated too carefully. With Landor he had warmed his hands many times before the fire of life, but this, rightly, was nobody's business: 'His life,' he said, 'was to be found in his books.'

He demonstrated with the élan of a boy playing cowboy how to throw the lazo and bolas; he drove me over 'Rest and Be Thankful', a mountain pass leading to Inveraray, and the highlands he loved; he praised the late Neil Munro as an excellent but neglected writer and we had tea at Dunderave (the original of Munro's well-known book *Doom Castle*); he told me about his role in the Scottish home rule movement, which was for him a future inevitability. We examined together many ancient Spanish books, bound in vellum, some of them illuminated, which were in his library and, while we looked at them, he told stories of writers he had known. If they were dead, it was always, 'Poor fellow', and of Conrad, 'He was the soul of honour'.

Don Roberto had a Gaelic housekeeper with whom he conversed in the ancient Erse language. I recall her only as a kindly creature with a taste for strong waters and a magnificent cook whose succulent roast mutton was something for the gods. A few months before my visit Cunninghame Graham had had a horse roll over on him, so he was not exactly in his most robust state. He ate sparingly, and drank only Vichy water. I was the hard liquor drinker, and he delighted in serving me choice Scotch, and it was he who introduced me to Drambuie. All Americans, he thought, were great whisky drinkers, and I naturally couldn't disillusion him.

My last link with him was the following letter which reached me ten days after he had died:

Plaza Hotel,
Buenos Aires.   March 1/36

Mi querido Heriberto:
    I found your letters on arriving in Buenos Aires ten days ago. Since

then I have lived in a whirl. Everyone has been my friend. Next week I go to see Tschiffely's two celebrated horses.[1]

Three days ago I was at Tujan where there is one of the most interesting museums I ever saw of the kind. Colonial furniture, horse gear, mostly silver, lace, jewellery, etc., etc., etc.

We are going through a heat wave, that is rather trying, and the sun has inflamed my eyes, which makes my writing worse than ever. However, it is nothing much and is passing off.

You must be rather lonely, with Dona Carina and Heriberto II away.[2]

I sail for home on the 26th in the *Almeda Star* (Blue Star Line). From Rio I came in an American boat *The American Legion*. She was very full of tourists.

With kindest regards,
Suyo amigo affmo– –
R. B. Cunninghame Graham.

P.S. My visit to Hudson's birthplace on the Pampa was extraordinarily interesting. It is a small 'rancho' near a wood, and the great plain surrounds it like a sea. Someday I hope to send you my account of it.

His body *did* return on the *Almeda Star* to be buried on the Island of Inchmahome in the Lake of Menteith in Perthshire. My memory easily carries me back to the day when Don Roberto took me there to see the grave of his wife. There between the ruined and ivied walls of an old priory they both now lie. It is a lovely spot far from the prying gaze of the curious. Only the voices of birds may be heard, and the sound of the wind sighing through the ruined walls.

I think Don Roberto was, in many respects, the greatest man I have ever known. Certainly his friendship meant a great deal to the callow young man who first saw him at Conrad's funeral. His memory will remain clear in my mind as long as I live. I was fortunate to get to know him well, and have affection for him which was, I think, reciprocated. He taught me a good deal, and from him I gained a little more stature, both mentally and spiritually.

[1] Mancha and Gato, two Creole horses, are celebrated in Tschiffely's book: *Tschiffely's Ride*. New York: Simon & Schuster, 1933.

[2] My wife had taken our son to Stockholm for a visit.

In his eighty-four years he passed, like some brilliant comet blazing in the heavens, through politics, and through literature. He had been a Member of Parliament (from Lanarkshire), leader of the Scottish National Party, traveller, ranchman, swordsman, horseman, laird, and friend.

He may well serve as an example of one who passionately loved life and all that it brings. Sympathetic, tolerant, shrewd in bursting the bubbles of pretentiousness, always open to new ideas and ways of life, ironic, charming as a companion, delightful as a conversationalist, fair in his dealings with others whatever station or rank they may have held, enemy of cruelty to man or beast, he represented the best of an old chivalric order of hidalgos, which, alas, seem to be entirely passing. I shall not look upon his like again.

From Cunninghame Graham it was a natural step to turn to the books of his friend Wilfrid Scawen Blunt. Some of Blunt's pamphlets offer some difficulty to the collector, but most of his books or poetry are not difficult to procure, and most of his autobiographical volumes may be bought at modest prices.

He is a most rewarding writer, and his *My Diaries*, 1884–1914, is a revealing and most interesting book—revealing of Blunt's fascinating and lordly personality (which greatly intrigued Lawrence of Arabia), and revealing, too, of the history of England during those momentous years which preceded World War I. *Gordon of Khartoum*, *The Future of Islam*, and *The Land War in Ireland* will not prove too difficult for the collector to find. They reveal an uncanny sense of prophecy in foretelling England's future as an Empire builder. It was not so much that Blunt knew history, which he did, but more important he knew human nature and diplomacy at first hand. Historians today could do worse than read Blunt to understand our own times.

I think it would not arouse serious dissent if one called Wilfrid Blunt one of the great individualists of his time. It is not enough to say that he was a poet, artist, sculptor, architect, breeder of Arabian horses, country squire, traveller, bitter opponent of his country's imperialistic policies, and friend of the most interesting luminaries of his day (the last of these, Hilaire Belloc, his neighbour, died in July 1953), nor to admire with H. W. Nevinson, 'so democratic a champion of freedom, so despotic an aristocrat at heart'. He was all of these, but more.

He was an intensely *interesting* individual. 'Born out of his generation,' Cunninghame Graham says of him, 'as are the most of men who achieve anything but mere material success, he yet was a true Englishman, a very English man of the Elizabethan breed, with something in him of the Renaissance in his love of sport and culture.'

This curious personality permeates everything Blunt writes and endows it with a flavour that is piquant, exciting, and seducing. Once enjoyed, one invariably returns to it, as I do.

Once on a quest for material about Blunt I sought out Newbuildings' Place in Southwater, Sussex. This large estate deep in the Sussex Weald gave Blunt the seclusion his autocratic nature demanded. It was a domain, where the poet, robed in Arabian garments, could and did reign as lord of the manor and of the Sussex Weald stretching from his garden to summit called Chanctonbury Ring, crowned with ancient entrenchments and a circle of beech trees. It is not difficult to imagine Blunt (as one of his old retainers told me) appearing before people on a lonely path to scare their simple souls dressed in his Arabian garments, and overawe them with his regal manner. He would sometimes order his carriage, keep the groom waiting three hours in the cold, and then, by some strange whim, dismiss it suddenly as unwanted. Here he was only exercising his ancient rights of domain as a feudal English squire; actually he was the kindest of men and proved this time and time again, as when he took in the dying poet Francis Thompson. The 1,000 or more acres of this part of his estate, about fifteen miles from Crabbett Park where he had his Arabian stud (later run by his daughter Judith, Lady Westworth), is well planned for privacy.

It was in 1870 that Blunt bought Newbuildings, which dates back authentically, as old prints prove, to about 1683, in the time of James II. The house, though modest in size, is as fine an example of a Jacobean manor house as can be found in all England. Here are ivy covered walls, roses, clipped trees, peacocks, gardens, birds and rabbits by the hundreds in the forests and copses nearby. And here lived the families who sheltered 'the harlots of the Pope' from brutal, if zealous, hands. A ruined chapel stands nearby with secret hiding places where anxious priests were thrust in with bread and cheese (and let us hope a flagon of ale) to sustain them. Even today the locality is still a Roman Catholic one.

The house used to entertain periodically the 'Crabbett Club', a group of Blunt's writing friends. They had but one rule, to wit, 'that anyone becoming a cabinet minister or Bishop ceases, *ipso facto*, to be a member'. A. E. Housman, Lady Gregory, W. H. Hudson, Robert Bontine Cunninghame Graham, C. M. Doughty, Arabi, William Morris, Wilfred Meynell, W. B. Yeats, and T. E. Lawrence were in the group.

The front hall, paved with Sussex stone, had in one corner an ostrich skin upon the head of which swallows had built a nest. In the panelled room to the left, which contains a great fireplace, there hung a portrait of Blunt, a self-portrait painted when he was twelve, and which showed such promise that the painter Watts was going to take him as a pupil save that his mother's death prevented, and gave the world a poet instead. On the wall opposite were two fine tapestries by his friend William Morris, and over the fireplace Arabian spears, bolas, lazos, and the more deadlier weapons of the more civilized countries. Peacock skins, brass coffee urns, and other Eastern mementos added to the exotic atmosphere and recalled his many winters spent at Shekh Obeyd, his winter home in Cairo.

For me, naturally, the most interesting room was the library. I can only single out for mention a few treasures of which he was particularly fond. Beside his own volumes of poetry bound in vellum by the Kelmscott Press stood a slim volume, *A Shropshire Lad*, inscribed : 'To Wilfrid Scawen Blunt from A. E. Housman, 1911.' There were copies of the first issue of Doughty's *Arabia Deserta* in two volumes, which Blunt helped to get published. Here, too, was an old Holinshed, and next to it an early edition of Machiavelli's *The Prince*, which Blunt knew by heart. Like 'Old Nick' Machiavel, Blunt, too, was an ironic realist when it came to politics. He saw through the pious and unctuous phrases which politicians employ in relieving us of our money, or in carrying 'the white man's burden'. Blunt wrote once: 'The white

man's burden, Lord, is the burden of his cash.' Blunt's wide experiences, beginning in the diplomatic service and ending as a
widely travelled country squire, had taught him that men's real
motives were not what they seem, being mainly acquisitive.
Moral and metaphysical claptrap never blinded him. This is to
his credit for he lived in an age which specialized in hypocrisy,
and, as the wily old man prophesied, finally reaped its whirlwind
in the First and Second World Wars.

In the library also was the original manuscript of Francis
Thompson's essay on Shelley, written in his stilted, child-like
handwriting. In the room beyond hung Neville Lytton's crayon
portrait of Thompson. For some weeks toward the miserable end
of his life, when Thompson lived in one of the cottages on the
estate, he came to the house for his meals. Blunt was well repaid
for his kindness, for had he not heard this unhappy poet read his
verses?

> Suffer me at your leafy feast
> To sit apart, a somewhat alien guest,
> And watch your mirth,
> Unsharing in the liberal laugh of Earth;
> Yet with a sympathy
> Begot of wholly sad and half-sweet memory—
> The little sweetness making life complete;
> Faint wind of wings from hours that distant beat,
> When I . . . I, too,
> Was once, Old wild companions, as are you—
> Ran with such wistful feet,
> Wraith of a recent day and dead,
> Risen wanly overhead,
> Frail, strengthless as a noon-belated moon,
> Or as the glazing eye of watery heaven,
> When the sick night sinks in a deathly swoon.

It was also in this library that T. E. Lawrence talked with the
redoubtable old warrior who had lived in Egypt before Lawrence
had ever heard of Arabia and the East. Both sympathized with
the Arabs. Both knew them as a wild but cultured people, living
a life of freedom which had been their birthright before 'ex-
pansion', and 'imperialism', or the lust for oil had been heard of.

Blunt must have recalled vividly, when talking with Lawrence, the trackless trails which he and Lady Anne had travelled over in their own caravans. Had he, too, been banished by the English Government from Arabia? Was it true that Lawrence had bearded the King? He might have thought, also, of the grave of his wife lying near Shekh Obeyd, once his own soul's oasis.

Upstairs, in the room where he died in 1922, placed on a chair facing the bed, stood a large photograph of Cardinal Manning, an early friend of his mother's. This stern and uncompromising figure, as relentless in his faith as his church, had an effect on Blunt, for, staring at it during his final years of pain, he came eventually to take the last rites of the Church. However, it is obvious that in his lifetime, as was the case with Conrad, he held lightly the orthodox tenets of his religion. Graham always spoke of him as a Hellenist or Pagan.

Sir Sidney Cockerell, in his *Friends of a Lifetime*, quotes Blunt as saying during his illness: 'During my worst time I read the Book of Job and it gave me a certain comfort of a desperate kind. The strength of Job for consolation is that it has no suggestion of that mockery of the soul, a future life. I never felt more strongly than in this illness the necessity of death, absolute, and for ever, as the end of pain, and the impotence of any other fancy as a branch by which to cling.'

To the back of the house Blunt, under the temporary influence of William Morris, had built the furniture for an additional sanctuary which houses the books of his most intimate friends. Conrad's work was there, though I was told Blunt never understood or sympathized with his foreign and strange personality, and they never met. In this place are first editions of Cunninghame Graham with whom he had a lot in common. Both had served jail sentences for espousing popular causes, Blunt in Ireland and Graham in London; one an English squire, the other a Scottish laird; both anti-imperialists, both great lovers of horses, both masters of irony, both gentlemen. On a lower shelf I noticed some of Hudson's books. Graham had introduced them and several times they had walked about the estate discussing the birds of the weald. One, a man who had known poverty and who had almost a prehensile feeling for nature, the other a wealthy

Tory squire who had been the spoiled darling of the best society in England. They must have been a curious pair together.

One still feels Blunt's presence at Newbuildings' Place. Indeed the old chieftain is buried there. I walked through the back garden into the forest, passing through rows of yew trees and beeches planted by the poet himself, and in the distance I saw a huge block of granite, under which, wrapped in his Arabian shawl, Blunt lies buried. Birds cry and rabbits lope casually by. He is alone for ever with nature.

On the stone is part of one of his own sonnets:

> Dear Checker-work of woods, the Sussex weald,
> If a name thrills me yet of things of earth
> That name is thine. How often I have fled
> To thy deep hedgerows and embrace each field,
> Each lag, each pasture—fields which gave me birth,
> And saw my youth, and which must hold me dead.

From Blunt's and Lady Anne's books on the Middle East it was logical, and indeed, inevitable, to turn to the greatest of modern English writers on Arabia, Charles Montagu Doughty (1843–1926), who conceived the curious idea of purifying English style by reviving the English of Chaucer, Spenser, and the Elizabethan age, and so spent his life in linguistic and anti-quarian study.

Doughty specialized in geology while he was at Caius College, Cambridge, but spent his life in travels and in authorship. He began his Arabian travels in 1876 and the first Arabian year he wandered from Damascus to Hayil, and in the second from Hayil to Jidda, taking plenty of time for archaeological observations, and finishing his journey in 1878. In those far off days, before jeeps and American Oil companies took over the country, it is safe to say that Arabia demanded more of a successful traveller, especially if he were a white man and a Christian (Nasrany), than any other country in the world, with the possible exception of the Danakil country in Abyssinia, and the vicinity of Cape Crozier in the Antarctic.

Doughty, supreme in his knowledge, and endowed with a temperament which had disciplined itself in Arabia to return contempt and insult with gentleness and forbearance, succeeded in his travels only after great handicaps and dangerous adventure.

Though Doughty worked nine years on his book, *Arabia Deserta*, no money came to him from publication of this masterpiece, and indeed he was fortunate that the Cambridge University Press did not try to recover some of their loss in publishing the book, which appeared in two volumes in 1888.

In May of that year Blunt wrote to Doughty: 'I have just finished reading your book, every page of which has been to me of deepest interest.' William Morris, Burne Jones the painter, Edward Garnett, Robert Bridges the poet, and Sidney Cockerell were others who at that time recognized the book's greatness. It became as Lawrence wrote in 1921, 'A book not like other books but something particular, a bible of its kind.'

Many people are still unaware that Doughty for the rest of his writing life wrote twelve volumes of poetry, one of which, *The Dawn in Britain*, was published in six volumes in 1906. He gives a clue to his writing: 'In writing the volumes, *Arabia Deserta*, my main intention was not so much the setting forth of personal wanderings, among a people of Biblical interest, as the ideal endeavour to continue the older tradition of Chaucer and Spenser, resisting to my power the decadence of the English language: so that whilst my work should be the mere verity for Orientalists, it should also be my life's contribution, so far, to literature.'

From 1894 to 1905 he worked on his great epic, *The Dawn in Britain*, which is the story of the growth of a national consciousness (Doughty was intensely patriotic in the best sense of the word), and which he tried to write in emulation of the tradition of the great English poets of an earlier age.

His first book of poetry, *Under Arms*, came out in 1900, and bears no publisher's imprint whatever, but I have it in two variations. This is perhaps his rarest book; his pamphlet entitled *Hogarth's 'Arabia'*, printed by him in an edition of twenty-five signed copies in April 1922, is scarce.

His 1866 pamphlet, *On The Jostedal-Brae Glaciers in Norway*, has resisted my search entirely, and the only copy I ever saw is in the British Museum.

Other volumes I collected were *Adam Cast Forth*, 1908, *The*

Cliffs, 1909, *The Clouds*, 1912, *The Titans*, 1916, *Mansoul*, 1920.
I have written considerably about W. H. Hudson and his books
elsewhere but I must add here that even the impecunious
amateur will find more difficulties with Hudson than with anybody I have so far mentioned. No one without considerable funds
can possess a first edition of *Fan*, issued as a three-decker novel
in 1892 under the pseudonym of 'Henry Harford',[1] or *The
Purple Land That England Lost*, 1885, *A Crystal Age*, 1887,
Green Mansions, 1904, or even Hudson and Sclater's earlier
Argentine Ornithology. However, it is not difficult nor very costly
to buy his truly magical books on the English countryside, the
most appealing of which, to me, is *The Shepherd's Life*. In fact,
he is better discovered and enjoyed in the cheaper and more ac-
cessible books such as *Hampshire Days*. *El Ombū, Far Away
And Long Ago, Birds in a Village, Birds in London, The Land's
End*, and *A Hind in Richmond Park*.

Perhaps the most enigmatic man I have ever met was introduced to me by Cunninghame Graham. This was Axel Munthe, a
genuine man of mystery, and the author of a then sensational
best seller, *The Story of San Michele*, which ran into innumerable editions both in England and the United States.

Doctor Munthe (1857–1949) was living in the spring of 1932
(when I met him) in Harrington Gardens, London, SW, quite
near Earl's Court tube station. Daily he was in consultation with
London doctors seeking his advice. He had been educated at
Uppsala, Sweden, and worked at the Salpétrière in Paris under
Dr Jean M. Charcot (1825–93) whose work in nervous diseases
and in such morbid conditions as hysteria in relation to hypnosis
was famous. Munthe left Charcot when he disagreed with his
theories on treatment by hypnotism. He practised for twelve
years as a gynaecologist in Paris. During periods of insomnia, he
wrote his successful book, in which he describes how he adopted
the term 'colitis' as a reasurring name for the imaginary ailments
of the fashionable patients of the Faubourg Saint-Germain. Perhaps today he would have used the term psychosomatis, which

[1] I bought my first copy from Maxwell Hunley in March 1964.
Many dealers have never seen it. This went to the Dobie collection of
Hudson in the University of Texas.

appears to cover a great many ailments, both real and imagined.

Munthe told me the first day I saw him that he was going to have to tell the mother of a shell-shocked army officer that her son was hopelessly insane and would have to be put in an asylum. I am confident that no one would have been able to convey this bad news with as little shock to the woman as Dr Munthe who had an almost hypnotic effect on women and animals, as his books indicate.

I found him a large man, heavily built, slightly stooped, and wearing thick glasses. Through the lens of one glass stared a mottled blue, unseeing eye, and the other was strained close to me so as to get the outlines of my features. At this time Dr Munthe was so blind that he had to be led about the city by a small Italian boy, whose father is the Capri fisherman in *The Story of San Michele*. His strong, heavily-lined face, with aquiline nose and aristocratic beard clipped to a point, was strongly reminiscent of Joseph Conrad. Munthe was then 73 years old. No one could be with him long before sensing his 'magnetism', and realizing that the long strain of dealing with neurotic people, and trying to combat death for a lifetime, had left its impress. He appeared to be a sad and tragic person. His simplicity and genuine kindness made me feel at home with him almost at once.

He wanted to know why I liked his book. I told him that I had found it interesting from start to finish, that I had liked the kindly cynicism, his ability to tell a story, his genuine love for birds and animals, his somewhat macabre humour, the salty wisdom displayed by a man of few illusions, and that like all really great works, even comedy, his book was permeated with a tragic sense of life. Furthermore, I found it charmingly written, and some of it, I felt, he had imagined and not experienced.

He was most taken with my phrase 'macabre humour', for to him this was the book's most essential characteristic.

He told me among other things that the late Stanford White, shot by Harry Thaw in a lurid love-nest affair these many years ago, had once offered him $50,000 for the column of Tiberius which he had fished out of the sea before his villa at Capri. It still adorns San Michele.

Very recently, so he told me, a titled English lady with a

famous name had come to him, reproaching him for putting her into his book and ended the conversation by bursting into tears. She was the woman depicted in the chapter 'Madame Requin' and 'John'. Nobody but Doctor Munthe knew her name, and her identity died with him. I mention this incident as the story is one which sceptical readers consider fictitious. Personally, I have no doubt the doctor saw the goblin in Lapland. As he has written himself, it is the only real thing that remains of all the people he knew there. Cursed are those without imagination.

After we talked a while, and had taken a walk towards Hyde Park, he asked me to read to him the preface for the twelfth English edition which had just appeared. As I read he sat with eyes closed, in rapt attention, with his chin in his hands, looking much like old prints of Mephistopheles. I remember that he chuckled audibly when I read:

Don Giacinto himself, the richest priest in Capri, who had never given a penny to the poor, is still resting in his coffin, and the ex-butcher of Anacapri, who blinded the quails with a red-hot needle, has had his own eyes stung out by the Devil in person in a fit of professional jealousy.

Was the doctor amused by the phrase 'professional jealousy', or at the recollection of how he got the better of the big-hearted butcher? Like most fundamentally kind men who are pagans, he is not without irony and pity when it comes to religious mongers.

The reading of his preface, which has to do with many characters in the book, provoked a question from him as to my own belief in immortality. He sat close to me, as he asked this question, peering into my eyes with his hand on my knee, and looking as if my answer would be terribly important to him. I replied bluntly with all the ignorance of my thirty-odd years that I had no faith whatever in the doctrine of personal immortality. His own reply delivered with an intense air of conviction was that he had no faith in it either, though his readers will recall that the idea seemed to obsess him as he wrote his book. Death was the end and that was that. Doctors, who have watched the cruel ways in which death too often comes, very often have no belief in immortality.

Were he to write another book he told me it would be called *The Doctor and Death*. Doctors, he believed, should help men to die as well as to live. The difficulties in doing this, however, were of course enormous. The ethics of the medical profession were against it. Christianity, regarding every human life as a direct miracle of God, was also necessarily unalterably opposed. One can't always believe the entreaties of a patient who begs to be eased out of his misery. People cling to life, as he did, with an amazing intensity, so that a doctor cannot put much weight in his patients' requests, for as soon as the pain eases they go on fighting instinctively for life. Morphine does not always decrease the patient's suffering. Most doctors shy at this idea of painlessly helping the patient, hopelessly ill, to die, but there are some who do and have practised 'mercy killing'. Munthe had had many quarrels with other doctors on this point. I nurse no belief, nor did I then, that Munthe's ideas would prevail for many years to come. Yet, if the human race should come to realize that death among their kind differs only in degree with that of animals, i.e. that man does not have an immortal soul, then possibly Munthe's reasonable ideas may be accepted.

When I last saw him he was leading a most simple and solitary life. He did not go out in the evening. He saw very few people in the daytime. He hoped to find someone who would return to San Michele to read to him. I got the impression of a tough-minded man with a great and kindly heart, who had seen more than his share of human suffering, who had fought all his life unsuccessfully with death, which fact haunted him, and who now remained a sad and somewhat lonely old man, with at times extreme depression of spirit. He told me again and again that he could not sleep, and that insomnia had been the curse of his life. He told me that he was going to return to San Michele to end his days and that he would travel no more.

I could visualize him in the bright sunlight of his Tower at San Michele. Timborio, as the peasants call him, had come home to stay. The brightness of the Capri sun and the gleam from the azure blue Mediterranean beneath his villa will not be his much longer, for daily the world gets darker and darker and soon he will know only the unending blackness of night. This was a moving thought, lightened only by the fact that he would still be able to hear the songs of the birds he loves, and the day when he would hear, perhaps not too regretfully, the mighty whirring of dark wings that he has heard so often before, though coming nearer, and nearer . . . was still far away.

Munthe died in the Royal Castle at Stockholm in 1949, aged ninety-one, after spending ten years in his gilded cage, planning, so I've been told, the journey back to Capri which he never made. His obituary notices were generous. He was called 'realist and mystic, scientist and poet, caustic philosopher and kindly essayist' and, above all, the 'apostle of pity'. Even greater than his devotion of psychiatry and writing was his love of animals, and his efforts to protect feathered and furred beasts from human cruelty earned him the sobriquet of 'the modern St Francis of Assisi'.

Cyril Connolly, an intelligent critic, wrote recently: 'Munthe is a European phenomenon like Rasputin or Keyserling or Jung or D'Annunzio. He had that gift of personal magnetism together with a belief in his destiny which is found both in great men and in charlatans, in all Europeans who are children of Greece and Rome and who believe in their star. Unlike some he was a good man—"good as the sea"—as the dying fisherman called him—and a natural healer with a Promethean hatred of cruelty and injustice, immense pity for suffering men and animals and the courage and energy to work for them. . . .

'This Swede, who was on our side in two wars and who married an English woman, who took his degree in France, migrated to the sun, had his island made a bird sanctuary, treated dogs and peasants free and gave away all his money, is a remarkable portent, for he might easily have gravitated to the Kaiser's court and drifted into mystical Nazism. If not quite a great man, he is certainly a great European.'

Morley Roberts (1857–1942), though not, perhaps, a great writer, is collected by some and deserves to be remembered not only for himself and his considerable accomplishments, but also as the friend of W. H. Hudson and George Gissing, and the author of one little classic of travel, *The Western Avernus*, 1887, which is now available in the Everyman Library.

I recall his telling me that if Hudson's regular heart specialist, Sir James MacKenzie, had been in town when Hudson was stricken, he might well have lived several years longer. However, this is pure conjecture, and perhaps his time had come as Hudson was over eighty when he died.

The Western Avernus described the adventures of Morley Roberts when, as a young man, he batted about the world seeking 'experience', and came to the golden west, but found there, with hundreds of others, not wealth, but only toil, hunger, hardships, but plenty of experience which proved good raw material for the many books he was to write later on. He started in Texas, went north to Minnesota, worked his way west to Manitoba as a labourer on the building of the transcontinental line of the Canadian Pacific Railway, fished in the Shushwap Lakes in British Columbia, and finally ended his Odyssey in that magical city, San Francisco.

Cunninghame Graham writes of him: 'One or two incidents declare the man, such as, for instance, when he found the abandoned pack-pony lying in a swamp, and though half-starved himself, and with his feet one great sore from walking, pulled out his fellow victim and set him on his legs.'

Roberts' best known novel is a thinly disguised fictional account of the life of George Gissing, *The Private Life of Henry Maitland*, 1912; other books of his well worth reading and collecting are *Rachel Marr*, 1903; *Time and Thomas Waring*, 1914; *A Humble Fisherman*, 1932, and a few others.

In the summer of 1953 there was a private dinner in London to celebrate the eightieth birthday of H. M. Tomlinson. Tributes to 'Tommy', as his friends knew him, came from all over England and from many parts of the world. It was fitting that this should be so, for as his friend Christopher Morley wrote for that occasion:

I still think the note I wrote in my copy of *Old Junk* is as concise a review as any the author has had; and few have deserved. I said:

'Here speaks the Lord God of prose.'

Tommy these many years has pretended the supreme privilege of deafness. But I remember that on the sun-gilded stone steps of a

Burgundian Chateau he could detect the faint bell-note of a lizard, far within the chinks of the sun-warmed blocks. Most of us had to strain every nerve to catch that tender tiny cry. Under the most hellish noises of history, Tommy has always had an ear attuned to the muffled voices of mortal anguish.

And yet, wise old eucalpyt, I think he has no notion how long, how deeply, he has been loved and honoured.

The curiously personal and gently anarchistic philosophy that an intelligent reader finds in Thoreau's *Essay on Civil Disobedience*, and especially in *Walden*, he will also find re-echoed in Tomlinson's prose, particularly in more recent years. For Tomlinson owes most, of all the great writers of the past, to the crotchety but kindly Thoreau. Thoreau's faith in mind as the ultimate reality finds echo in Tomlinson's: 'The world is what we think it is. . . . If we can change our thoughts we can change the world, and that is our hope', and again in, 'The mind is all that matters'. Thoreau and Tomlinson indulge in outbursts of personal and social indignation; both are philosophically inclined in their thinking, which is to say that both are preponderantly reflective; both reveal in their writing their own unique personalities; both knew and sympathized with the life of the poor; both may be called old-fashioned liberals. Tomlinson does not like governments, and he sees, as did Thoreau, that they are the enemy of all that each individualist holds most dear—the dictates of his own conscience. The charm of Tomlinson's writing, as of Thoreau's, is enhanced by a sublimity which the ancient Longinus defined as 'the echo of a great soul'.

H. M. Tomlinson was a man of the people. He was born in 1873, in the East End of London, where the road to China begins, and his first lessons of life were learned among the poor. He was brought up among the wharves and docks, and, although a landsman, early came to know ships. He had little formal education, but his parents, although they were unable to lift him above the class to which he was born, nevertheless offered him a very decent intellectual background. From his father he inherited a knowledge of and love for music, and his father's books filled his mind with the rational theories of Darwin and Huxley. He was set to work at the age of twelve, and soon, as a shipping clerk, found himself making out bills of lading for, among others, the now legendary clipper ship, the *Cutty Sark*. His keen physical senses absorbed the odours of the docks, of the sea, and of ships and their often exotic cargoes. He began as a child to register his impressions on paper. Years later he said, 'I work so slowly', and though he seemed to write, to use Conrad's phrase of Hudson, 'as the green grass grows', actually it was the result of many years of constant effort. He always disliked office routine. Like many another before him, Charles Lamb for one, his mind was far away from the ledgers and bills of lading—following the ships to the Americas, to China, to the Dutch East Indies, where the sweet-smelling spices came from, to the lands with strange names and inhabited by curious peoples. His spare time was spent in reading in various London libraries. 'I was familiar with all of Emerson's work before I was twenty,' he said, and 'I was not much older before I became acquainted with a greater teacher in Thoreau, whose *Walden* I carried constantly in my pocket.' Later on he read Whitman, characterized by Thoreau as 'apparently the greatest democrat the world has seen', and Herman Melville. It was not long before he began to have contributions accepted by the London *Morning Leader*, and by Ford Madox Hueffer's *English Review*, and he finally landed a full time job as a newspaper man. He joined the *Morning Leader* in 1904, and later the *Daily News*, when the two papers amalgamated. Even before his first book was published he wrote prose of distinction and, to those who knew his writing, his finest book *The Sea and the Jungle* was not a surprise.

Many know the story of how Tomlinson, a victim with other millions of the 8.35 to London, started on a fantastic trip to the heart of the Amazonian jungle. It all happened on one fateful day when 'the sky was waterlogged and the grey ceiling, over-strained, had sagged and dropped to the level of the chimneys'. For one who passionately loved freedom, and who instinctively rebelled against a conventional and futile routine, the daily life of 'dutifully climbing the revolving wheel like the squirrel' could only become irksome. Fate, in the person of a skipper (according to Frank Swinnerton he was Tomlinson's brother-in-law) and the Putney bus, intervened in the up-to-then casual course of Tom-

146

linson's life. The skipper met Tomlinson on that foggy morning, and mentioned a trip to Para, and thence 2,000 miles up the Amazon and Madeira Rivers. What a dream for one who had so loved the ships! What an escape for one who had always loved the names of far off places . . . of Manaos, Obydos, Santarem, Ita-coatiara! The skipper, knowing his man, said: 'Then why don't you chuck it? Give it up and come with me. Look there . . . see that Putney bus? If it takes up two more passengers before it passes this spot then you've got to come.' Tomlinson agreed. One man jumped on the bus; it almost reached them, but before it did the skipper hopped aboard, and held up two fingers with a grin. Thus the decision was made and a new freedom came to one who had been so long a captive of the revolving wheel.

The *Capella*, later sunk by a submarine, was a 3,000-ton freighter, 300 feet long, with a 23-foot draught, and 'with derrick supports fore and aft, and a funnel; and the three of them are so fearful of seeming rakish that they overdo the effect of stern utility, and appear to lean ahead'.

Even before Lundy was reached shortly out of the Bristol Channel came a violent storm (it was December 1910), and 'a lump of soap made a flying leap from the washstand, and then slithered about the floor like something haunted and panic-stricken'. To a landsman there was something startling in a sea that didn't behave when you were scarcely out of sight of land. Strong misgivings soon struck our purser (signed on at a shilling a month), and he reflected on the sea: 'Perhaps it is better not to live with it, if you would love it.' Doubts percolated in his mind. Ships had been lost in December gales, but now a very human thought, quite reassuring, came to him: 'Besides, I had already commenced a letter which was to be posted at Para. The letter would have to be posted. They were waiting for it at home.' The pure trust of a simple man. Everything would be all right. It was.

The reader soon knows that *Capella* well. Here is the saloon: 'It had curious marine odours then, with which I was not friendly till long after, odours that lamps, burnished brass, newly polished wood, food, and the steward's store-room behind it, never fully accounted for; and I remember it as I found it in the still heat of the Amazon, when it had the air of the oven; when, writing in it,

147

the sweat ran off the fingers to soil the paper, strange insects crawling everywhere on its green baize table cover, and banging against the lamp,' and always, 'There was the warm oily gush of air from the engine-room entrance.' We know the jungle: 'Still the forest glides by. It is a shadow on the mind . . . and as day is dying it is still there, paramount, enigmatic, silent, its question implied in its mere persistence—meeting me again on the next day, still with its mute interrogation.' We know the river: 'The river was merely a drain burrowing under the jungle.' There is excellent characterization, as, for instance, O'Brien, who like Thoreau, was a free man: 'He was outside any authority but his own. . . . I puzzled much over this phenomenon of a free man, took his freedom so quietly and naturally that he never even discussed the subject, as we do with enthusiasm in England.'

If the reader is curious about why the Capella should have pushed its way into the heart of the Amazonian jungle, let him study closely a modern map of Brazil and he will see a thin double line, marking the railroad running from Porto Velho (the destination of the ship) to Abuna, and then southward to Guajara Minim. This engineering feat was the final outcome of Tomlinson's famous voyage.

If the reader wants to know why this railroad, built at heavy cost of human life, was obsolete even before it was finished he will find it told in the late Peter Grieve's delightful book, *A Wilderness Voyage*, which follows Tomlinson's route almost exactly.

But the world of which the *Capella* was such a vital part was soon to end, and the war brought Tomlinson 'no inspiration, only horror'. It produced, however, some of Tomlinson's finest work. He became a war correspondent in Belgium and France from August 1914. Later he was made an Official Correspondent with G.H.Q. of the British Armies in France from 1915–17. From 1917 to 1923 he served under H. W. Massingham on the *Nation and Athenaeum*. This is the bare record.

Tomlinson really never recovered from the war. The acid of death and destruction corroded the man's spirit. He believed, as did Thoreau, that a man must speak the truth that is within him, and his dispatches soon ran him into difficulties. Everyone knows now how many lives were wasted in futile and stupid offences such as the Battle of the Somme and Passchendale, but then the truth could not be told. Neither could Tomlinson betray his spiritual integrity, remembering Emerson's: 'Nothing is at last sacred but the integrity of our own mind.' And he became a sad and at times bitter man.

A blue-bell at Thiepval became for him, midst the welter of mass suicide going on about him, a symbol of something stable, of a force in nature that not even man could quite destroy. It provided for him also, as it did for many others, a saving grace, a slight margin for belief in the permanence of lovely things. Although the smells of cordite and rotting corpses soon obliterated the smell of grass, the smell of pines and fir, the blue-bells still bloomed at Thiepval. Nature offered him an anchor for 'his purest thoughts' and kept him sane.

His best war writing will be found, I think, not in his war novel, but in his essays. Especially in his volume entitled *Waiting for Daylight*. Here one gets what Tomlinson really thought about the statesman, about Tommy Atkins, who is immortalized in the essay 'The Nobodies', and about those who led the common troops to their slaughter. He is at his best in his descriptive passages and, in one essay, the once ghostly city of Ypres is preserved once and for all by the magic of Tomlinson's pen. Who has written anything finer about the war than his *Illusion*, 1915? The unreality of the Western Front, as if it were really another, and stranger pock-marked planet, is conceived with perfection. In his novel *All Our Yesterdays*, as I have hinted, he is not quite so happy. The war, I have sometimes fancied, hurt Tomlinson as a writer, for it turned him more and more in upon himself. In the place of the perfect fact one finds more and more a feeling for abstractions, for vague generalities. It has never crushed the innate serenity of his own nature, but actually the scenes of horror, and the conviction of war's utter futility, lacerated almost beyond repair the spirit of this essentially kind and tender-minded man.

When H. W. Massingham left the *Nation*, Tomlinson left also, and he got a roving commission from *Harpers* to travel in the East Indies. For nine months he explored the Moluccas, Malaya, and Ceylon, and he has left his impression in another superb travel book: *Tidemarks*. This book, together with *Old Junk*, *London River*, *Under The Red Ensign*, and *Gifts of Fortune*, give us his sharpest work.

His best novel is probably *Gallions Reach*, in which he depicts the scenes of his youth, The Royal Albert Docks, and in which there is a fine description of a sinking ship. 'Every novel,' he says, 'is autobiographical; it can't help it.' But his Arcadian novel, *Snows of Helicon*, is a failure because it chases a vague dream and never becomes real.

South of Cadiz shows, too, a falling off in descriptive power, not because he has lost his feeling for the concrete, but because his interest has shifted more acutely to the things of the spirit, and when he vaporizes into romantic yearnings for Platonic Ideals he is not equal to his master Thoreau.

On his own admission he has not read widely, but what he has read he has made his own. He liked Hardy (the pessimistic but gentle soul), Dickens (the humanitarian), the Brontës (ardent individualists), Meredith and Tshekhov (literary artists), Samuel Clemens and Sinclair Lewis (writers on the United States).

He knew a great deal about the literature of the war, and I owe to him my introduction to Duhmel's terrible and truthful book of sketches called *Civilization:* 1914–18.

Though Mr Tomlinson died years ago I have never forgotten him. He used to speak with a ghostly, far-away voice and, as he was becoming deaf even then, put his hand to his ear to catch one's reply. He had a somewhat sad smile, as if he had seen the bottom of things, as indeed he had, but he nurtured to the end, I think, a faith in man, in his reason, and in his essential goodness. Tomlinson was sceptical and ironical, but was at heart a kind and gentle humanitarian of the nineteenth century, quite unable to reconcile himself to a Dreiserian naturalistic universe.

He deserves a revival.

CHAPTER V

The Bookman and the Friends of Dartmouth Library

Studies serve for delight, for ornament, and for ability.
Bacon: *Of Studies*

In January 1938, when Basil O'Connor gave me $500 to help launch the organization *The Friends of the Dartmouth Library*, nobody knew what the results would be. Now that more than a quarter of a century has passed one may say that they have been remarkable. Thousands of rare books, letters, manuscripts, paintings, and prints have been donated by people to the College many of whom have no connection with Dartmouth.

I was well advised at the start by the Yale librarian, James T. Babb, who was a book collector like myself. Then President Ernest Martin Hopkins, the late Thomas W. Streeter, Harold G. Rugg, Richard H. Mandel, George Matthew Adams, Bella C. Landauer, Marston E. Drake, Thomas M. Beers, Basil O'Connor, William J. Bryant, and others quickly rallied around.

Our aim was simple: 'The purpose . . . should be to get, when and where possible, complete collections, single rare volumes, manuscripts, diaries, letters, books and pamphlets which throw light on the cultural history of this or other countries; in other words, any original or rare material the library could not be expected to buy with its own funds.'

Later we extended our interests to include paintings and sculpture. For instance, when an opportunity arose to buy Chester Harding's portrait of Mrs Daniel Webster, one of his best pictures, a phone call from me to Mr. W. J. Bryant of Springfield, Vermont, was all that was needed to obtain the portrait which now hangs in Baker Library.

This brings up an important point: that the Friends of the Library have contributed many original paintings, prints, etchings and lithographs to the great art collections at Dartmouth, as well as innumerable art objects, Chinese, Pre-Columbian, Mexican, etc. It would be impossible to enumerate here the quantity and quality of these paintings and other artistic gifts, but they include many works of moderns given by Mr and Mrs William B. Jaffee, along with paintings by Maxfield Parrish, J. M. W. Turner, William Thackeray and George Cruikshank drawings, and literally hundreds of others, including works by Paul Sample, the well-known American painter.

When we started our organization I was Assistant Professor of Comparative Literature at Dartmouth and had no connection whatever officially with the Library. In fact, I have never had any, and I regard this, with no offence meant to the Library, as one of the reasons for such success as we have had.

The Dartmouth College Library is the best *college* library in the United States. Soon after its founding in 1769, the College had a few books, and by 1774 it had perhaps 300 volumes. By 1800 the collection was nearly 3,000 volumes. I suppose today we have nearly a million books.

Owing to a new library building in 1928 given by George F. Baker, and the important donation by Edwin W. Sanborn, as an endowment for the purchase of books, in memory of his father, Edwin B. Sanborn of the class of 1882, Dartmouth was firmly established as a library with infinite possibilities.

The point of view of the professional librarian and the rare bookman is generally poles apart. The librarian has to think of basic material in all scholarly fields, and he usually has no feeling whatever for first editions, finely printed books and manuscripts, unless they serve a practical purpose.

Today with the advent of microfilms and electronic devices it is possible to visualize a library without any books at all. This I did in my satire on the American college *Here's to Togetherness*.

Throughout the twenty-six years I directed the organization I have had the co-operation of about 400 people who have paid yearly dues and have given rare material to the library. This is not a great number and with a little more effort we could have had more.

The Friends have always, perhaps because of my own natural

distaste for bureaucracy, been an extremely simple organization.

We have cost the college nothing except the expense of cataloguing the material we have acquired. We paid our own way either through membership fees or special gifts from certain people who believed in what we are doing.

We have no constitution or by-laws, we are not incorporated, and we never have any minutes for any meetings. Generally we had no meetings. When I retired in June 1964, there was really nothing to retire from, and nothing but a membership list to turn over. We always worked independently, had no official connection with the College. However, the Comptroller's office did receive and disburse our funds.

For a few years we had an executive committee which met once a year in New York City, and later on in Hanover. During the war, from 1939 to 1945, we felt that we couldn't justifiably solicit funds when there were other, far more deserving causes such as the Red Cross, British Relief, and so on, so during these years we coasted along as well as we could without financial backing.

I felt then, and still feel, that the College itself should have encouraged and supported us far more than it did. For several years we had an annual dinner in Hanover which attracted several important bookmen as well as many financially able to help the library. Our meetings were high spots, and most successful, but they were never attended by the President of the College, and never had any official recognition from the administration. The Executive Committee might have been treated with more courtesy and also those friends who might have wished to give more to the College.

I soon realized the fact that the administration took a dim view of our dinners and meetings. We were getting too big, too important, and too successful. I am certain we aroused jealousy in certain quarters and, instead of getting support, we merely got a grudging acquiescence to our existence.

This is spite of the fact that a great library adds prestige to any educational institution, and that the Friends were of immeasurable help in building up Baker Library's special collections which have attracted, and are increasingly attracting, both European and

American scholars, as well as furnishing valuable materials for the faculty and student body of Dartmouth.

Hence it was that all the work gradually fell on me alone. The Executive Committee soon ceased to exist except on paper, although the individual members consistently supported me. However, we were never able to put up a very strong organization such as Princeton has, as no one wanted us to have one, least of all the Administration.

So in a way the 'Friends' at Dartmouth has been a peculiarly one-man job. I have had only half a day a week secretarial help, no special office, no files, and nearly everything was carried in my head.

It is important that the director of such an organization as ours knows books and loves them as well. He should have a wide acquaintance with book dealers, both in the United States and abroad, who will notify him when they have something suitable for the library's special collections. Also the more book collectors he knows the better. He must, above all, be free of the Philistine approach so often taken by trustees and some librarians.

At one point the Trustees of Dartmouth proposed that the College sell some of the rare books I had succeeded in getting in order to raise money. This infuriated me so that I wrote an angry letter to the treasurer saying that even if it were a good thing to sell such books, it was poor form as many had been given in memory of the dead. It is not uncommon in libraries to run up against this Philistine attitude, though the situation is becoming much better in this regard. Note the head of the University of Texas' solicitude for its great library! And Chancellor Tolley's at Syracuse.

I always found it helpful in my work to visit, and even work at times, in certain American libraries.

I did a year's graduate work at Harvard, and so became acquainted with its magnificent library. I have visited the Clements' Library at the University of Michigan. I know the head of special collections at the University of North Carolina. I am familiar with the University of Texas libraries and only last spring saw the rooms dedicated to Dobie and Tinker. I have worked at the Huntington Library, the Bancroft Library in Berkeley, and I was happily present at the opening of C. Waller Barrett's famous collection in the Alderman Library at the University of Virginia. I am familiar with the collections at Indiana and New York University.

Dartmouth has a lot to aim for but we have made a good, if modest, start.

During our time we have received many great author collections, many great individual classics, many fine paintings, many manuscripts, and many great letters.

The late George Matthew Adams, one of America's recent great book collectors, I think, was a personal friend of mine whom I visited both in New York City and at his island camp on Grand Lake near Halifax, Nova Scotia. As a matter of fact, the twenty-five years have included a great deal of travel, some of it difficult, most of it pleasant, and often resulting in great collections for Dartmouth.

This island paradise of Mr Adams I was especially fond of and during our talks before the fire at night he planned great things for Baker Library. I can only list without much explanation some of his donations, several of which I think are definitive collections. It is not possible here to describe these collections at any great length but suffice it to say that they offer for research to any student, undergraduate or graduate, much material—not only published books but also manuscripts, letters, and much ephemera.

Among the great collections that Mr Adams gave Dartmouth was the Joseph Conrad collection to which we later added all but two of Conrad's letters to Cunninghame Graham, and other interesting accessions. As a matter of fact, it might be well to state here that no collection is considered complete and all are being continually expanded.

Mr Adams' tastes were wide, and most of his collections here also include prints, etchings, lithographs, and so forth. Although our Conrad collection cannot compete with that at Yale, given by our friend Mr George T. Keating, nevertheless there is much to be said for it.

The same could be said of Mr Adams' collection of Stephen Crane, Vachel Lindsay, Katherine Mansfield, Ambrose Bierce,

Herman Melville, Walt Whitman, and Richard Jefferies, as well as the early collection of Edward Thomas: Robert Frost's English friend who died in the First World War, and which was augmented by my own collection of Thomas. Perhaps less important collections given by him are those of Francis Brett Young, E. D. Howe, Roark Bradford, Michael Fairless, and Jesse Stuart. Besides these collections, Mr Adams gave generously of funds toward certain purchases such as Rupert Brooke's letters, single valuable editions of Rupert Brooke, George Meredith, T. E. Lawrence and others. All in all, Mr Adams left a permanent mark on the Dartmouth Library.

The United States is fortunate in its income tax laws which enable one to deduct gifts to institutional libraries. This is the main reason that we get as many gifts as we do. The donor is generally favoured by as high an appraisal as the income tax people will allow. There is not as much danger in the appraisal of books as there is in paintings. With the popularity of modern painting, abstractions, pop art, and what-not, it is possible to be the recipient of a painting which consists of nothing but a single coat of black paint (labelled Despair?) or of two or three bright colours hurled on to a canvas by a spray gun, a donkey's tail, or a BB gun. The appraisal value of such may be many thousands of dollars though it actually is not worth storage room.

It can be seen that this could, and probably has, become a racket. I think that college officials must scrutinize with great care the paintings and sculpture, so-called, that they accept in the field of modern art, and check carefully the appraisal figures. It is possible to conceive that if this privilege is widely abused the income tax laws might be changed so that even books might not be deductible. If this should happen the stream of gifts would nearly run dry in a short period of time.

My position as Director was an unsalaried one but I did have a travel and entertainment allowance which made it possible to do my job.

At the beginning the library had to be educated. When a gift was received all too often no letter of thanks whatever went out, not even an acknowledgment of the gift. This happened to me for several months after I had given valuable collections. I

156

realized that this was no way to encourage gifts, and many times I had to insist that letters be written to people who had given books or letters. Naturally this did not endear me to those responsible.

However, as time went on and with slow changes of library personnel, the situation changed completely. Now anyone who gives anything today finds his gift promptly and politely acknowledged by a letter from the librarian or someone connected with special collections.

Though our administrative costs were kept at a minimum we never had enough money to do what we would have liked to do. We had to pass up the opportunity all too often to buy some valuable book that would fit into our collections. Our general income has been between $6,000 and $10,000 a year. Of this perhaps $1,500 would be used for travel and entertainment. I strongly believe that the amount of money spent this way should be left entirely to the discretion of the director. He should have money to go to Europe, to travel in the United States, for unless he does travel and visit collectors and dealers, winning their good will and interest, he cannot do his job properly.

On the other hand, I believe that the organization should remain small and avoid bureaucracy at all costs.

Among the rewards of the position I held for so long were the friends I made.

Thus, when Charles Jackson, who then lived in Orford, New Hampshire, became a friend of mine, he presented Dartmouth with the manuscript of his famous book about an alcoholic, *The Lost Weekend*. I was able also to get Henry Beston, another friend who used to speak in my Nature Writers course every year, to give us the manuscript of his finest book, *The Outermost House*, a classic in nature writing about Cape Cod. Then too through friendship with Kenneth Roberts, but mainly owing to his close friendship with Mr Hopkins, we were able to get his manuscript *Rabble in Arms*, one of his finest books. Ben Ames Williams gave his manuscript of *A House Divided*, and eventually all his papers.

A familiar figure in Hanover for many years, and a born collector, was the late Mrs Bella C. Landauer, who proved to be a great friend of the Dartmouth Library. She is remembered also for her collections at the New York Historical Society and she generously gave to other institutions as well. We have been the recipient of innumerable magnificent gifts from her, only a few of which I can mention here. She began with a collection of Benjamin Franklin engravings, a fine collection of Tennessee Williams, a tremendous collection of sheet music concerning Kipling, Dickens, Barrie, Tennyson, and also a fine collection of Eugene O'Neill, booksellers' broadsides, theatre items, many first editions, and she contributed money for the purchase of Rupert Brooke letters, and other material.

In the Spring of 1961 I visited Henry Williamson once again in North Devonshire, then working on his novel, *A Test of Destruction*, for the purpose of persuading him to give Dartmouth the manuscript of one of his books.

He chose for us the manuscript of one of his non-fiction books, *A Clear Water Stream*, and I carried this away with me.

He has put so high a price on his manuscripts, so the London dealers tell me, that not even the University of Texas has met his price. We were more fortunate.

Mr Williamson recently gave them to Exeter, in England.

It always seemed to me that we could never compete with the great university libraries in collecting the great books of the past, so under my aegis we specialized in modern writers. We must have one of the best collections in America of writers of the last century or so. As an example of what a small college can do I will write here mainly on one of our great collections: that of Henry L. Mencken.

It all began when one of my former students, Richard H. Mandel, gave to Dartmouth his Mencken collection.

The Henry L. Mencken collection in Baker Library at Dartmouth received publicity recently because Dartmouth was the only college or university to benefit by Mr Mencken's will to the extent of being left seven volumes of his books (four of *My Life As Author and Editor*, and three of *35 Years of Newspaper Work*), enclosed in seven wooden boxes, painted with green stripes and bound with metal bands and labelled: 'Papers of Henry L. Mencken, not to be opened until January 29, 1991.' One of the conditions of the gift was that the College should agree that the boxes not be opened until that date. This legacy seemed to us at Dartmouth final proof of the importance of our Mencken collection. The original collection given by Mr Mandel consisted of all of Mr Mencken's books, including a fine copy of *Ventures into Verse*, but lacking at the time many of the pamphlets, editorials, ephemeral material, and so on.

My own friendship with Mr Mencken dates back slightly previous to 1930. Graduating from college as I had in the 'twenties, I had become an admirer of Mr Mencken because of his forthrightness, clear style, lack of humbug, and unique method of puncturing American follies and foibles. Like many others of my generation I was considerably influenced by the 'Baltimore Bombshell'. We enjoyed his cracks at the 'booberai', his digs at the antisaloon league, bogus politicians, and other montebanks. I began corresponding with Mr Mencken and continued to do so until his death. We dined together at the Maryland Club and he became interested in our collection. He understood that we were buying everything we could find, including the rare *A Monograph of the New Baltimore Court House*, issued in 1899. So from the very beginning Mr Mencken sent us many pamphlets, editorials, all of these signed or inscribed, so that our collection, at his death, was about as complete as it was possible to be (and no Mencken collection can ever be complete, owing to the profuseness of the minutiae involved in reaching the absolute).

There are several boxes in the collection labelled 'Pamphlets presented by H. L. Mencken'. It would not be possible here to list these, but they include such diverse material as the announcement of his marriage to Sara Haardt on August 27, 1930, together with such pamphlets as *The Anatomy of Quackery*, published in Cleveland in 1935; a signed copy of *Erez Israel*, one of twenty-five copies issued in New York, privately printed in 1935; 'What Mencken Thinks of El Paso and Juraez', a copy of *From the Nordic Blond Renaissance*: and German edition of *Heliogabal*.

After *A New Dictionary of Quotations* came out, Mr Mencken presented us with twenty-eight drawers of 3×5 cards which made up the original manuscript of this book.

159

He also gave us a large slip case or box full of 'Hat Rack' case material. Many will remember the issue of Mencken's *American Mercury* which contained the article on a woman of easy virtue who dispensed her favours in empty freight cars—Box Car Molly, I think, was her name. 'Hat Rack', another story of a miss who chose a cemetery for her love affairs, aroused the wrath of the Watch and Ward Society in Boston. Mencken, always a great antagonist of 'Comstockery' and the Watch and Ward Society, decided to make a test case of this, and was arrested selling a copy of his issue on the Boston Common. Vindicated in court, he had his triumph, and this large case contains all the material on 'Hat Rack' which Mr Mencken was able to get together.

Among the manuscripts and typescripts which Dartmouth possesses, one would mention the corrected carbon of *Supplement One of the American Language*, corrected typescripts of *Happy Days, Heathen Days*, as well as the first draft and revised typescript of *Newspaper Days*. It seems to this writer that these three books are among those of Mr Mencken's which will endure. Also the typescript of *Notes on Democracy*, together with fragments of the first draft and typescript with author's corrections of his *Treatise on Right and Wrong*. Mr Mencken also presented us with a miscellaneous collection of sixteen typescripts including his 'Notes on Conscription', his essay on Raymond Pearl (incidentally, a Dartmouth man, and one of Mencken's most intimate friends).

Carroll Frey gave us the manuscript Foreword to his bibliography of Mencken, together with the original drawing of Mencken used in that book.

On a trip to the West Coast in 1955, the well-known American collector, George T. Keating, then living in Los Altos, California, generously gave to me for our collection all his Mencken books. These were all inscribed and included among them was almost certainly the best copy in existence of *Ventures into Verse*, which is heavily annotated.

From my own Mencken collection I presented about 150 letters from Mencken to me, written from 1930 to 1956. I added to this gift later letters from his devoted secretary, Miss Lohrfinck, which I received from her after his illness and death.

I have been asked to give the reasons why Mencken chose Dartmouth as the only college or university library to receive his memoirs, previously described and not to be opened until 1991. Although I have not written Miss Lohrfinck about this, my own guess would be that it was owing to a combination of things. I suspect that his friendship with Raymond Pearl had much to do with it, and perhaps was the most important reason. I think, also, the fact that we were given the definitive Huneker collection impressed him. I suspect, too, that he was generally impressed with the fact that Dartmouth was enthusiastic enough about his collection to make it as perfect as possible. Mr Mencken was also aware that his friend George T. Keating had given us his collection. This obviously meant that we had a great collection of his books—some of them duplicated several times, and all inscribed and unique copies.

I can only say that I felt elated and proud of the Friends of the Library when I learned that he had chosen us for this legacy. It was natural that the New York Public Library (which, I believe, received his correspondence) and the Enoch Pratt Library in Baltimore should also receive his memoirs. Other great university libraries possess fine Mencken collections—such as Harvard and Yale—but, nonetheless, Dartmouth received his special blessing. I regret exceedingly that I will not be here when the boxes are opened, and used by scholars.

Many people do not realize that Dartmouth already has a great research library. Only a few people are aware that we have perhaps the finest collection in the country of modern first editions, of at least 100 author collections, each of which is being built up year by year to reach as near perfection as possible. Already Dartmouth, still a college but rapidly becoming a university, has attracted international scholars who must come here if they are to write definite books on such men as Cunninghame Graham, Huneker, Stephen Crane, Frost, and other modern writers. I cannot predict what Dartmouth's plans will be for utilizing the Mencken papers when they are opened in 1991, but I can be reasonably sure that they will be available to all scholars interested in assessing Mr Mencken's place as editor and writer in American literature. I am willing to assume that his remarks on many American writers, some of whom by that time may well be forgotten, will be—to say the least—forthright and penetrating.

It is too early to assess Mr Mencken's place in American literature, but I have heard Robert Frost say that he was our greatest American essayist, and I expressed my personal opinion in my book *The Mind On The Wing*.

'Mencken has unquestionably been a vital force in contemporary letters. . . . For those of us who attended college in the early 'twenties, and in fact for the whole post-war generation, he made a genuine impact on our intellectual point of view. Reading him we became slightly more civilized. He seemed to us then, as he still does to me, one of the most forthright men of letters we have ever had—a man who with wit and with clarity wrote the truth as he saw it about these United States, about its laws (especially the prohibition law), its clubs and societies, its language, its writers, and its standards of criticism. He wrote with an urbane, cosmopolitan point of view, with an Olympian outlook, and his sole object seemed to be to expose American quackery, whether he found it in our politics, in our philosophers, in our education (the Scopes trial in Tennessee), or in our writers and critics.

'For him life has been a gaudy and extravagant show to be exploited and enjoyed. His biggest guns have been aimed at quacks and reformers, who abound in the great American Bible belt, and he has aroused their fury to such a pitch that a volume of their vituperations was actually collected and issued by Mencken in 1928. . . .

'By training and inclination Mencken is a newspaperman, one trained to respect the fact, to be suspicious always of bombast and hokum. He is a thorough-going empiricist, a pragmatist in morale, and a hedonist in philosophy. He is what William James called a "tough-minded" man. In short, he is one of our few really civilized men.' (When these paragraphs were written, Mr Mencken was living—hence the tense.)

Although Mr Mencken enjoyed taking cracks at pedagogues, most of them I am certain well deserved, he was nonetheless himself a good scholar and while his volumes on the American language may not remain the last word, they certainly represent a real scholarly contribution to a most interesting subject. It

could also be that the future will judge Mr Mencken for his auto-
graphical books and some of his criticism rather than for his great
pioneer work on the American language.

Early in my career as head of the Friends of the Dartmouth
Library, I felt that I could not ask other alumni to give books
unless I were willing to give them too, and so over the years many
collections I had made as an 'impecunious amateur' went to
Dartmouth. These included the best collection in the world of
Robert Bontine Cunninghame Graham, with hundreds of letters
and manuscripts. This has already brought scholars from Europe
and many in this country to Dartmouth and no doubt will continue to do so. I also gave collections including all books, letters,
manuscripts, etc., of the famous English critic, Edward Garnett,
the nature writer Henry Williamson, Edward Thomas, early
friend of Robert Frost, Richard Curle, who once stayed with me
in Hanover, as well as an amazingly fine collection of the now
popular writer Henry Miller. I also gave a collection of Wilfrid
Scawen Blunt which included the corrected proofs of his collected
poems given to me one afternoon in Cambridge, England, by the
late Sir Sidney Cockerell, as well as letters, etc. Also books by
George Santayana, Edward Thompson, the Scottish writer,
George Blake, collections of Auden, Sean O'Faolain, and
others.

The Cunninghame Graham collection is, I think, probably the
finest there is anywhere. It has been added to every year. Through
a connection in London I was able to purchase a magnificent collection of Joseph Conrad and W. H. Hudson letters to Cunninghame Graham. There were seventy-seven Conrad and fifty
Hudson letters. Mrs A. F. Tschiffely was willing to part with
them knowing they were going to a great library which already
had a collection of the books of her husband and his friend
Cunninghame Graham. One Conrad letter recently brought $200
so we were very lucky indeed in getting these at a very moderate
price some years ago. It is fair to say that the money the Friends
raised over the years has been used with discrimination and taste
in adding to great collections already in the possession of the
Library. We were able to buy things that the Library could not
justifiably buy with its own funds. This has been I think our

great contribution and if all the books were seen together they would I am sure fill a building.

Probably the most famous living bookman at the moment, with the possible exception of Waller Barrett, is Thomas W. Streeter, of Morristown, New Jersey.[1]

His collection of Texiana is at Yale, but Dartmouth has been the recipient over the years of many fine books as well as financial aid. Among these I must note many early English tracts, many valuable railroad pamphlets, particularly concerning New England, the rare second edition of Lucretus' *De Rerum Natura*, books by Melville, early western books, copies of his famous bibliography of Texas, generous financial aid toward the purchase of Rupert Brooke material as well as the 1499 Hypneratomachae which contains the first use of woodcuts.

Since 1958 Gilbert Verney of Bennington, New Hampshire, has been another most generous donor to Dartmouth having presented us with many first editions of Ruskin and fifty rare books from the library of the late Governor Winant. In 1961 he commissioned me to examine the Verney family papers at Claydon House in Buckinghamshire, England, which resulted in a gift of more than $6,000 to have these papers microfilmed. The result was a microfilm more than a mile long, 30,000 exposures of historical papers going back to the Long Parliament. Through the generosity of Mr Verney the Friends were able to give a copy of this microfilm to the British Museum, the Buckingham County Seat at Aylesbury, a copy to Yale, the Library of Congress and also to Dartmouth. I think this may be the Friends' most significant contribution to knowledge as most of these papers were virtually unknown to scholars previous to this microfilming, though four volumes of them had been published by Lady Verney, a sister of Florence Nightingale, in the nineteenth century.

The only collection at Dartmouth which the College itself publicized was the Stefansson collection given by a Trustee of the college. Our collections got very little, if any, publicity. Consequently few people know of what we have and our book treasures are not used as much as they should be. Now that the Friends are

[1] He died soon after this was written.

run by the Library itself, perhaps it will no longer hide its light under a bushel.

The most perfect organization would be run something like this: First, the Director should be a man who genuinely loves rare books and who knows a lot about them. He should also be a man of some personality who can get on with people, and who has won recognition for his accomplishments as a collector, and who can raise a certain amount of money each year. Secondly, there should be an annual dinner to which all the Friends are invited; the chairman of this dinner should be some prominent bookman, and the dinner should be warmly supported by the administration and the library. Thirdly, there should be several annual exhibits, and one large one at Commencement time. Lastly, there should be published a book THE DARTMOUTH COLLECTIONS so that the world and community would know what we have to offer.

Perhaps, too, the Library should do something once in a while for the friends who support it. We did this at times by sending an occasional book. (We also always at Christmas sent a J. J. Lankes Christmas card.)

One of our publications was an unpublished Ralph Waldo Emerson poem, *Indian Superstition*, edited by Kenneth W. Cameron of Trinity College. We also did a bibliography of Stephen Crane, one of Vachel Lindsay, both to honour gifts from George Matthew Adams. We published a whaling book, *In A Sperm Whale's Jaws*, telling of a remarkable episode in the life of the grandfather of Professor George C. Wood, a one-time colleague of mine on the Dartmouth faculty. Then we published *Thoreau and the Wild Appetite* with the Thoreau Society, a delightful essay by Kenneth Alan Robinson, as well as the previously mentioned *Three Fugitive Pieces* by Cunninghame Graham.

It is always wise to give donors some recognition once in a while in appreciation of their interest.

Over the years the greatest single benefactor to the Library was a gentleman from California who recently died. It was lucky indeed for the Friends and Dartmouth to become the recipient of the great library collected by Perc S. Brown of Orinda, California. I first got in touch with Mr Brown when he was living in New

Jersey through Marston E. Drake of the well-known book firm in New York of James F. Drake, Inc. It was owing to Mr Drake's great stimulus that Mr Brown started giving us books.

It would be impossible to list the major first editions in English literature which Mr Brown has given us. These include all the great writers but I will mention only a few: Robert Louis Stevenson, Mary Webb, Samuel T. Coleridge, Tobias George Smolett, William Makepeace Thackeray, Charles Dickens, Lawrence Sterne, Thomas Gray, Oscar Wilde, Walt Whitman, Alfred Tennyson, William Wordsworth, and Oliver Goldsmith, as well as modern writers Ernest Hemingway, Thomas Wolfe and William Faulkner. Also included are many oil paintings, statuary, letters and manuscripts of Dickens. Among the great books might be mentioned Tristram Shandy, a presentation copy of Dickens' *Bleak House*, the rare 1926 *Seven Pillars of Wisdom*, and an immaculate first edition of Gray's *Elegy*.

I might interject here that the rare book market shows no signs of falling off and most of the gifts we have had are now worth much more than they were when presented.

I think perhaps the most important single gift of Mr Brown's consists of numerous magnificent documents of American history including letters of Benjamin Franklin, Thomas Jefferson and, above all, George Washington. One letter of Washington's recently brought in New York $17,000, and Mr Brown has given us numerous ones, including an engineering survey made when Washington was eighteen years old. I think it is fair to say that as long as the college endures, future scholars and students will be indebted to the late Perc S. Brown for his genius as a collector.

Our collecting interests were varied and among our many gifts I recall that the late Judge Walter L. Hetfield, Jr, of Plainfield, New Jersey, gave us eleven volumes consisting of the *State of New Jersey versus Hauptmann*, a trial over which Judge Hetfield presided.

CHAPTER VI

The Bookman in England

Oh lovely England . . .
Walter de la Mare

Memorable to me was my first visit to England after 'my short period there as a soldier when I passed through on my way to the front in 1918.

On July 12, 1924, at 1.00 in the morning, after a pleasant voyage from Quebec, I arrived in London from Liverpool.

If Bloomsbury, where I lived for the next three months, was the backwater of sandals and beards, introverts and extroverts, homosexuals and lesbians, long-haired writers and neglected geniuses, ivory-towered isolationists, and 'bottle parties', this was not the Bloomsbury I knew.

The Bloomsbury that I got to know was a rather dowdy district, whose centre for me was the British Museum. It was an area bounded on the west by Tottenham Court Road, one of the dingiest of London streets and the scene of Gissing's *New Grub Street*, and on the east by Gray's Inn Road. In those days it consisted of a region of somewhat formal streets and squares dating mainly from the eighteenth and early nineteenth centuries. Jonathan Cape, the up-and-coming publisher, was then located near my quarters at 11 Gower Street. At one time Bloomsbury was a fashionable and even aristocratic quarter, but in my time it had literary associations and the gloss had long since worn off. It is even dingier today.

It is trite to say that there is nothing as lonely as a great city in which one is a complete stranger. For days I wandered the streets alone, read alone, ate alone, until one day in semi-desperation I bought a canary in the Tottenham Court Road. From then on, as if the bird were a talisman, my fortunes changed, and my spirits soared.

167

What is the infinite and nostalgic charm of London? What was it that before the summer had passed bound me to it with ties which are even stronger forty years later? There is a spell about London, but of writers I know, only DeQuincey, James Bone, and Thomas Burke (possibly E. V. Lucas and Harold P. Clunn may be mentioned here, too) have come near to describing what this unique quality is.

London has that dingy and haunting beauty given it by Sir Christopher Wren's use of that 'great and magical' Portland stone, which I am told is a marine deposit of the Jurassic period laid down before Britain arose from the sea. As a city it is vastly rich in historical tradition and association, going back even beyond the Romans. It is peopled with the ghosts of many, many great men; its atmosphere of coal smoke and mist rising from the river creates a beauty (and sometimes a hazard) which is peculiarly its own; it is full of bookshops; and it was once the home of Sherlock Holmes. It has given me some of my happiest days, and when I revisited it in the spring of 1955, my old ecstasy returned as if my youth had not gone and the Blitz had never happened.

I love and venerate London and heartily agree with Samuel Johnson's 'No, Sir, when a man is tired of London he is tired of life; for there is in London all that life can afford.'

London's beauty appears sometimes almost in spite of itself. It is a city of evening mists which give it an almost eerie quality; it is a city where the sun's gleam at intervals transfigures St Paul's with an almost unearthly glow.

Then there is the Thames, which Whistler made his own, a river which, like the Seine in Paris, leaves an indelible mark on the city.

There is a pretty story I like to think of when I am by the river. Pepys in his diary tells how, while being rowed to Deptford, he began to sing a song, and a stranger following in another wherry took up the song singing seconds, and in this pleasant manner they made their way. The sight of Shakespeare's Globe Theatre, Christopher Wren's house, Billingsgate, Traitors' Gate at the Tower, and other historical sights may be observed well from the river boat which runs from the Tower to Westminster Bridge. The fare is only twenty-eight cents.

168

The streets are full of the types and nationalities that make London the great cosmopolitan city it is. Men from all parts of the Commonwealth, in all kinds of dress, are so common that nobody (the English are a polite race) notices them, and if one did notice them he would not reveal the fact. The apprentice of Dickens is the office boy of today. Bardolph and Nym, Dame Ursula, Will Honeycomb, Beau Tibbs, Sam Weller, Mr Guppy, Dick Swiveller, all honest Londoners, all in different guises and vocations, still roam the London streets.

The Londoner's speech form, which at first is so bewildering to visitors, is, according to Professor Ernest Weekley, a 'noble blend of East Mercian, Kentish, and East Anglian, which, written by Chaucer, printed by Caxton, spoken by Spenser and Milton—has in modified form and with artificial pronunciation, given us the literary English of the present day'. Hence the honest Londoner who speaks with a light cockney accent has no need to be ashamed and to acquire in its stead the false 'refayned' tone that makes 'How now brown cow' into a 'hoow noow brewn coow'. Good, honest, deep cockney, 'Ahr nah breahn cah' is far preferable, though the American has as hard a time understanding what the true cockney is saying, as if he were hearing a Swedish dialect for the first time.

It is its age and the somewhat mellow carelessness of London which makes it so fascinating for me. Regent Street, once reminiscent of the best of the eighteenth century, has now so changed that its early beauty has been almost completely destroyed, and yet it is always a thrill to see it again. The Café Royal when I was first there still had about the same atmosphere it had when it was frequented by the small giants of the 'nineties.

I never knew the London that rumbled with horse buses, tinkled with hansoms, and shrilled with cab whistles and old street cries, though the latter had not entirely vanished when I was first there.

However, I was fortunate enough to know London before Hitler's blitz: the London of the Middle Temple and of St Clement Danes, a London which differed only slightly from the London of Sherlock Holmes made so real in Sir Arthur's immortal, if somewhat naïve, stories.

For many, and I am one, Sherlock Holmes is as real a person as any who ever lived in London. Often I walked past 221b Baker Street, now housing the Abbey National Building Society, where Holmes and Watson lived. Experts in Holmesian lore seem to agree that the house which best approximates Mrs Hudson's lodging is the blitzed frontage still numbered 111 Baker Street, but there are others who believe it is at 221b Upper Baker Street, where the Holmes exhibition was held a few years ago.

Paternoster Row used to run nearly parallel with the north side of St Paul's churchyard. Its name was derived from the breviaries and rosaries that were once sold in it, and its ecclesiastical character is further indicated by such names as Amen Corner and Ave Maria and Sermon Lanes. It used to haunt this district as I found bargains there in publishers' remainders in Simpkin Marshall's showrooms.

Bertram Rota took me there on my first return to London in nineteen years, in April 1955, and nothing remained but empty cellar holes overflowing with weeds and flowers. There were walls still standing, and buildings still full of rubble. Had not St Paul's been nearby I would not have known where I was. The smell of destruction still lingered. Simpkin Marshall's was and is no more.

One of the landmarks destroyed was the Chapter Coffee House, about which Thomas Chatterton wrote glowingly and misleadingly to his mother while he was starving in a London garret. On the night of the fire that made most of the book trade temporarily homeless, Amen House, the London headquarters of the Oxford University Press, remained unscathed. So, too, did Old Bailey, the Central Criminal Court, which was once Newgate Prison, and which was torn down in 1902. I sat several times at Old Bailey trials, and found the Court inexorable in its dispensing of justice. However, Christ Church on Newgate Street was one of the many wrecked St Christopher Wren churches.

The immediate and obvious fact about London is its bulk and magnitude. There are about 7,235 people to the square mile, and more than 9,000,000 people living within a twenty-mile radius of St Paul's Cathedral. London is the largest aggregation of human beings ever to live in a single community. One becomes aware of this as he travels around by Underground, bus, and car.

One of my favourite places is Gough Square, where in No. 17 had lived the great and justly famous Dr Johnson. Here he wrote his *Dictionary*, but instead, of being remembered by any of his literary remains, Samuel Johnson is remembered and loved because of the rugged quality of his mind and character, not in spite of his prejudices, but because of them. His good English common sense is reflected in many of his most pithy sayings, some of which emanated from these quarters in Gough Square, still intact, I was glad to see, in the summer of 1956. (A. E. Newton's shade haunts the place, too.)

Of Lord Chesterfield's letters: 'They teach the morals of a whore, and the manners of a dancing master.'

Of Scotsmen: 'The noblest prospect which a Scotsman ever sees, is the high road that leads him to England.'

Of free will: 'Sire, we *know* the will is free, and there's an end to it.'

On McCarthyism: 'Patriotism is the last refuge of a scoundrel.'

On writing: 'No man but a blockhead ever wrote except for money.'

On thinking: 'My dear friend, clear your mind of cant. You may *talk* as other people do: you may say to a man, "Sir, I am your most humble servant." You are *not* his most humble servant.'

On re-marriage: 'The triumph of hope over experience.'

I am grateful that I knew the beauty of Adelphi Terrace before the wreckers took over. Since 1768 the lovely Adam houses, with magnificent ceilings and mantelpieces, which adorned the noble terrace giving upon the Victorian Embankment, have housed many of the great in the arts. There was Garrick's house at Number 5, the Savage Club at Number 6, Thomas Hardy had lived at Number 8, and the houses where Shaw and Barrie lived gave it contemporary fame.

The Adelphi Arches underneath were once infested with the choicest thieves and cut-throats of an earlier London, and we avoided them at night, even in the 'twenties.

In the terrace also lived at one time or another John Galsworthy, Herbert G. Wells, and William Butler Yeats. Long before

171

them there were Dr Johnson, Oliver Goldsmith, and their circle. Edward Gibbon came here to finish his *The Decline And Fall Of The Roman Empire*. Benjamin Disraeli was born at Number 16a John Street. Charles Dickens lived for a time at the Adelphi House, and here, in one of its comfortable sitting-rooms, the Fat Boy in *Pickwick* came suddenly upon Mr Snodgrass when that gentleman had tenderly encircled the waist of Emily Wardle.

I am glad also that I knew the Middle Temple on the South side of Fleet Street before it was blitzed. Particularly I recall the stately Elizabethan chamber of Middle Temple Hall with its fine hammer-beam roof and pendants. The large oak table had been given to the Hall by Queen Elizabeth, and Shakespeare himself is said to have taken part in a performance of *Twelfth Night*, which, according to a zealous group, was written by a couple of other fellows, in this hall on February 2, 1601–2.

The Church, the Halls, the Middle Temple Library with thousands of volumes, and many of the suites of chambers surrounding the Courts were destroyed or severely damaged in World War II. In fact, when I returned there in May 1955, I had difficulty in recognizing the place. Oliver Goldsmith's home on Brick Court and Lamb's birthplace are gone, though memories of them linger. Much of the London of Inigo Jones, Christopher Wren and the brothers Adam no longer exists. However, the reconstruction of Pump Court is especially good and the place is now beginning to look its own self again but the sense of violation remains.

Near the Embankment there were streets which Samuel Pepys had walked. It is curious how powerfully the personality of this 'right hand of the Navy' stamped itself on London, especially for anyone who has read his long diary. Although he was born in Salisbury Court, Fleet Street, and lived in Axe Yard, Westminster, and in York Buildings, I could never find any building that had actually housed him. However, there were streets which he described which had changed little since he passed, thinking probably of some pretty wench, over their cobbles. I have always venerated the memory of this doughty, clever, human, humorous, and above all honest man.

The Poets' Corner in Westminster Abbey recalls the names and works of Hakluyt, Chaucer, Tennyson, Browning, Edmund

172

Spenser, Samuel Johnson, Rudyard Kipling, Thomas Hardy, and many others. As I have a romantic feeling for the past, and for the graves of many who lived long ago, I often return to the Abbey.

Once I found the grave, extremely simple, of William Penn at Jordans in Buckinghamshire. This is a spot I want to revisit. It is only a short trip from London. His resting place and gravestone reveal the essential purity and simplicity of the man.

Chelsea Old Church, first mentioned in history in 1290, was almost completely destroyed by bombs, except for the St Thomas More Chapel. It has now been rebuilt. Carlyle's house in Cheyne Row I knew, as much for the room where Ralph Waldo Emerson used to stay as for the old historian himself, at the moment a much underrated literary figure. I lived near there on Sidney Street at one period, and eventually got to know Chelsea well.

In spite of two wars the British Museum Reading Room is still substantially the same as it was in 1857, when it was redesigned by its director, Sir Anthony Panizzi. One still sits in the great circular room under the most spacious dome in the world, except for St Peter's in Rome. If I close my eyes I can smell its dusty atmosphere of leather, old books, and stale air. It is a clearing house for knowledge and God only knows how many volumes have originated here. However, many of its readers never produce books. They simply sit, year in and year out, and read! They remind me of some of the candidates for the PhD degree at Harvard who spend a lifetime in and around the 'yard', working for their phantom degree.

As one passes through the swinging doors into the reading room one is faced squarely with the word SILENCE, and this mandate governs the whole atmosphere and activities of this great library. I had made application through the proper channels for one of its 485 seats, and as a professional scholar had no difficulty in obtaining a ticket. The superintendent's raised desk occupied the centre, and ringing it were 1,000 volumes of catalogues, many of which I assiduously consulted.

If one desires one of the several million books all he has to do is to ransack the catalogues for the particular one he wants, enter it on a slip which he hands in at the central counter, and return to his seat. The book arrives in about twenty minutes on a small, noiseless, rubber-tyred truck, from which an accompanying porter hands it to the reader. I have never done research in a more congenial, or a better managed, library anywhere, though I have no complaints to make concerning the Huntington or the Bancroft Libraries in California. There were special rooms where the reader went if he wanted to look at a rare book or a valuable manuscript.

The questions asked and the remarks made at the circular desk would amuse and perhaps baffle any librarian. 'Please give me all the editions of the works of Joshua Poole', 'Who was the heroine of Lytton's novel *Rienzi*?', 'Have you any Polish pamphlets printed in Jersey in 1832?', 'Where can I find an account of a hamlet in Flintshire?', 'Do you have the 1922 Egyptian census?', 'What kind of an oven was used in a herb gatherer's hut in Sherwood Forest in 1644?', 'What was the name of King Cophetua's beggar maid?', and so on. The librarian and his assistants have developed an air of insouciance and politeness which carries all before it.

It was not unusual that summer some thirty years ago to find oneself sitting not far from Bernard Shaw, Harold Nicholson, the lean condor like Lytton Strachey, or next to an African chieftain with white hair who wore a plug hat through all his meditations. In fact, I used to think this hat must have been a talisman to ward off the evil spirits of the place, for I never saw him remove it. The room was indeed haunted by the ghosts of many who had made history: Karl Marx, Lenin, Mazzini, Disraeli, Dickens, Carlyle, John Stuart Mill, Thomas Huxley, John Wesley, and many others. I was completely happy there.

As I look through my notebooks of that summer I am astonished at my industry. With Darwin I might have written: 'I have steadily endeavoured to keep my mind free so as to give up any hypothesis, however much beloved, as soon as facts are shown to be opposed to it.' I read many books besides the essential ones in my study of American ideas: *The Last Years of H. M. Hyndman*, about Socialism; several books by Cunninghame Graham; Balzac's *At The Sign Of The Cat* and *Racquet*; H. W. Nevinson's *Books and Personalities* as well as his *Changes and Chances*;

174

Joseph Conrad's *Under Western Eyes*; Boswell's life of Johnson
in three volumes; Anatole France's *Thais* (he was shortly to die in
Paris); Voltaire's *Zadig*; James Agate's *Half Past Eight*; Bernard
Shaw's *Saint Joan* (which I also saw on the stage with Sybil
Thorndike); and Thackeray's *Book of Snobs* and *London Sketches*.

When does the temper of one's mind become fixed, if ever?
My early and seemingly natural penchant for doubting was increased rather than diminished by my London sojourn, and by
my summer's travel and reading in the British Museum. I came
to suspect emotional thinking and I came to believe in intelligence.
I soon realized that nothing could be known without 'blood,
sweat, and tears'. The English mind on the whole is, as far as I
have observed, a more mature and better tempered instrument
than is ours. England's spirit of compromise, its genius for understatement and irony, its light touch, so often missing in our
pundits, delighted me. I was thoroughly happy among the English and got on very well with them, and they with me. Even now,
I must confess, that in foreign affairs and in literary criticism I
tend to think more like the English than like most Americans. I
find their journals and broadcasts more intelligent and far more
critical than our own.

Work at the British Museum was interrupted in late August
when an American friend, Joseph Brewer, then St Loe Strachey's
secretary on the *Spectator*, and I drove an old Morris-Cowley
around the British Isles.

The car was a museum piece even then. An open roadster, it
had a canvas top that could be raised and lowered without slowing
down. As we passed through many showers this often proved a
boon. When it was fair weather, all we had to do was to unscrew
two screws above the windshield, grab the canvas top and reach
over our heads with it. When it rained, as it often did, we reversed
the process. The engine had two cylinders, and when they were
both hitting, we sounded a little like a steamroller. We carried
petrol in spare gallon tins strapped to the mudguards. Our lights
were unreliable, so we never drove at night if we could avoid it.
One night we were reduced to burning candles in the lamps, and
once we entered Durham with no lights at all. To stall off a
policeman we asked him as politely as we knew how if he would

recommend a hotel. He, equally polite, did so and graciously over-looked our lack of lights.

I never enjoyed a trip as much. We drove about 1,200 miles and visited cathedrals, abbeys, castles, graves, bookshops, villages famous for something or somebody, ancient houses, and we stayed, whenever possible, in very old and picturesque inns.

In the short time we were on our trip, thirteen days I think it was, we drove through the Lake Country, saw the Trossachs to-gether with Loch Lomond and Loch Katrine, crossed the Cheviot Hills, the Scottish lowlands and some of the highlands, as well as the Northumbrian moors. We visited Ecclefechan where Carlyle was born; Dove Cottage where Wordsworth had lived. We saw the Wessex of Hardy, the Winchester of Jane Austin. We visited many bookshops in Lincoln, Durham, Edinburgh, Keswick, Chester, Bath, Tiverton, Winchester (where we slept at the God-Begot Hostel), and finally Princes Risborough, where our trip be-gan and ended.

We agreed with Mr H. G. Wells in *Mr Polly*: 'There is no countryside like the English countryside for those who have learned to love it; its firm yet gentle lines of hill and dale, its ordered confusion of features, its deer park and downland, its castles and stately houses, its hamlets and old churches, its farms and ricks and great barns and ancient trees, its pools and ponds and shining threads of rivers, its flower-starred hedgerows, its orchards and woodland patches, its village greens and kindly inns. Other countrysides have their pleasant aspects, but none such variety, none that shine so steadfastly throughout the year.'

On August 29 we were in John Bunyan's Bedford; then we drove north through Huntingdon to Peterborough where we saw a magnificent cathedral, and on to Lincoln where we saw another. The next day we spent in York and Durham. On a Sunday, of all days, we crossed from Newcastle into Scotland, driving over the bleak and lonely Cheviot Hills into Jedburgh (quiet as a grave on Sunday), and finally through Galashiels and Dalkeith to Edin-burgh. Though we stopped at Melrose Abbey we did not visit Abbotsford.

Many of the towns and villages we passed through appeared to be morosely lethargic and dull to the point of imbecility. There

176

were a few exceptions, but never on a Sunday, when the whole country seemed to fall into a torpor that was stupefying. Each one had what Cunninghame Graham used to call 'God boxes', grim and dreary churches which expounded on Sundays, and weekdays, too, for all I know, the unholy joys of Calvinism. Indeed, I was told that these churches and their attitude toward sins of the flesh had changed little since Burns wrote *Holy Willie's Prayer*. One could better understand Cunninghame Graham's unforgettable characterization of the Scots, that 'they fornicated gravely and without conviction'.

It was a relief to get to Edinburgh, a city built upon a rock, and a city of bookshops. The old town sits on a ridge which runs from Holyrood to the castle on the hill, and is, perhaps, from a visitor's point of view, the most interesting part of the city. On the other side to the east rise the two shapes of the Salisbury Crag and Arthur's Seat. Princes Street, with its single line of buildings, has this magnificent panorama as its missing side. It did not take long to fall in love with Edinburgh.

The houses of Edinburgh are built of a hard, grey stone, cut at her doors, with a front of brick or painted plaster to break the rock-like monotony. Most of her roads appear to run headlong down hill like salmon rivers in spate. East of Princes Street one notices choppy waves of tenements soaring out toward the hills. To take leave of a friend who is walking north on this street is like walking straight into clouds. The same illusion may also be observed in San Francisco, the only city I know in the United States which can rival Edinburgh in its charm and beauty.

There is no great cathedral in Edinburgh save St Giles, and this, though it goes back to the twelfth century, cannot rival the great cathedrals we had admired in Peterborough, Lincoln, York and Durham. Indeed the claims of Edinburgh do not lie in her ancient architecture, which, owing to her turbulent history, is full of interesting anachronism and curiosities.

What gives Edinburgh its fascination is its magnificent site, its castle on the hill, its historical associations and memories, Princes Street, the antique look of the old town, its bookshops, a few individual buildings such as Holyrood and Melrose Abbey nearby, its people, and last and not least its wonderful whisky.

The Gaelic *uisge-beatha*, 'water of life', or whisky to the reader, is distilled from fermented barley water. Read what the author Neil Gunn has to say in his *Whisky and Scotland*, 1935:

The distiller's aim is to ensure that a large mass of starch, held together by proportionately small quantities of albuminous matter, of which all grain is composed, is changed from insoluble to a soluble condition; second, that this soluble starch is converted into sugar in order that it be fermented or turned into alcohol; and, third, that the alcoholic wash so formed be boiled off into whisky; these three divisions of labour he calls, respectively, malting, brewing, and distilling.

No one but the Scotch distillers have the secret of making good Scotch whisky, and until one has tasted something like Lumsden's Travelled Whisky (which crosses the equator twice in casks), or some real Pot Still Whisky, he has not tasted the best.

Whisky is only one of many drinks which are capable of moving man 'to the intense lucidity of inexplicable utterance'. With the climate Scotland possesses, where a heavy rain may be called a mist, we soon found whisky a necessity, though as the bard says:

> It matters not what drink is ta'en,
> The barley bree, ambition, love,
> Or Guid or Evil workin' in's,
> Sae lang's we feel like souls set free
> Frae mortal coils and speakin' tongues
> We dinna ken and never wull . . .

Whisky cost us 12s 6d in those days, and of this the government took 8s 6d, which left 4s, or roughly $1 a bottle (when the pound was $4.80) out of which came the profits of the distiller, the wholesaler, and the retailer. The whisky itself cost less than 2s a bottle to produce.

To the grey city of the north, as Edinburgh is known, I pay my homage and sing her praises:

> Reikie farewell! I never part
> Wi' thee but wi' a dowie heart.

There is probably an atavistic strain in the blood which can be stirred by visiting scenes well known to one's ancestors. I only

178

know that in my veins run Scottish and English strains, and whenever I return to any part of the British Isles I feel as if I were coming home. And though great cities are always changing, perhaps not more so than the eyes that see them. Nonetheless, no matter how dingy London or Edinburgh may look to the returning visitor, their rare grandeurs and beauties finally, if almost reluctantly, disclose themselves.

After the natural beauties of Derwentwater and Windermere in Cumberland, the dreary and ugly towns of Preston and Wigan in Lancashire offered a vivid and almost terrifying contrast. Wherever industry has taken over in England and Scotland (and it must if they survive), unspeakable ugliness prevails. This need not necessarily be so, as modern city planning has shown, but after her nineteenth-century profits were dissipated by two great wars England cannot afford the luxury of much city planning.

It was a relief to come to ancient Chester, with its justly famous rows of timber houses and its fine cathedral. This was the most medieval town we had seen in England. The red sandstone walls which entirely enclose the city are not older than the fourteenth century, though they follow the line of Roman walls built centuries earlier.

Through Shropshire, Hereford, and Gloucester our little car merrily brought us the next day into Somerset to the wonderful city of Bath. There is, so far as I know, no more beautiful sight in England than the whole panorama of Bath viewed from the lofty summit of Beechen Cliff. The winding Avon, the old abbey, grey, massive, and somehow terrible in its majesty, terrace after terrace of lovely houses built in a dignified Palladian style and rising in perfect symmetry from the valley to the hill caused Landor to call the city 'the Florence of England'. Certainly its houses are the most beautiful I have ever seen.

Another factor that adds to the charm of Bath is its ancient history. It dates back to the Romans, and was probably famed for its hot mineral springs long before the conquering Roman legions came. Remains of Celtic camps and earthworks have been discovered in the neighborhood. It is to be remembered, too, that Stonehenge, most mysterious and aged of all, is not far from Bath.

179

The Bath waters gush hot and bubbling to the surface from a great depth and with a volume of 500,000 gallons a day. We did not try their efficacy, though we visited the famous Pump Room and took the stairs to the east of the building to the remains of the Roman baths.

From Bath we drove through Wells and Glastonbury, swung north at Taunton through delightfully named villages like Crowcombe and Stogumber to our next destination which, after failing to make Porlock Hill, the highest prominence in Exmoor, brought us to Exeter.

Nowhere are greys and greens juxtaposed with such wonderful contrasts as at Oxford, where I spent as much time as I could spare the rest of the summer. The lawns of Trinity or Magdalen are of a wonderful green that is unmatched. These lawns are hundreds of years old which explain their near perfection. The work of the ancient architects conspires with the air of Oxford to cast a benign dignity over the place that is overwhelming in its appeal. If one turns into almost any gate he will find himself in a cloistral calm that is most restful.

Alas, there has been change, too, at Oxford, and for the worse. The motor car has nearly ruined Oxford as it has London.

I spent a lot of hours in Blackwell's on Broad Street and bought books which face me from my shelves as I write these pages. I have been a customer there for nearly forty years.

When John Henry Newman returned to Oxford as an old man, Emmett Lavery, the dramatist, quotes him as saying: 'I can utter no higher wish than that you may have in your hearts, as I have in mine, the love of God and the love of man, the love of truth and the love of beauty, the love of country and the love of Oxford. Oxford! In it and in you I gather up and bear in memory all the brave names that have served this our university from the earliest times until now. *Dominus Illuminatio mea* was the great medieval motto which she gave to the world and so it must be our motto today. The Lord is my light. . . . I give you my blessing . . . the blessing of an old man who has loved, and still loves, Oxford as he has loved no other place on earth.'

I finally returned almost reluctantly to London, 'overwhelmed by the ugliness of the architecture, the gloom of the people, the drabness of the September sky, the obedience to authority,' but yet aware that, 'There is more honesty, affection, good sense, justice and tolerance to be found here than in most countries in the world.' I began working once again in the British Museum Reading Room. I read Josiah Royce's *The Philosophy of Loyalty* and *The World and the Individual*. I learned 'that loyalty is the will to manifest, as far as is possible, the Eternal, that is, the conscious and superhuman unity of life, in the form of the acts of an individual self'. After this metaphysical nonsense it was with relief that I read Santayana's *The Sense of Beauty* and particularly his *Life of Reason*.

My real life as a book collector actually started in London. Here I made life-long friends among booksellers. Here I had my first two books published, one on Henry Williamson, and the other on Robert Bontine Cunninghame Graham. Here I was the happiest I had ever been.

After more than forty years London still holds more charm for me than any other city I know. As a book dealer I see it once a year. It did not take me long to learn that rare book selling is a highly specialized business and if one wandered out of his field of interest he was apt to make serious mistakes.

I am fortunate to be a member of the American Club at 95 Piccadilly which has large bedrooms, a shower bath, an excellent bar, a decent table, and a fine view of Green Park across the street.

I often begin my book buying day by walking up through Shepherd's Market to Curzon Street where, at Number 10, G. Heywood Hill has an excellent bookshop.

It was here a couple of summers ago that I bought one of the finest books I ever briefly owned. This was Colonel T. E. Lawrence's copy of the signed limited edition of Joyce's *Ulysses*. Lawrence had had it bound and his initials were inked in the right-hand corner. I had never before paid as much as £200 for a book ($560) which is, of course, nothing at all in the rare book trade.

Each year I go to this book shop as there are almost always some fine books by Henry James, in which Mr Hill specializes, and other books I can easily sell.

It is but a short walk from here to Berkeley Square where the well-known firm Maggs Brothers Ltd is located. The prestige of this firm is so immense, and it has such a grand appearance, that for many years I did not dare enter its doors. Now I go there every year and buy fine Winston Churchills, books by T. E. Lawrence, fine press books, and at times even a Robert Frost first edition.

From Berkeley Square it is not far to walk back to Piccadilly and then toward the Circus to Albany, at the other end of which, on Vigo Street, is Bertram Rota's shop. He is the best-known dealer in London for modern first editions.[1]

When I first knew Mr Rota he was at 76a Davies Street but his shop now is John Lane's the old Bodley Head, which was once the haunt of Beardsley, Wilde, Dowson, and other contributors to the *Yellow Book* and the *Savoy Magazine*.

As a collector I bought modestly for many years from Mr Rota but now I buy much the same type of book as a dealer. I still find myself buying the books I like rather than simply the books I think I can sell. Alan Hancox in Cheltenham once told me that I was his favourite book dealer for this very reason. This may not be a compliment as the book business like any other has to be run realistically.

It is not very far from Mr Rota's to Charing Cross Road and Cecil Court where Bill Fletcher holds court at Number 27. Mr Fletcher is a very knowledgeable bookman and though he does not specialize in my type of book I generally find something there. Last year it was an *Alice in Wonderland*, 1866, I got for a friend in Tulsa, Oklahoma.

All along both sides of Cecil Court there are many bookshops worth a visit, but many of the books are in just fair second-hand condition. To the collector conditon is everything, and if the book has the dust wrapper on it and is MINT condition, which for many is the prime requisite, so much the better. I seldom find bargains among old books of which Foyles is said to have 1,000,000 volumes. Still there are many bargains to be found there. However, my own practice is that it saves time and effort to go to the best shops, pay their high prices for the good books, and then try to make a fair profit.

[1] Now moved to Savile Row.

After leaving Cecil Court I take a taxi to Smithfield Market. Here the last religious martyrs were burned at the stake, the great Scottish hero Wallace met his fate 500 or so years ago, and nearby is St Bartholomew's, the oldest church in London.

On a little street called Cloth Fair is the shop of Frank Hollings, run now by my friend Dusty Miller.

Mr Miller has a fine sense of humour, is wise in his field, and we always have a lot of fun together.

The best story I heard in 1964 came from him. It seems that a bishop was being shown through a maternity ward of a charity hospital. He noticed that most of the infants were in fine shape but there was one little baby who looked rather frail. He inquired of the nurse as to what was wrong with that particular child. The nurse replied: 'That child is the product of artificial insemination.' 'Oh,' said the bishop, 'just another case of sparing the rod and spoiling the child.'

Last year I bought from Dusty a fine presentation T. S. Eliot to a fellow poet, a presentation of Dylan Thomas' first book to another Welsh poet, a marvellous T. E. Lawrence letter, a collection of Morley Roberts' books inscribed to A. D. McCormick, the illustrator for some of Hudson's books, and many other fine modern first editions. This past June (1964) Dusty casually handed me a unique Robert Frost item which consisted of preliminary specimen sheets, dated 1912, of his first book, *A Boy's Will*, 1913, the printer's estimate (amazingly low), early Nutt catalogue which advertised the book at 1s 6d, and so on. I immediately ordered a slip case and felt that somebody in America would be a lucky collector!

I have never been to 45 Cloth Fair without finding good books. I know such books are exceedingly hard to come by and that this is a time to buy and not let the opportunity slip by. I missed some fine Henry James presentation copies some years ago from Heywood Hill because I lacked the proper imagination. A rare book is much harder to find than money.

What a book is worth depends on what someone will pay for it. There is no logical sense in the cost of a book except that scarcity, condition, and demand dictate the price. No rules can be made as to what to pay for a book. I have sold a book one year for a certain price, and bought another copy later for more than I sold it for.

This is especially true right now of the books by T. E. Lawrence. Undoubtedly the Lawrence film started a new group of collectors, but he had always been desired by the discriminating collector. I see no reason to think he will soon fall from grace.

If I were going to spend the rest of the day buying books I might, after lunch, take a cab to Francis Edwards in Upper Marylebone Street. This shop is especially rich in travel books but there are also press books and first editions to be had. It is here that I generally buy my books on Arabia. Upstairs I found Cunninghame Graham books, others by W. H. Hudson, the curious figure Paul Fountain (the one with the Hudson introduction is the most illusive), and other writers of exploration and travel.

Sometimes from the Green Park Underground, which is the nearest tube station to my club, I go to South Kensington where I browse around a few bookshops.

Many American book dealers tend to go to London during the Antiquarian Book Fair which is generally held in June in the premises of the National Book League on Albemarle Street.

At this fair more than forty dealers show their books. I have found that it is essential to have an invitation to the preview on the night before the opening as the better things are snapped up at that time. In fact the really best things may go while the dealers are arranging their exhibits. Maybe this is one of the main reasons for exhibiting. However, several great London dealers do not exhibit as they attract visitors to their own shops. Maggs, Dusty Miller, and Heywood Hill did not exhibit this current year.

However, last year, just by chance I was able to buy a book I had long been seeking in fine condition. This was the first issue of Robert Frost's first book: *A Boy's Will*. I had cabled twice for it and lost it, and suddenly the same copy I had been seeking appeared under the glass of R. A. Brimmell's case. I bought it at sight. Several of the better known New York dealers wanted it, but, by passing up a drink, I had found it first. It is an 'unopened' copy! Pristine!!

I went about my business that evening and bought both for

myself and for the Friends of the Dartmouth Library, which I then directed, several fine things. These included a Jean Jacques Rousseau manuscript, *Le Gouvernement des Femmes*, a corrected proof of a poem by Rupert Brookes, entitled 'The Busy Heart', and a rare map of the British Antarctic Expedition of 1907–9, signed by its commander, Ernest Shackleton, and every member of the shore party, for the Dartmouth Stefansson collection; the manuscript of John Cowper Powys' *The Art of Happiness*, and other things.

All of the items mentioned above are in the Dartmouth College rare book collections.

When I am in London I generally attend the auctions at Sotheby's on New Bond Street, or at Christie's on King Street.

I was lucky enough to be invited to the auction at Christie's on June 22, 1960, when modern literary manuscripts were sold on behalf of the London Library. The important dealers from England and the United States were there. Many distinguished writers were in attendance. In fact, it was one of the most famous book auctions of our time.

One is familiar with the high prices of modern paintings (there is a scandal brewing behind all this) and some of the prices of this auction were also high.

June 22 was a hot night and I was fanning myself most of the time when someone on my left whispered, 'Be careful of your fanning as it might be understood as a bid!'

During the sale over $75,000 was raised for the London Library. The highest price was for the manuscript of E. M. Forster's *A Passage to India*, which ultimately went to Texas for $18,200. At this time this was the highest price ever paid for a living author's manuscript. The amazing sum of $10,640 was paid for three small T. E. Lawrence items which consisted merely of manuscript notes regarding the subscription sale of copies of the privately printed edition of *Seven Pillars of Wisdom* in 1926. T. S. Eliot had written out for the occasion a manuscript copy of *The Wasteland* and this brought nearly $8,000.

I heard as late as the summer of 1964 from a London bookseller who shall be nameless that the RING is still working now and again in the London auction rooms.

Not to mince words this practice of a group of greedy antiquarian bookmen is a thoroughly dishonest one in which the seller gets bilked by the English dealers involved.

Certain of these book dealers got together in a scheme to keep the bidding down to about TEN PER CENT of the real value of the items involved. They then would adjourn somewhere where they would hold a private auction of their own, selling the books somewhere near their real value, to one of their own number, and sharing the difference between the rigged price and the true price.

Having been in the auction rooms in recent years in London when L. D. Feldman of New York City was bidding, I am quite certain the RING was not working on these occasions as the prices Mr Feldman paid were fabulously high, often far above the market price, so that the London dealers simply couldn't compete. The fact that he aleady had a purchaser who was willing to pay high prices made it nice for all hands.

I must say that I do not recall ever having been cheated myself by any London book dealer, but I have yet to bid on a book at a London auction—simply from lack of experience.

There are many fine books shops scattered through England but I personally see only a small number of them.

Alan Hancox, in Cheltenham (an interesting town in itself), has built up a fine reputation in modern books and author collections. George Sims, in Hurst, near Reading, is one of the most astute dealers I know. His catalogues and stock are always fresh and exciting. Boris Harding-Edgar has moved from London to Kent to a charming old house and always has desirable books. Perhaps the best loved dealer in all of England is Harry Pratley in Tunbridge Wells. His prices are always reasonable and he constantly gets new stock. I shall never fail to visit him when I go to England.

George's in Bristol, Heffers in Cambridge, Blackwell's in Oxford, Howes in Hastings, and Alan Thomas in Bournemouth are well known in the trade.

One of my good friends is Timothy D'Arch Smith who directs the rare book section of the Times Bookshop on Wigmore Street in London: well worth a visit!

Years ago I recall getting some Edward Garnett Letters to me bound by Riviere, but alas, Riviere is no more, and when I want a fine slip case, or a book bound in Levant, I go to Sangorski and Sutcliffe whose place of business is 1–5 Poland Street in the neighbourhood of William Blake's London home. Since I have become a friend of Kenneth Hobson I seldom fail to go and watch their craftsmen who work entirely by hand to produce their work. One of the firm's difficulties today is to get apprentices willing to learn their craft. Higher wages lure them away. There are thirty-six different operations required in binding a book by hand. No machine has yet been invented which can do the job as well. The only machine at Sangorski's is one which trims paper.

Sangorski and Sutcliffe have been in business since 1897. During these years they have bound for royalty, for famous exhibitions, and other special occasions. There is one of their most elaborate bindings in the Seventh Regiment Armory in New York. Mr Hobson is himself a fine artist and engraver, and his bookplates are known all over the world. I believe Yale has a collection of them.

Each June I go to see my friend George D. Painter, the biographer of Proust: a shy, modest civil servant with a vast knowledge of his subject, who works in the British Museum.

In the summer of 1963 there was to be an exhibit of great books in London and through his kindness I was able to have a preview. For one who loves books it was almost a religious experience as he showed me some of their treasures. Although during the blitz many books were lost, the really great ones were safe underground in one of the London tube stations. Here was the Gutenberg Bible on vellum, printed in 1455, the first and still one of the finest books ever printed on movable type. This is a so-called forty-two line Bible type and there are forty-nine known copies extant. Harvard and Yale have copies and there are many others in the United States. However, the thirty-six line Bible type, also probably done by Gutenberg in 1458, is much rarer as there are only thirteen known copies. None of these are in the United States though the Morgan Library has some pages from it.

Another book Mr Painter showed me was the 1462 Bible printed near Mainz. Gutenberg had fallen into financial difficulties, and a man named Fust, unable to collect from Gutenberg, took his equipment together with Schoeffer, Gutenberg's trusted foreman, and founded a new company, and printed this Bible from specially made type. Schoeffer had been a calligraphy expert who was educated at the University of Paris, and who later went into printing.

Thomas Grenville's collection of some 12,000 books are also in the British Museum and are famous for their superb condition. Their pages were as fresh, Mr Painter explained, as if they had been printed yesterday. One of the books in this collection was the Catholicon printing in Mainz in 1460, probably the work of Gutenberg, and another was Caxton's famous edition of Chaucer's *Canterbury Tales* printed about 1478.

We have many Caxtons in America but I was able to see one of the three known Caxtons on vellum. This was a life of Christ printed with wood-cuts in 1489. Caxton learned printing in Cologne in 1472 and then moved to Bruges in Belgium where he worked three years at his trade, whence in 1476 he returned to England and in the precincts of Westminster Abbey printed his famous books. One might get one today for $10,000 but it would not be one of his best.

Before I left that day I handled a first edition of Ptolemy's *Geography* printed on vellum at Ulm in 1482; then a first edition of Homer in Greek printed in Florence in 1488 by a printer who is not well known. Other treasures were a first of Villon printed in Paris in 1489, and finally the Subiaco, 1465, the first book containing Greek printing which was done on Roman type.

One Monday at a Savoy Luncheon Club I was able to hear Sir Frank Francis speak concerning the future of the British Museum. He said that the ordinary visitor found it a vast, anomalous and somewhat irrational sort of place. For the first time since the bombing the British Museum now has an up-to-date constitution. The Trustees are now appointed by the Prime Minister, the Royal Academy, and so on, and much of the old-fashioned and out-moded procedures have been done away with. A new library building is going to be built in which they will be able to store books outside the British Museum and even lend them out. The new plans provide that objects may be seen more readily. The galleries are being repainted, the dome repaired and strengthened and the approximately seven museums will be better organized. Manuscripts are always on exhibit. I generally seek out Captain Robert Falcon Scott's last words written just before he died returning from the South Pole in 1912.

I manage to get to Ascot Heath as the guest of friends who live in Sunningdale about every June. This past year it was rained out.

Few go to Ascot who do not bet on the horses and no one knows less about the horses, the odds, what a tote treble or a daily double is, than I. Everyone studies racing forms, reads the daily paper, and gets all the information he can on the horses before placing his bets. This process I waived. I invented my own system which in 1963 worked out very well. I simply picked the names of the horses that had for me the most fascination such as Conmucho-gusto, Nautch Dance, Ship's Biscuit, Horse Radish (a sure winner), Utrillo, London Gazette, and Young Lochinvar. I doubt if any of these horses were the favourites but in the four races I bet on I won in three. The system is anybody's for the asking.

There are of course changes in London: new buildings, new blocks of flats, streets torn up (Piccadilly this past summer was a bedlam), but there are still many areas where the changes are scarcely noticeable. Fleet Street looks much the same, around the Abbey there are few changes, St James is about as it was, Lancaster House still shines in radiance at night, and it will take a good many years yet before the London I knew forty years ago disappears. From a bridge in St James Park on a misty day last summer the towers of Whitehall reminded me of Camelot.

No matter how many times one may visit London there is always something new to see.

In 1964 the Tate Gallery was having a modern exhibition with an elaborate catalogue covering the last decade, 1954–64. Frankly what I saw was appalling. Among the exhibits there were three panels about ten feet tall and three or four feet wide, numbered, I recall, 74, 75, and 76, which consisted of nothing but black paint. Even the frames were black. Then there were several by an *avant-garde* German painter which were painted with a blow-torch. I had been told that Sir Herbert Reade had called this man's work the sonic break-through in modern painting. I can well believe it.

I suspect that the end of the Western world as we know it is at hand.

CHAPTER VII

The Bookman as Publisher

'When I am all Ha-Ha with Gay it is always in the French.'
Mademoiselle Hepzibah

I suspect that almost every book collector wishes that he might have been a publisher.

However, the publishing business needs much capital, and the way of issuing printed books for commercial sale is strewn with risk and possible financial disaster.

In our own time many small publishers have been swallowed up by larger corporations in business to make money.

I think it was nearly ten years ago that I read in the London *Times Literary Supplement* that there had been expressed at that time a desire for a revival of small semi-amateur presses and publishing enterprises of the type common in the 'twenties. This intrigued me and I decided to take a risk.

As all collectors know even the great presses come and go: even such famous printing houses as the Kelmscott, the Ashendene, the Gregynog, and Doves, are now but memories and their books are eagerly sought after.

Nonetheless, the urge to print is a fairly common one, and there are many private presses still in existence throughout this country and England whose books the average collector may never see.

There is a Lloyd Haberley in England who writes, prints, binds, and sells his own books. Some of them are handsome examples of typographical and binding art.

Mr Norman Strouse, an advertising executive, has for his pleasure a private press at 2 Beekman Place in New York City.

In Berkeley Heights, New Jersey, Mr Joseph Ishill has the Oriole Press, and he issues for his friends charming and delightful books which have found a place in several famous libraries.

Recently, I believe, Mr Ishill has moved as printer in residence to the University of Florida at Gainesville.

I corresponded for years with the late Edwin B. Hill, who began printing in Illinois and then moved his private press to Ysleta, Texas, and then to Tempe, Arizona, where he died. Mr Hill published many small brochures of things he liked written by Henry Thoreau, Ralph Waldo Emerson, and other favourite writers of his.[1] My own collection of his imprints I gave to Harvard, and my duplicates to Dartmouth. They seldom appear in the rare book market, but when they do they are eagerly snapped up by connoisseurs of printing and by the seekers of the curious in literature.

Hal Trovillion and his wife, of Herrin, Illinois, have over the years published many delightful books. I believe that his press, at the Sign of the Silver Horse, is now the oldest private press in the country since the death of Mr Hill.

About ten years ago I decided that the impecunious amateur in collecting was to become the impecunious amateur in publishing. At that time teaching at Dartmouth, writing, painting, speaking, writing reviews for the *New York Times Book Review*, running the Friends of the Dartmouth Library, were not sufficient to consume my energy so I decided to start a small publishing business called *Westholm Publications* (Westholm is the name of my home), unique in the fact that there was to be no office, files, staff, sales force, or visible overhead.

It has been amusing at times to receive advertising material directed to Westholm Publications, Hanover, New Hampshire, trying to sell me heavy office equipment, new presses, and other mechanical devices, as if I had a big plant and a big staff.

As a matter of fact, I do everything myself. I choose the manuscripts, edit them, write the necessary introductions, do all the correspondence, write some of the books, get them printed by various fine presses, advertise them, and finally sell them.

I issued my first announcement optimistically saying: 'Though making a profit is not frowned upon very much in these United States, it is suspected that Westholm Publications will be lucky

[1] One of his titles was *The Alchemy of Books* written by the present writer!

to break even, but if the miracle occurs, and there is a small profit, as much as possible of it will go into the pocket of the publisher. In any case he thinks it will be a lot of fun.' It has been.

I did borrow $400 from a friend for my first book but since then I have been solvent, and on some of the books have made a small profit. Almost all of them have quickly gone out of print and many now sell at a premium. Several won awards at the Mid-Western Book Fair and my last one became one of the *Fifty Books of the Year*!

I decided that my publications would consist of small, limited editions, signed when possible, and I hoped to issue two or three books a year. Each book would be printed by a good press, and would sell for as small a price as possible. It proved in several cases that with the dealer's discount there was no appreciable difference between the cost and the selling price of the book. In one instance I lost on each book sold to a dealer.

I had to wait until April 28, 1955, to fulfil a long-felt and intense desire to visit the grave of my old friend Cunninghame Graham, buried, almost to the day, nineteen years before between the ancient priory walls of the Augustinian monastery of Inchmahome on the Lake of Menteith in Perthshire, Scotland, not far from the ancestral home of the Grahams of Gartmore. The daffodils were swinging audaciously in the face of a cold wind which was driving, between spurts of sunshine, an icy rain in our faces. While the waves slapped against our boat recollections of a previous visit there with Cunninghame Graham to see the grave of his wife, Gabriella, became vivid.

Altogether I spent an hour there thinking of my friend lying under his simple slab of stone. This was inscribed ROBERT BONTINE CUNNINGHAME GRAHAM of GARTMORE, and below his name was chiselled the brand he had used for his cattle and horses during the exciting days of his youth in South America. No more fitting spot could be imagined for the last resting place of this remarkable Scotsman. Before leaving I placed a lone daffodil on his grave.

It was the next day at Ardoch, on the Clyde near Cardross, which I had visited for a week a quarter of a century before with Don Roberto, now the home of my host, his nephew Admiral Sir

Angus Cunninghame Graham, KBE, CB, that I found among Cunninghame Graham's letters, notebooks, and manuscripts a letter on 'the senseless destruction of this noble bird',[1] the albatross on a P & O liner, which he had written with great indignation from Gartmore more than half a century before.

When I got home I looked up in the Dartmouth Library the printed version of Cunninghame Graham's letter in the December 1, 1900, issue of the English *Saturday Review* (I had spent a couple of hours trying to decipher his spidery and difficult handwriting), together with W. H. Hudson's letter written from 40 St Luke's Road in London where he then lived, and the original statement in *Nature* magazine for October 25, 1900, which had precipitated Hudson's and Cunninghame Graham's angry and implacable stand.

I obtained permission from Admiral Cunninghame Graham and the Royal Society for the Protection of Birds in London to reprint these two fiery letters and the first WESTHOLM PUBLICATION appeared in the fall of 1955 with the title *Two Letters on an Albatross* by W. H. Hudson and R. B. Cunninghame Graham. I wrote the foreword, and William Stone of the Sequoia Press in Kalamazoo, Michigan, did the book. Although handsomely designed it was actually done by offset lithography which offended the purists who demand fine books set in type. I did not offend my customers again and my next Sequoia Press book was printed in Linotype Janson.

There were only 200 copies and it has long been out of print.

It has been the general policy of Westholm Publications to print editions of from 200 to 400 copies, though in two instances this policy has not been followed. *The Coronary Club*, 1956, has sold 1,300 copies in paper and hard cover, and *Here's to Togetherness*, 1961, was printed in an edition of 1,000 copies, and is almost sold out.

Working as I did on the proverbial shoestring I was unable to print the second book until the first had been sold and paid for. However, this did not take long, and my second book, called *Emerson at Dartmouth* in an edition of 300 copies, was printed by

[1] The phrase is Hudson's.

the Lane Press in Burlington, Vermont, early in 1956. This contained in full his oration given at Dartmouth in 1838.

For twenty-five years I wrote a book column, 'Hanover Browsing', in the *Dartmouth Alumni Magazine*, and on the hundredth anniversary of Emerson's famous speech, *Literary Ethics*, given before the Dartmouth Literary Societies and their friends, on June 24, 1838, I reprinted parts of this in the magazine.

Some Emerson critics and admirers, including Thomas Carlyle, have said that this essay was nobler in utterance than the better-known Harvard Divinity School Address, *The American Scholar*.

Note this famous passage:

Why should you renounce your right to traverse the starlit deserts of truth, for the premature comforts of an acre, house and barn? Truth also has its roof, and bed, and board. . . . Thought is all light, and publishes itself to the universe. It will speak, though you were dumb, by its own miraculous organ. It will flow out of your actions, your manners, and your face. It will bring you friendships. It will impledge you to truth by the love and expectation of generous minds. By virtue of the laws of that Nature which is one and perfect, it shall yield every sincere good that is in the soul to the scholar beloved of earth and heaven.

However, one student noted at the time: 'Mr Emerson's oration is either too deep or too dark, or at least, it was something which I was not able to comprehend.'

In an age when the big lie (or the small one for that matter) has become an instrument of policy among nations, as well as among far too many individuals, when the liberty to read and to think for oneself is not only questioned, but becomes a hazardous occupation in some colleges and universities, it is refreshing to turn once again to the 'Sage of Concord', and to read once more his impassioned and lyrical prose which, like all lasting writing, somehow carries with it the quality of nobility, sadly missing in most of the writing of our own times.

My life-long interest in W. H. Hudson has led to correspondence with many Hudsonians including George Matthew Adams, David Dewar of London, Raymond Wasson of New York, Eric

S. Whittle of Wakefield, England, Dr Jorge Casares of the Argentine, and others. Hours of conversation with Cunning-hame Graham, Morley Roberts, and Edward Garnett about this still enigmatic person added fire to my enthusiasm. It was natural, then, to turn to Hudson in my publishing interests.

My friend, the late Don Jorge Casares, of Buenos Aires, sent me the manuscript of Hudson's Diary written during his trip from South America to England in the year 1874. Up to this time books on Hudson invariably repeated the error that he had left Buenos Aires in 1869. This book set the record straight as the diary was written from April 1, 1874, to May 3, which was the time required for the *Ebro* to make this voyage.

Dr Casares got the manuscript from Hudson's only living relative in South America, his great nephew, Hubert Rockwood Hudson. This 'diary' was written in the form of five long letters, the first of which is dated April 14, 1874 (from 'Atlantic Ocean'), and the fifth dated May 5, 6, and 8, from Southampton, England.

Albert Merriam Hudson, to whom these letters were written, was the fifth child of Daniel Hudson (1804–68), of Marblehead, Massachusetts, and Caroline Augusta Kimble (1804–59) of Berwick, Maine. Albert M. Hudson was born in Quilmes (in the House of the Twenty-Five Ombu Trees) on October 10, 1843, married, became a teacher, begot a family, and died at fifty on February 8, 1893. The owner of these letters is his grandson.

In 1958 J. J. Lankes, a friend of many years, was still living and I got him to do a tailpiece of a ship under sail for the book which was printed by the Stinehour Press in Lunenberg, Vermont, in a small edition of 250 copies. The frontispiece consisted of a previously unknown portrait of Hudson when he was about thirty-three years of age, taken after he got to England.

There is still some mystery as to why Hudson left South America at this time, where he got the money to do so, whether he had to flee from the dictator Rosas, or what . . . no one today knows.

His diary runs to only twenty-one pages. Here we find his first descriptive nature writing about England, the country he came to love with a passion, and which he has described in his finest books such as *A Shepherd's Life* with a magic none has equalled.

My edition was the first printing in book form and the Stinehour Press did its usual excellent printing job. There was no advertising, no review copies, and only a postcard describing the book was sent to a few libraries. A few copies remain.

I have never visited Hudson's grave in Broadwater, Sussex, near the burial place of another naturalist, Richard Jefferies. However, I have traced his homes in London; at Leinster Square, and later the place where he lived in Southwick Crescent where Mrs Hudson kept a boarding house. At 40 St Luke Road, Westbourne Park, Hudson spent forty years in this dingy and dreary place called the Tower House. After seeing it, one can understand his many trips to the country. Never do I see New Forest without visualizing a tall, stooped man, listening to the cry of some bird.

Violet Hunt well described this at the time of Hudson's last illness in August 1922; she writes:

I got down at Westbourne Park Station, turned a corner, and walked along a row of gaunt and decaying, stuccoed and Victorian houses, standing back, with what they call a garden, from a straw and paper bestrewn street. This is where he lived and had died, in the tall house at the corner of another dreadful street bisecting it. 'Huddie' was his own landlord: I had been told he owned the whole row, but my impression is that only one house was his, which he had converted into three flats and basement for his housekeeper. For himself he had retained the first floor: his tenants, he told me, were preferably ladies.

I vividly recall several meetings I had in London, introduced by Cunninghame Graham, with Hudson's friend Morley Roberts. On one occasion visiting his house where he lived with his stepdaughter, he showed me stowed under his bed a box of Hudson letters published by him under the title *Men, Books and Birds*. He offered to sell them to me, as he was a poor man, but, alas, I could not afford them, and I lacked the sense to borrow the money and secure them. I forget the asking price but they later went for somewhat more to a New York collector.

However, some years after Morley Roberts' death I was able to secure the letters of Morley Roberts and Hudson's housekeeper, Mrs Jessie McDougall, which concern Hudson's death. This led me to write in the summer of 1958 a little book called *For A*

Hudson Biographer. My monograph ran to something over thirty pages. It contained a copy of Hudson's will, printed here for the first time, together with a genealogy of his family: hence the title.

This book won commendation at the Midwest and Chicago Book Fairs for excellence in design. Only 221 copies were printed. I suspect it is generally unknown to most Hudsonians.

My third and last Hudson book appeared in 1963. This was *Gauchos of the Pampas and their Horses.* I had known J. Frank Dobie for many years and had visited with him every now and then in Austin, Texas, and on his ranch nearby. I knew of his interest and admiration for Hudson and Cunninghame Graham and we had discussed the possibility of a small book which would consist of four or five of their best stories about the horses and gauchos of the Argentine pampas. Months, even years, passed and nothing happened as Mr Dobie was for a time quite ill from pneumonia and its aftermath. However, in the fall of 1962, Mr Dobie's manuscript finally came, with his choice of four of their pieces together with a magnificent introduction on the two writers.

I believe the genesis of his foreword was a piece which appeared in one of his columns in a Houston paper, but he spent many hours revising it. I know of no better essay on these two great writers.

Mr Dobie selected W. H. Hudson's 'Story of a Piebald Horse' from *Tales of the Pampas,* and 'Christiano: The Sentinel Horse' from *The Book of a Naturalist.* From the works of Cunninghame Graham he chose 'The Horses of the Pampas', from *Father Archangel of Scotland,* and 'San José' from *Progress.*

The book was hand set by Carroll Coleman in Garamond in an edition of 400 copies. It sold out within a matter of weeks and its success was assured when it was chosen one of the *Fifty Books of the Year.*

The biggest sales in my publishing ventures came from a small booklet of forty-five pages called *The Coronary Club,* 1956, which told of an amazing recovery from a severe heart attack and embolism the writer suffered in 1947 after fourteen years of exhausting teaching. Out of nine weeks in bed, with a year to recuperate, came a new attitude toward life, a part-time career as a watercolour painter, and the conviction that this attack had probably saved my life. Later on Dorothy Thompson, who died finally of a heart attack herself, told me that I had written about it as if it had really been a boon.

Carroll Coleman hand set the first edition of 500 copies in wrappers.

The great Dr Herman L. Blumgart, heart specialist at the Harvard Medical School, now retired, had written glowingly to me how happy I must be that my little book had helped so many people who had also suffered heart attacks.

Sherman Adams gave a copy to President Eisenhower and I had a friendly letter from him about it.

In any case I made an exception to my general rule not to reprint and had 500 more copies done offset by a New Hampshire firm in Franconia.

In 1962 I had another edition of 300 copies reset with a frontispiece in colour of one of my own watercolours in a handsome hard-bound book again designed by Mr Coleman. I was happy that this book, too, won printing awards at the Chicago and the Midwest Book Fairs.

This little book interested also Robert Frost collectors inasmuch as it described a meeting I had arranged between Robert Frost and John Sloan, the American painter who had come from New Mexico to settle in New Hampshire. I took Mr Frost, who shortly before had had an operation for skin cancer on his face, to see John Sloan who was also in the Mary Hitchcock Memorial Hospital for an operation. They were somewhat shy with each other, but exchanged pleasantries. Obviously both admired each other, and Frost said as we left, 'I came to admire.' They did not meet again as John Sloan died shortly after.

In 1957 I wrote a small book of about fifty pages about college teaching as I had known it called *What Price Teaching?* I attempted almost for the first time to tell the real truth about a teacher's career in a small liberal arts college like Dartmouth. Naturally it raised a certain amount of controversy and made me a few enemies. There was very little of Mr Chips in this story.

At any rate the Shenval Press, 58 Frith Street, London, printed the edition of 200 copies, which I numbered and signed. It was oversubscribed several times and is now almost unobtainable. It sold for $6, and I would gladly pay twice as much for a fine copy today.

The same year I also published two other small books, both relatively important, I think, in American literature.

The first was a magnificent essay by the late Professor Kenneth Alan Robinson titled *Thoreau and the Wild Appetite* which was illustrated with woodcuts by J. J. Lankes. As the second President of the Thoreau Society I had to find a speaker for the annual July meeting in Concord, Massachusetts. Kenneth Robinson, one of the great lecturers and teachers at Dartmouth, had a life-long interest in Thoreau. Everything that Thoreau had written or said about food was in this address, which was considered to be one of the finest ever given before the Society.

The Friends of the Dartmouth Library and the Thoreau Society joined and issued 500 copies in wrappers. Later I had 150 hardbound for Westholm Publications once again printed by the Stinehour Press. Both of these editions soon went out of print.

I hoped to publish an article on the Alamo by Mr Frank Dobie who had written it for *Collier's Magazine*. However, before it came out, *Collier's* folded, and for one reason or another, perhaps because its present shape did not satisfy the author, I never was allowed to publish the article.

I had better luck with Kenneth Roberts who had published in the same magazine his story on the battle of Cowpens. He gave me permission to publish it and also agreed to make it a real collector's item by signing the copies. However, his sudden and lamentable death on July 21, 1957, prevented this, but nevertheless the Sequoia Press went ahead and printed 400 copies with the title: *Cowpens: The Great Morale-Builder*.

Mr Roberts' vigour of style, his most painstaking respect for fact, and his ability to paint vast canvases of characters and scenes in American history, made this a memorable little book.

With Mr Roberts' death his publishers, Doubleday and Company, naturally wanted his last book but their edition came out about five months after mine, so mine became the real first edition of his last book.

Owing to lack of capital my advertising had to be of the most meagre sort. I did advertise, and still do, in the London *Book Collector*, edited by John Hayward, and now in the American *Book Collector*.

Once in a while I get some free publicity as, for instance, once from Uncle Dudley in the *Boston Globe*.[1] In the February 11, 1957, issue of the *Globe* he wrote a long editorial called 'Second Wind' on *The Coronary Club*. In part he wrote:

What was it that convinced Professor West that a coronary attack is almost to be welcomed? 'First, I have, relatively speaking, fewer fears. Conquering one's fears is the very secret of happiness. I've had it, and whatever happens to me now is in the nature of a dividend.' The experience was, for him, at heart a religious one and he is able to communicate much of its true inwardness. 'I find life wonderful; people interesting, the natural world beautiful beyond dreams, and if I should die tomorrow, I can honestly say that life has been a joyous experience.'

My general selling plan was to send out a broadside on each book to a mailing list consisting of libraries and collectors which I had been building up for some time. I bought no lists but painstakingly built up my own.

Following Kenneth Roberts' book I issued a sequel to *What Price Teaching?* which I called *Learning my ABC's*. This was a kind of summing up in a succinct form of my philosophy of life: A for Art, C for Communism, D for doubt, and so on.

Like its predecessor it expressed a minority view, likely to be anathema to all right thinking people. Some of it was controversial: a fighting word in 1957.

On June 28 the *Times Literary Supplement* had an admirable article called 'Loyalties', and among other things it said: 'A time of strained and breaking loyalties all over the world—in politics, nationalities, religions, moralities and families—is certainly a time of trouble. . . . In such a time, it is natural that the powers-that-be, the Establishments of the various tensed societies, should think and act in terms of "security": security for ancient ways and familiar forms, for customary institutions, and the vested interests in them. . . . It is understandable that, among us in the West,

---

[1] The late Mr Lucien Price, author of several fine books.

uncertain of ourselves and fearful of what we may become, *independent thinking* is at a discount, originality is hard to come by, and old opponents (menaced alike by the unfamiliar) close the ranks and appear indistinguishable. . . . Old and young, governors and the governed, all strive for security; and security means perpetuation of the familiar.'

I had written this book for the individualists of our time: editorial writers, teachers, artists, and so on: the last vanguard of free men who will not be pushed against their will into the channels of conformity.

One example will suffice:

D for Doubt

It was Winwood Reade (1838–75) in his controversial book *The Martyrdom of Man*, really an introduction to universal history, who wrote: 'What a state of society is this in which free thinker is a term of abuse, and in which doubt is regarded as a sin!'

This appears, at times, to apply equally well three-quarters of a century later, and I am not unhappy to report that I am a grievous sinner, as I am a born doubter, and believe with the English poet Lord Tennyson that there is 'more faith in honest doubt than in half the creeds'.

Doubt, I believe, is the beginning of wisdom, but it is not an attitude that pays off well in worldly terms. It is the professional man of faith who gets big television fees, who writes well-paid newspaper columns, and whose books reach the best-seller lists. The doubter retains his intellectual integrity, continues to venerate such men as Montaigne and Lucretius, and he must be content with the infinitesimal audience capable of admiring such writers as Swift and Thoreau.

Out of my teaching in Comparative Literature, which deals mainly with ideas, the subject of naturalism, the doctrine that religious truth is derived from nature and not from divine revelation, has become a philosophy for many people living today.

I have always found my students were fascinated by two remarkable essays which reflect the naturalistic trend: Bertrand Russell's *A Free Man's Worship*, which he wrote some sixty-odd years ago in 1903, and John Burrough's *The Faith of a Naturalist*, which appeared just before his death in 1921.

202

In 1927 Bertrand Russell had written:

Fundamentally, my view of man's place in the cosmos remains unchanged. I still believe that the major processes of the universe proceed according to the laws of physics; that they have no reference to our wishes, and are likely to involve the extinction of life on this planet; that there is no good reason for expecting life after death, and that good and evil are ideas which throw no light upon the non-human world. I still believe that, in times of moral difficulty and emotional stress, the attitude expressed in this essay is, at any rate for temperaments like my own, the one which gives most help in avoiding moral shipwreck.

If you read John Burroughs' essay you will note how far the naturalist has progressed from orthodoxy since Henry Thoreau, a great poetic naturalist, who died in 1862. John Burroughs, who was a great American, and who was a symbol in his day of rugged Americanism, as Robert Frost has been in ours, faced life with fortitude and courageously retained the integrity of his own mind. His 'The Faith of a Naturalist', which was printed first in his book, *Accepting the Universe*, is not always easy to find so I got permission from the proper people and called my book *Two Modern Essays on Religion* which the Lane Press in Burlington printed in an edition of 300 copies. Owing mainly to student interest this book almost immediately went out of print.

I hope some other publisher takes up the idea and reissues this.

Mr Walter Hart Blumenthal, who lives in Philadelphia, is an indefatigable scholar who has devoted a lifetime to several special fields of research: bibliomania, interesting facets in American history, and on the question of the authorship of the plays attributed to William Shakespeare.

In 1959 Westholm Publications printed his essay, *The Mermaid Myth*, in which Mr Blumenthal attempts to prove, and I think with some success, that William Shakespeare was not known to those who frequented the Mermaid Tavern. Mr Blumenthal quotes from books about Shakespeare which mention as frequenters of this tavern Shakespeare, Ben Jonson, Thomas Carew, John Donne, Walter Raleigh, and others. Then Mr Blumenthal

goes on to argue that there is no proof whatever of these statements, nor is Shakespeare's name linked to the Mermaid by any
of the writers of his day.

I have never wanted to be drawn into this controversy as I
have never studied the matter, and I couldn't care less as to
whom the authorship rightly belongs, but Mr Blumenthal's re-
searches are thorough and appear unassailable.

Another book with which I had little to do except to have
my firm's name on the title-page was when a friend of mine,
an erudite businessman and amateur archaeologist, William J.
Bryant, had arranged through Tuttles of Rutland and Tokyo to
have a book of his essays and photographs, *Flames of Life*, printed
in Japan. I was not consulted as to the number of copies done,
there was no editorial work on the book, nor did I see the format
until the book appeared. Some of the sixty full-page coloured
illustrations were not up to standard and some of the letterpress
was imperfect. However, the book itself contained much shrewd
Yankee wisdom and had it been priced a little lower, and published by someone with sales apparatus, it might have sold better
than it did.

Naturally I have long been concerned with the decline of the
small liberal arts college in America and with it the concomitant
decline of a humanistic education. This has led me to question
seriously whether the quality of our education today is any better
than it was, say, in the time of Daniel Webster, or even my own
time at Dartmouth more than forty years ago.

Whatever may be the answer to this I have taken a dim view
of the take-over by IBM machines, computers, machine tested
examinations, and the almost complete triumph of the sciences
over the humanities.

I had often joked with my classes about an imaginary SPARK-
PLUG U, founded by Ezra Sparkplug, a Connecticut minister, a
couple of centuries ago.

My friend Corey Ford and I frequently discussed Dartmouth
with a certain amount of amused animation and as the term 'togetherness' was much in use at that time by the administration he
suggested we call the book *Here's to Togetherness*. As this word
has always seemed to me to have a cheap, commercial, and bogus

connotation, I accepted his advice, though perhaps the title
SPARKPLUG U might have been more effective.

Mr Ford wrote a theme song for the book which was actually
sung at one of the spring fraternity hums. The song was supposedly written by Dr Luke Warm, my imaginary president of
Sparkplug U.

I reproduce it here as it seems to set the tone of the book:

> Hail to togetherness
> and our Alma Mater true.
> In unison we cheer
> For we're all together here
> At dear Old Sparkplug U.
> (Rah! Rah! Rah!)
> Allness is Oneness
> And everyone's the same.
> So let us all conform
> To the norm of Dr Warm
> Sparkplug, bless her name!

The book was dedicated to 'the memory of Henry L. Mencken
and Irving Babbitt, two friends who might have been amused'.

The Shenval Press of London did 1,000 copies which I numbered and signed. It was bought by many universities and
colleges. Many outsiders thought it was about their own colleges
and I believe that today education has gone in some respects far
beyond the absurdities expressed in the book.

On June 12, 1959, I was invited by Douglas Young and the
Scottish PEN Society to give an address in Edinburgh (at Preston-
field) on my old friend Robert Bontine Cunninghame Graham. I
used notes for this address and on my return I wrote this up and
used it as a foreword to another Westholm Publication called
Three Fugitive Pieces by Cunninghame Graham.

These papers I found at Ardoch Cottage in Dunbartonshire
after my lecture while staying with Admiral Sir Angus.

They consisted of a review by Cunninghame Graham of a book
on Garibaldi which was published in London in 1931. The second
fugitive piece was Cunninghame Graham's report to the British
Board of Trade in 1917 on the horse and cattle resources of the
Republic of Colombia. He had been sent to Cartagena by the

British War Office to make this report. The third fugitive piece was a prologue to W. H. Hudson's *The Purple Land* which had been first published in 1885; 500 copies of this were printed by the Sequoia Press for the Friends of the Dartmouth Library, and 100 hardbound copies were done for me.

I have no immediate plans for Westholm Publications but hope to do at least one book a year in a small printing which reflects my own taste.

Although not much money has been made, neither has any been lost. I have been able in my own few books to say what I think, not always possible these days with a commercial publisher, and at the same time to publish a few books in which I believe. This is one of them.

It has been fun.

Postlude

Logan Pearsall Smith once wrote:

Some people say life is the thing
but I prefer reading.

I prefer life, but reading has had its place. My life spans from the horse and buggy age to the jet age of today: an age of violence, of astronauts, of scientific wonders.

Still I venture to think that human nature is about as it always has been.

Except today life is more dangerous as man now has the means to destroy life totally. I would not want to bet much either way.

With Thomas Jefferson, Ralph Waldo Emerson, and Henry David Thoreau I am, when it comes to government, a philosophical anarchist.

Though I realize that Jefferson's position is untenable in the complex, violent societies of today, nevertheless, in *principle*, I agree with his:

A little rebellion now and then is a good thing . . . an observation of this truth should render honest republican governors so mild in their punishment of rebellions as not to discourage them too much.

Societies exist under three forms: (1) without government, as among our Indians, (2) under governments wherein the will of everyone has a just influence, (3) under governments of force. It is a problem not clear in my mind that the first condition is not the best.

The first condition, in my opinion, is undoubtedly the best. However, when one realizes the truth of W. H. Hudson's remark in his *Idle Days in Patagonia* (p. 58) (1893): 'In spite of what we have been taught, it is sometimes borne in on us that man is a little lower than the brutes,' one is therefore forced to the conclusion that powerful central governments, such as we have, have

207

come to stay, until through their dubious scheming life is reduced once more to a few men struggling to survive in caves.

We are seeing in our own time a major division in our land, perhaps the greatest since the Civil War, between those who, in the fear and hatred of Communism, would sacrifice all our traditional liberties, and would abrogate the freedom of the individual mind, the soul, and conscience, and those who would retain them.

Not to mention the Civil Right's war, murder most foul in Mississippi and Alabama, and the Bobby Baker case.

Not all politicians are scoundrels, but the majority of them will do anything for a vote: compromise, lie, evade the real issues, and steal. They make, in fact, quite a lot of money posing as patriots. We, the people, honour them, flatter them, and re-elect them; colleges too often give them honorary degrees. It seems to me curious that more young men, on the make, do not seek a career in so obviously profitable a game as American politics.

An honest politician is practically a contradiction in terms in this country. If he doesn't sell out for money, he loses most of his decent principles. We have been living, and still are, through as dishonest and cynical an era as modern times has known. And, like the iceberg, only a fraction of the crime and corruption in higher circles ever appears in the light, and much of that is suppressed by our courts. It is quite evident that crime controls the courts in a large measure, as it seems literally impossible to stamp it out. The 'little man', caught in between, has little chance. There have been many times in the past few years when I have felt that what we had in Washington was the Department of Injustice which white-washed every political crook if he happened to be a party member, which accepted bribes from wealthy men so far as income tax evasions were concerned, but which assiduously never gave the 'little man' a break. Influence was peddled like popcorn at a circus, and it became a recognized part of the Washington scene.

R. M. Lockley, an English naturalist and ornithologist, after a recent trip through Europe writes as follows of politicians and the countryman everywhere: 'Politically the countryman is the same the world over; in the common meaning of the word he has no

208

politics, asking only to be left in peace to till his soil and tend his animals. As one French cultivateur said to us: the garrulous politician easily finds the right answer for taking the wrong action, but the inarticulate peasant has no choice—in his trade he must always find the right answers, for it is he who must carry the serious burden of feeding the world while the politicians play their party games, declare their hot and cold wars, and make their mockeries of peace. The countryman has not time for these tricks, no leisure for planning or taking part in gigantic political evils. While shells rain on his hay meadows he moves over and grows wheat in his cornfield, like the bird which sings and builds its nest in the heart of a cannonade. A day of fine weather is more important to the peasant than a month of bloody battles.'

It is such people who have been exploited by the Stalins, Hitlers, Francos, Perons, and other governments with more honourable heads, from time immemorial. The little man everywhere is at last awakening and may eventually push his exploiters into the sea, but it will take a long time. We are now suffering from the dislocations of a giant revolution which began as far back as 1600. We shall continue to suffer unless we try, with all the intelligence we possess, to understand what is going on. Instead of this we listen to the medicine men, to ignoramuses who infest the Washington scene and fiddle and faddle while the world explodes in a nuclear cloud of an atomic disaster. We scarcely deserve to survive.

In view of fairly recent events in my own State of New Hampshire, in which its officials badgered and persecuted a harmless, in fact, very decent old lady, a Mrs Nelson, who once, years before, had, with my late friend Thomas Boyd, dared legally to run for Governor of her State on the Communist ticket, I take my stand with them. I can only reiterate with Thoreau: 'I saw that the State was half-witted, that it was as timid as a lone woman with her silver spoons, and that it did not know its friends from its foes, and I lost all my remaining respect for it and pitied it.'

Truly, as Thoreau once stated, what is called politics is comparatively so superficial, so cheap, so vulgar, so dishonest, so inhuman, that I cannot recognize that politics concerns me in any way whatever.

It is the politicians who deprive us of so many of our freedoms:

209

to think, to read certain books, to see certain films. This is not always due to ignorance or intolerance. It generally results from a bid for votes, a commodity without which the politician cannot survive.

Shortly after I retired as Emeritus Professor of Comparative Literature in June 1964, I was asked by the *Daily Dartmouth*, which claims to be the oldest college newspaper in America, to write a weekly column in which I could say what I thought without censorship. This lasted ten issues and by this time it seemed appropriate to stop, as I didn't want to repeat myself, and I had irritated the college administration enough with my criticism.

I took a tip from H. D. Thoreau and called my column 'A Different Drummer', and began by quoting that marvellous statement from the last chapter of *Walden*: 'If a man does not keep pace with his companions, perhaps it is because he hears a different drummer. Let him step to the music which he hears. . . .'

This could be my epitaph.

On my sixty-seventh birthday I finished the last chapter of this bookman's autobiography by quoting from certain pertinent passages from these columns which, briefly, sum up my point of view as a college teacher in the humanities.

September 30, 1964

The other day I happened to hear Judge Amos N. Blandin, Jr, address the Grand Jury in Woodsville, New Hampshire. He spiced his talk with an apt quotation from Heraclitus of Ephesus, a pessimistic Greek philosopher of the six–fifth century B.C., which was as follows: 'The major problem of human society is to combine that degree of liberty without which law is tyranny with that degree of law without which liberty becomes licence.' Then he went on to quote one of his great law school professors who said: 'The perfection of knowledge is to be able to say true things in a few plain words.'

It is good to know that we have a Supreme Court Justice in this State who has a background of classical and liberal arts learning. Few lawyers or judges, I feel sure, ever heard of Heraclitus of Ephesus. Judge Blandin is a graduate of Dartmouth in the Class of 1918. I hope we are turning out men like him.

NEED FOR CLASSICAL EDUCATION

After a lifetime in education I am of the belief, now stronger than ever, that the undergraduate liberal arts college should provide a broad, liberal, and classical education. Specialization is for the graduate schools. I feel quite sure that Harvard Law School would rather have a Latin or Greek major than one who had majored in government or economics, or physics or chemistry.

We should have a truer balance between the science and the computers with the humanities, which teach literature and life, and in a liberal arts college the scales should be weighted a little more on the humanities side. An oasis, as it were, in the arid desert of science.

The modern Dartmouth student should take as many courses as he can get (and they are all too few), in the basic humanistic studies. He should learn to read great books and to *understand* them; he should learn to write well and clearly 'in a few plain words'. (It was Thoreau who said that 'the essence of a great style is to tell the truth'.) He should learn at least one foreign language, he should know something about our Greek and Roman civilizations so that his point of view from which at last he judges the world should be a reasonably civilized one. He should have intellectual curiosity, and an insatiable desire for knowledge of himself, the world, and nature. He should understand, or at least feel sometime in the college career, the intellectual ecstasy possible in the educational process on the college level.

AN INDEPENDENT MIND

As the new president of Vassar recently said: 'The educator's whole business is to stimulate an independent mind. This is especially true in our twentieth-century world. The achievements in the physical universe, the surge into outer space, the mass effort to eliminate poverty—all this has to be in the terms of radical institutions. This is an age of extra-rapid change. Yet physical power can become a lethal weapon. We can stand on a pinnacle of promise and peril. This requires a versatile, flexible wisdom—it cannot be met by a conformist mind. . . . The college exists for the students and isn't doing its rightful job unless it continues to keep in close touch with them.'

211

This is what the excellent teacher does. This is why he is teaching. This is his mission in life.

If there is a deadly apathy among all together too many students, and there certainly was last year, at Dartmouth it may well be the fault of the College.

It behoves each student to get what he is paying for and be satisfied with nothing less.

October 7, 1964

I see that AuH_2O is accusing Mr Johnson, owner of $3,487,999·23¼ in cash, stocks, radio stations, and Texas heifers, and whose chemical formula is $Fe\ NaC1+SO_4=SO$, of being soft on Communism, of wishing to eradicate poverty, of providing medical care for emeritus professors, who certainly need it, and other sundry imbecilities.

On the other hand AuH_2O is for American motherhood, a 24-hour day, Arizona sunshine, the American Legion, and a bulging cash box (with approximately $1,563,444·31½ expanding the sides and both the ends of said box).

Furthermore AuH_2O would have us use our fleets of obsolete bombers, PFFT 606s, the US Marines (PAX VOBISCUM) to show these commies, all two billions of them, where to get off. (Claremont Junction?) He would bomb them with TNT, Wheaties dipped in Honegar, pamphlets entitled 'Why I Was for McCarthy', and other fissionable material. He would have us bomb Viet Nam, Nam Viet, TaiPeh, and PehTai, Chou En-lai, and lay on Chou; in fact it is rumoured that he would also tell the BEARDED WONDER where to get off. (I recommend in this case Bellows Falls, a fate worse than death.)

He would save the world for General Motors, who already own half of it, the Republican Hope Chest, and all good American stockholders.

THINNER BUT SIMILAR

It has always been difficult for me to hate the Chinese or even the Viet Kong (I like a K here better than a High or Low C). The latter are a little thinner than the Vietnamese, as they consume less rice, fewer bananas, tins of SPAM left over from World War

212

II, and on the whole it is diffcult to tell them apart, especially when they lie grotesquely stretched out dead in the burdock, gorse, pine cones, or tumble weed, which I am told abounds in Vietnam. In death they all look alike. The word Communism doesn't really explain matters to them. Few of them have enough to eat, and they are not fighting for democracy (a word which is a sham at the moment for many Americans), but for a full bowl of rice for their millions of offspring, for some general with an unpronounceable name, Phlegm-mgelhp, who has promised them all a FORD Mustang, a roof for the W.C. which has the habit of floating off during each monsoon (eleven months of the year), a WIENER SCHNITZEL, well done, for Christmas, and an opportunity to elect Government One in Sparkplug U.

BIRTH CONTROL PILLS

The Vietnamese, the Chinese, Burmese, Balinese and the Hindustani in far away NEPAL, and in fact most East Asians, and West Asians, too, for that matter, have not yet had the advantages of birth control pills, and other such paraphernalia sold by our leading druggists and pool hall proprietors. As the English would say, 'A pity'. So the Asians are always hungry with that lean and hungry look of YON Cassius (Yon for John) . . . billions of them.

The thought of SEVEN HUNDRED MILLION Chinese coming over the top with a Tommy Gun in one hand, a banner labelled EXCELSIOR in the other, and chanting in unison to the tune of AS THE BACKS GO TEARING BY, 'NO TICKEE NO WASHEE', has always scared me.

MORE PRUDENCE

Were I AuH_2O I would be a little more careful about the verbiage I scatter like water, willy nilly flowing, over the political scene. I would use more computers, more Gallop Poles (from Southern Silesia), and more Arizona ticks . . . far less dangerous, and less idiotic, than the political speeches written by illiterates who teach political science in Oconomowoc, which have already given the world the cold robbies.

If we can survive the next few weeks we are indeed a powerful nation.

I still prefer *C6 H22 O11*, in moderate quantities when the sun reaches the yard arm, and even after it passes it, and so I will leave it at that.

October 21, 1964

Men are ambitious, vindictive and rapacious. These words representing the view of human nature held by Alexander Hamilton who was a political theorist of giant proportions. He had read Thomas Hobbes.

There is no reason to change these words today as men are still vindictive, ambitious, and rapacious. As we are living in a jungle, Hamilton believed in the necessity of a strong central government, a strong executive, and he further believed that the government should be energetic, should do things, that the constitution should be loosely interpreted, and that the Union must be strong.

On the other hand the Democratic Government under Thomas Jefferson believed in State's Rights, in a weak federal government, in the strict construction of the constitution, and a belief that the Union should be a weak confederacy of states.

IDIOTIC POLICIES

Both parties respected the Judicial side of the government.

It is a little curious today that the Democratic party, forced perhaps by historical trends and events, represents the views of Hamilton, while the Goldwater party represents the view of Jefferson.

In Illinois in August my host flew the state flag, though to give him credit it flew under the American flag.

With the events in China and Russia in mind it is tragic and pathetic that the quality of our leadership in one party is represented by Goldwater, Miller, and Slippery Dick. (One has learned not to expect much from Eisenhower.)

Nor, to be fair, could one consider Johnson and Humphrey as giants of the intellect or of principle. Still they are the best we can offer at the moment.

A President should be a man of intellectual attainments, a man of principle, an honest and truth-telling man, a man with political sagacity, and one who by sheer force of character can carry the

214

country along with him. There have been few such in our history.

MUST SHED IDEALS

Should such a man exist under our political system it would be almost impossible for him to retain these qualities and become a Presidential candidate. He must shed whatever ideals he may have and become a wheeler-dealer, a party man, a compromiser. In fact, he must become a kind of bounder, a ward-heeler, sometimes nothing better than a crook if he is to go very far in American politics today.

Look what happened to Adlai Stevenson, not to mention Scranton and Rockefeller.

In Russia, of course, they do things differently.

If Khrushchev, by any chance, decides to go under or over the WALL, we should make him professor of political science, or Government, make him a Ph.D by ukase, and give him a banner labelled Excelsior.

Our head in the sand policy with China, and with every other Communist Government, is almost incredible today and yet we are carrying it on. No wonder they despise us. Events will certainly force a change but by that time we will be playing from weakness, not strength.

RESPECT FOR JUDICIARY

Powerful lobbies, some Christian, all commercial, have forced us into policies which are, to say the least, idiotic. In China, in Vietnam, in Laos, in Africa, in Cuba . . . everywhere we have been absolutely idiotic. Hear Willem Oltmans in November in Great Issues, I hope he speaks out. Being a European his view will be detached. He has been everywhere, knows everybody, and is not afraid to say what he thinks. His lecture will justify the whole course.

As Cromwell said, 'By the bowels of Christ I beseech thee,' to remember a few fundamentals:

1. Men are ambitious, vindictive and rapacious.
2. Patriotism is the last refuge of a scoundrel.
3. A statesman is a dead politician.

H   215

4. We must recover some of our personal and political integrity in our national life or we are indeed lost.

October 24, 1964

I seldom get a chance to offer a positive suggestion to the administration or trustees, as I haven't seen any of them to talk to for several years now.

However, I offer them today a suggestion absolutely free of charge.

One of the really amateur Dartmouth teams is the Rugby team, which won two games against Princeton last Saturday, while the Dartmouth varsity was losing. The rugby teams play for the love of it; there is little, if any, coaching. There are no field telephones, cameras, strategists pacing up and down the side lines, bands, cheer leaders, or banners. Just a few guys having fun in an ancient and honourable game.

The rugby team, for one reason or another (one of the main reasons is that they bring no money to anyone's coffers), have to play their games in West Lebanon.

I suggest that they play from now on on Memorial Field (lest we forget, this field was dedicated to the Dartmouth men who died in World War I) where those who like English rugby can watch in some kind of comfort.

This would necessitate the building, badly needed, of what I once called facetiously in describing an imaginary Sparkplug U, the 'Golden Bowl'. Golden, because at $5 a seat, with 50,000 or more seats to sell, the Golden Bowl would soon be paid for. Now that we are going to have home and home games with the Big Three in the Ivy League, not to mention the smaller five, and teams of far lesser calibre, we should be able to accommodate our generous alumni and their friends, when we are host to a good football team.

Also their cars. The price for parking has jumped from 25 cents to $1. Why shouldn't the college pick up an extra $10,000 or $20,000 a game just for car parking?

There is a natural sight for this bowl. On the right as one drives out Lyme Road, now a big broad highway, there is, before one gets to La Bounty's Service Station, a huge field, owned

216

I am told by the Dartmouth trustees, with a natural declevity which will save costs of excavating, and with a lot of parking space where the cows now roam and cheerfully, I am told, chew their cud. (Old Hickory.)

The Trustees need not hire Mr Rockefeller's architect, nor Mr Nervi, Nurmi, or even Ed Stone. The design need only be a concrete bowl, adequately reinforced, big enough to enclose a football field of regulation length, and seat forty or fifty or more thousand paying spectators.

The drawing plans could be done at Thayer School, or I could do them for that matter, and all the blueprints needed could be done in a Thayer seminar for engineering students. If necessary the 'new' maths department could be drawn into any discussion of stresses and strains. I realize that a lot of blueprints would be needed, but after all the College does own a couple of Xerox machines.

Nearby there would be a gigantic Nissen hut, complete with showers, field kitchens, etc, which also doesn't need an architect, as everyone knows what a Nissen Hut looks like (we see one of them frequently), for the serving of barbecued chicken, giant burgers, a tossed salad, and dry toast. This could be a real money maker. The work could be done by Thayer Hall employees who would be glad to serve with time and a half pay for working on a Saturday afternoon.

Naturally there would have to be other facilities but these need not be described.

A Singapore-like bar in the Nissen hut would increase the revenue, and it would also concentrate the drinking where it belongs, instead of under the stands, behind trees, or under one's topcoat.

I would remind my readers that we did not have such a bar in the Golden Bowl at Sparkplug U, but then we didn't need that much money in those days.

We did have pretty girl Sparkettes who did dances between plays and between the halves, which added gaiety and beauty to the scene.

We also had tom-toms to help the rhythm of a forward pass, and in fact one of the coaches was a band leader, who could, at a pinch, teach rhythmic dancing. We found at Sparkplug U that this kind of coaching did help considerably in the wide open game of today.

Although a bowl is not in itself a thing of beauty, on the Lyme Road, if the bowl was sunk well into the ground, the beauty of Balch Hill or Oak Hill on an autumn day would not be too badly impaired. My plans do call for the bowl really sunk into the ground. I understand from Geology I that there is no inland lake under that particular spot of ground, so the bowl could be sunk to the land level. Obviously there would have to be signs posted, on days when there were no games, to warn people not to fall into the bowl. This is a real problem easily solved for we could, if necessary, surround the bowl with a tall Inland Steel fence, so that not only could the bowl be protected, but it would also serve to prevent school boys, or indigent college employees, from getting in free during the third or fourth quarter. We really must have the fence.

I trust that at the next Trustees' meeting several committees may be appointed to look into this matter. The more committees the better, though of course they will slow down matters, and CONSTRUCTION SHOULD SOON BEGIN.

It is a pleasure to offer these ideas to the Trustees for free.

Possunt qui volunt.

October 28, 1964

The big question for the Republicans is not the election which they have already lost, but how can the moderates and sane ones regain control of the party machinery? The extreme conservatives and the John Birchers are not going to let go except under the pressure of a fire hose.

It is now obvious that the right wing extremists have been using Mr Goldwater: 'He's just the best we could do—this time.' Poor fellow, they have already written him off; I can almost feel sorry for him, though he should have known better. All along he has just been a stooge for the radical, lunatic right.

For some weeks now Mr Goldwater has reminded me more and more of Mortimer Snerd, though I would admit under slight pressure that he has somewhat more pulchritude than the little dummy familiar to all.

218

Mr Goldwater says something, then takes it back, reverses his field, and all of this dreadful stuff is fed to him by the shrewder people back of him. The water runs, is turned off, and then a new mixture is run through the microphones. What can a poor voter do? This time vote democratic. Overwhelmingly so.

Take a look at his advisers: Leonard W. Hall, Everett M. Dirksen (a senator's senator), William F. Knowland, temporarily marooned in the land of the Giantburger, Stephen Shadegg, Dean Burch, Denison Kitchel, Harry Rosenzweig, Ray Bliss, William J. Baroody, not to mention Slippery Dick.

NO PARTY BARRIERS

To think of our great country being taken over by such a lot is to go out to the nearest pine tree and quietly vomit. Especially now. These people dare raise the morality and corruption issue when even a MORON knows that corruption knows no party barriers. Think of the Tea Pot Dome scandal under poor Gamaliel Harding; think of McCarthy.

Only a day or two ago an intelligence officer admitted to me, what I already knew, that Washington is full of sexual deviates, as is every big city, and there are more lesbians than homosexuals in the world capitals. Moscow, London, Paris, Rome: sexual deviation is an indoor sport.

And then I read of a film backed by, believe it or not, an organization which calls itself THE MOTHERS FOR A MORAL AMERICA. Financed by Mr Humphrey? The Birchers? or the mothers of America? It would be revealing to know if any party funds paid for the film.

Choice it was called. Cost a mere hundred grand which included $35,000 network time. Certain scenes were thought to be 'unduly suggestive', and were deleted. These included a girl posing in a topless bathing suit, and a man wearing only a fig leaf at a cocktail party. Tush. Tush.

The picture was meant to suggest to the TV audience that the democrats, Mr Johnson in particular, were responsible for our current low moral state.

The last headline I have seen announced that GOLDWATER CANCELS GOP FILM.

No wonder the world gapes at our claim to moral world leadership.

We have become ridiculous.

When I was a boy I once heard Theodore Roosevelt speak from the back of a train platform in Beverly, Massachusetts. He castigated the 'malefactors of great wealth', and had bolted his party, the Republican, because it was so shoddy. Today, though it wears custom made clothes, sports crew cuts, and works from plush offices, it is shoddier still.

Democrats called the film *Choice* the 'sickest political programme to be conceived since television became a factor in American politics', and then went on to say 'that it was an outrage for a major political party to descend to such a level'.

Pundits had predicted it would be a hateful campaign.

Before this column appears again the election will be over.

I trust that many honourable and decent Republicans everywhere will be able to pick up the pieces and build something better than the reeking hysterical edifice created last summer in San Francisco.

I have always thought that you could fool all of the people all of the time, but perhaps this election will show that I have been wrong.

I resigned from the Republican Party during the disgraceful McCarthy era. McCarthyism is a state of mind, and is, of course, still with us and, human nature being what it is, stupid and unbelievably greedy, it will always be with us. But the people next Tuesday will be able to scotch it, temporarily at least, and perhaps good sense and a better ethic may bring back the GOP to something resembling good taste and decency.

I feel sorry for the Keatings, Pillsburys and Clevelands, forced to submit to the gang back of Barry Goldwater.

May God Save the Republic.

November 5, 1964

I came across a spirited letter from Dame Edith Sitwell the other day which referred to an 'appalling passage about a pony on its way to the slaughter-houses of Belgium, who, after a lifetime of service, was to have a hoof returned to the family of its

owners "as a memento of its fidelity".' She goes on to say: 'I was
made sick with horror and grief of that work-worn, trusting body,
and that betrayed heart. But, as St John said, "my father's
house hath many mansions", and I hope that little creature has
found its rest there. As for the master and his family: I only have
one hope for them, and that is that they may never know one
moment of sleep again—either in this life or in the eternal hell
that so surely awaits them.'

This reminded me, though of course to a somewhat lesser
degree of revulsion, of the modern vandalism that goes on here in
the name of progress.

WEEP NO MORE

Let us weep no more about college finances or for the alumni fund
when the College can afford to tear down ruthlessly a fine greenhouse, functional and handsome as well, next to Webster Cottage
which is to be moved. This greenhouse gave pleasure to many,
and represented life.

I can imagine the day when Baker Library will be torn down
to give way to a modern mausoleum harbouring micro-films.

Eventually, if this destruction goes on, a handsome village will
have been destroyed and we will look exactly like Boy's Town,
Nebraska.

Though I am not a professional city planner I do have a few
ideas as to how I would change Hanover.

I would do away, almost entirely, with the Main Street, which
I would replace with grassy plots, flower beds, and trees. I
would retain the sidewalks, but would remove the hideous lights
and replace them with softer ones. Many of the shops I would
retain. We need an apothecary or two, several haberdashers, a
bookstore, and a few fine eating places, now sadly lacking.

All of these buildings would have Colonial exteriors with
modern interiors, such as the Dillon Bank has in Morristown, N.J.

I would leave Tanzis as it is as a reminder of a better and more
friendly Hanover.

SHOPPING CENTRE

This arcade, or whatever you choose to call it (there is a handsome one in Tunbridge Wells), would extend as far as the Gulf

221

Station. I would tend to develop shopping districts out on the Lyme Road beyond the Golden Bowl, let us say, opposite the Deep Freeze.

I would reverse the fire station and have the trucks come out the back of the building. New roads and parking spaces could be constructed in that general vicinity.

I would put a moat around Hopkins Centre. This could be used for swans in the summer, and skating in the winter. It would also tend to absorb some of the moisture underneath the structure.

Then I would turn it into a productive building, tax wise, and with a few changes it could be turned into a brewery or a grain elevator which was obviously what it was designed for.

So instead of consuming money by the bucketful every day, it would produce some.

Then there wouldn't have to be so much pressure put on the alumni for funds. We, as a College, might even become self-supporting.

ADMINISTRATIVE ROW

I would connect Parkhurst, McNutt, and Robinson into one large building with naturally underground connections wide enough to move pianos, computers, and boa constrictors. This would naturally have a colonial façade and the entrance would be a handsome greenhouse where each administrator on entering could pick a daisy, a buttercup, a dandelion, or a carnation for his buttonhole. This would also give off a pleasant odour.

On the site of College Hall I would construct a new student union complete with Post Office, a soda fountain, and bowling alleys. This could be connected to Thayer Hall where food would be consumed on a voluntary basis. As I intimated, the Mall would have a few good eating places.

The Inn can stay where it is.

I would also install a new curriculum which would guarantee to teach men life and literature, and how to read and write. All computers, IBM machines, and higher mathematics, the 'new' mathematics, would be moved across the river.

Classes would be voluntary.

I would emblazon across the new administration building in large letters the word EXCELSIOR.

November 11, 1964

Now that the alarums and excursions are quieting down it is time to sober up, and look seriously into some of our difficulties.

One grave problem is, of course, Southeast Asia, where we are hopelessly mired down, and where the Vietkong daily make us look like toy soldiers.

I suspect that not even the Vietnamese are happy with us there. Why we are there at all is one of the most interesting questions one could posit. Why?

Let's look at the giant China with a new atomic weapon.

I quote: 'In the nineteen-twenties and 'thirties, when Japanese pressure, interference, and encroachment were continuing and accelerating, China's official and unofficial spokesmen were careful not to disturb the American illusion that the Chinese disliked all foreigners but made an exception of the American as democratic and anti-imperialistic. The truth was that the Chinese thought the Americans too were imperialistic, but enough less active in their imperialism, and enough the rivals of Britain and especially of Japan, to offer a chance of splitting the imperialistic front.'

'Still later, I myself can vividly remember sitting in dug-outs during the intensive Japanese bombings of Chungking in 1941, in the months before Pearl Harbour, and listening to men who were high in the government and in the personal confidence of Chiang Kai-shek denouncing the hypocrisy of America which was making loans to China, and continuing to supply Japan with strategic raw materials and the petrol that fuelled the bombers. A great many Americans, though they were hazy about the ins and outs of high policy, had an uneasy feeling that something was wrong. It was an emotional relief, after Pearl Harbour, to have a new, simple, black-and-white definition—China was the friend, Japan the enemy.

PERSON AS SYMBOL

'Unfortunately, the less the political workings and social structure of a country are understood, the easier it is to substitute a person as the symbol of a nation. Wartime propaganda soon personified Chiang Kai-shek as "China". In the Press, on the wireless, in political speeches, it was not China but Chiang Kai-shek who had

223

become "our most faithful ally". The clamour was raised for Washington not to support Chiang was the same thing as "betraying China". The scene was set for the excesses of the late Senator McCarthy....

'One of the developments that could lead to a saner American policy would be an increase in the economic prosperity and stability of China. Once industrialization really gets going, there will be a market for heavy machinery from which American manufacturers and exporters will not want to be excluded. At present, two vast processes of international decentralization are going on—one, of the malignant autocracy created by Stalin; the other, of the over-centralized Juggernaut of unheeding, thick-skinned power which the late John Foster Dulles almost succeeded in perfecting.

'The process of these decentralizations put a premium on diplomacy. It has been said of the late President Kennedy that his diplomacy demanded cold courage and strong nerves, but that he did not believe in backing the opponent into a corner; some room for adjustment must always be allowed. There are signs that the diplomacy of President Johnson is of the same kind. If he is elected in November to begin a new term, with a strong mandate, he might even be able to begin to repair the weakest facet in America's world position, by substituting flexibility for rigidity in America's China policy.'

AMERICAN IN EXILE

The above was written by Owen Lattimore, now an exile in Leeds University, England, driven there by stupid and hostile America. He knows more about China than all the State Department put together and it is a crime against nature that he doesn't have an important job there himself. POLITICS makes this impossible ... politics, ignorance, and prejudice.

Let us remember it was people like Senator McCarthy, William Knowland, now sulking in California, Wyman of New Hampshire, Loeb of the *Manchester Union* (though he is no more important than a flea), the late Senator Bridges, who did incalcuable harm in Washington, and who created our stupid and ever increasing dangerous position in regard to China and the Far East.

We equate China with Mao, or Chou En-lai, when as a matter of fact China is a country of heavens knows how many hundreds of millions of people all looking for a bowl of rice (heaping) and a Hoover vacuum cleaner or Maytag washing machine (no advertisement). Nice people most of them, or at least as nice as most of the human race.

Communism is but a word that means different things to different people. We should not be terrified by the word.

We better get along with it. The ironical thing is that the institution that will adapt itself the quickest to it, when it becomes evident, as it is now, that it is here to stay, that creeping Socialism is going to break into a gallop in all backward nations, is the Roman Catholic Church.

Our mistake as a nation has been to back the dictators, the people with money, to a point that is frightfully dangerous to the safety of our descendants. No wonder we are called imperialists which we have been. Worse than this, we have been incredibly stupid, as witness our treatment of Owen Lattimore.

My own guess is that Alger Hiss was also rail-roaded. I lived through the Sacco-Vanzetti case and know how strong prejudice can mar our judicial proceedings.

As I have said before we need more intellectuals, not less, in our foreign service, and in our State Department, and in our politics.

Now that L.B.J. has the mandate I can only pray that he also has the intelligence needed to get us out of the mess the old line conservative Republicans got us into.

November 20, 1964
What I want to write about here is something else again. Even the news item said of him: 'Internationally known humorist and scholar of Texas folklore.'

The citation, read by President Lyndon Johnson when Mr Dobie received the Presidential Medal of Freedom on September 14, 1964, said of him: 'Folklorist, teacher, writer, he has recaptured the treasure of our rich regional heritage in the Southwest from Conquistadores to Cowboys.'

He succeeded Henry Steele Commager as professor of American history at Cambridge, England, in 1943–4.

He has written eighteen fine books, some of them approaching greatness.

The writer of a standard book on the Alamo, Lon Tinkle, recently wrote of him: 'Posterity will, I believe, take him more seriously than he was taken in his lifetime. It will keep his books alive as long as any written by Texans or about Texas since Cabeza de Vaca's *Relacion* of 1542. . . . So long as story patterns convey meanings, as they have since the dawn of literature, in a way unlike that of other forms of expressing truth, Dobie will remain one of the few Texas "immortals".'

Now for my story.

Some years ago when Mr Dobie was in fine health I tried to get him up to Dartmouth to lecture to the student body. I am quite confident, for I have heard him tell stories on two of his Texas ranches, that in all their four years at Dartmouth the students would not have heard a speaker as fascinating, as full of warmth, and humour, as full of knowledge of life and literature, of people, as the late J. Frank Dobie.

And yet the COMMITTEE, stupider than most committees, for reasons which certainly can make no sense, refused to have him up.

Either they were (A) completely ignorant of the life and work of Mr Dobie, or (B) arbitrarily refused to give the undergraduates the experience of a lifetime, perhaps because it was I who proposed him.

I was, to say the least, slightly astonished after hearing some of the speakers the College does get up, and I wrote to Mr Dickey to see if he would overrule the committee. Naturally, in this case, he refused to do so. I must admit I expected nothing from him.

When Henry Steel Commager wrote me expressing his own astonishment that Dartmouth would not have Mr Dobie, he queried 'What is wrong at Dartmouth?' that it could turn down one of America's greatest men.

My reply to Mr Commager was to the effect that I couldn't possibly answer his question in a letter for lack of time and space. We let it go at that.

Incidentally he had enormous classes at Texas, but got in trouble with the authorities, even as you and I have.

Now this great man, incidentally a friend of Robert Frost, but much more generous in his nature, lies buried among the great of the Lone Star State, not far from the grave of Stephen F. Austin (1793–1836), an honour given very few indeed.

I am proud to have been his friend, and to have won his friendship, and one of these days I hope to return to Austin to pay my respects at his grave.

His latest book is *Cow People* and I hope some of my readers may read it.

My Dobie had a passion for freedom, and expresses it so in his fine book *Tales of the Mustang*:

> So sometimes yet, in the realities of silence and solitude
> For a few people unhampered a while with things,
> The mustangs walk out with dawn, stand high, then
> Sweep away, wild with sheer life, free, free, free—
> Free of all confines of time and flesh.

Hale to a great spirit: Frank Dobie, hail and farewell.

December 2, 1964
It is always a sight for the gods when a college tries to do something drastic, and forward looking, about its curriculum.

Self interest rears its pretty little head, and the faculty engage in a battle to preserve departmental interests that would make a Tammany Sachem look like Red Riding Hood.

In all my forty-two years at Dartmouth the student's interests (as today at Hopkins Center) were scarcely, if ever, considered. The curriculum was always designed for the interests primarily of the faculty.

Everybody has known for years that the first two years at Dartmouth have been, for the good students, generally a mere repetition of what he has already taken. He gets bored, his intellectual curiosity, if he has any, lies dormant, he becomes apathetic, never thinks for himself (and if he does he gets stepped on for it). He merely walks the academic treadmill of required courses, many of which are duller than a wet dish of cold robbies.

Carborundum II must not be dropped. It must be kept a re-

227

quired course for every freshman must be taught how to sharpen a pencil.

Great Tissues must have compulsory attendance lest the speakers drone on to an empty lecture hall.

The major must start in prep school else the student won't be a specialist by his sophomore year.

A POPULAR TEACHER

I know something of what I speak for I was a popular teacher in a department of two men and we incurred resentment from our inferiors sharp enough to open a safe. Last year when I taught 1,060 students (enough to kill a man, especially a badly paid one), and the biggest lecture class of its kind in the history of Dartmouth, there was a black cloud on the horizon which brought real trouble to my successor, a kind of innocent bystander, Professor Vernon Hall.

If I hadn't finished my career in June, something would have had to be done about me and my department, and sure enough, after I was retired we folded, and by a legal process, lethal in its efficiency, Professor Hall was forced out, and Dartmouth lost another fine teacher.

The college news service, with calculation inspired from above, gave no publicity to a record unique in Dartmouth history, and if it hadn't been for the *Daily Dartmouth* my last class, again unique, would not have been mentioned.

Instead of being proud of one of their teachers, they exhibited a petty, mean, and ungenerous spirit.

Even worse they censored my last lecture, which is something an Ivy League College is not supposed to do. The last word on this has not been spoken.

It is easy to go on record as being against the three (or four) term system. It is a killing process, an intellectual rat race which destroys the very thing it is supposed to preserve, which is the liberal education of the Dartmouth undergraduate. Today the student has no leisure to read, or to think for himself, or to listen quietly to great music, or just to relax. He must pass innumerable tests, write innumerable papers instead of one excellent one which he might have time to develop.

228

This process over the years has led me to state publicly that a student at Dartmouth gets an education, such as it is, in spite of and not because of the college.

The college could have a two term system, and a summer school if it wants one, and so keep some semblance of good sense.

It would be difficult, indeed, to prove that the Dartmouth graduate of today is as well educated as one in Daniel Webster's class.

I would have fewer regulations rather than more. I would allow more freedom rather than less. I would allow a student to grow up somewhat in his own way and time, guided by stimulating courses and stimulating teachers.

I would see to it that a student learns to read, and love reading and to write well. I would help him to a zest for life.

RUN LIKE PREP SCHOOL

The other day a bright young faculty member, who shall be nameless, said that we are being run like a prep school.

The deadly apathy now prevalent might be changed. The students themselves should have a voice in what they should study, and the methods which prevail. They at least should be heard.

The administration wants nothing which will disturb the smooth emanations of its news service and the image projected by its public relations department.

It is devoted to raising money, and all too often truth is lost in the shuffle. If it has any startling ideas about education they seldom appear in print except in frightful banalities which make Lyndon Johnson resemble a modern Socrates.

Actually we are turning out every year a lot of nice young men, but to call them educated is to use the word farcically. There are, to be sure, a few exceptions: possibly 10 per cent, and some of these have already flunked out or left college. This has all been said before in *The Education of Henry Adams*.

I trust the men trying now to revitalize the Dartmouth curriculum may succeed in spite of faculty politics, log rolling, self interest, and a rather indifferent administration.

Like the State Department we have far too much Christian endeavour spirit, and not enough classical good sense.

Index of Names

231

This is a signed and
limited edition of
500 copies